TRIPS Compliance, National Patent Regimes and Innovation

TRIPS Compliance, National Patent Regimes and Innovation

Evidence and Experience from Developing Countries

Edited by

Sunil Mani

Professor and Planning Commission Chair, Centre for Development Studies, Trivandrum, Kerala, India

Richard R. Nelson

Columbia University, USA

Edward Elgar
Cheltenham, UK • Northampton, MA, USA

Published by
Edward Elgar Publishing Limited
The Lypiatts
15 Lansdown Road
Cheltenham
Glos GL50 2JA
UK

Edward Elgar Publishing, Inc.
William Pratt House
9 Dewey Court
Northampton
Massachusetts 01060
USA

A catalogue record for this book
is available from the British Library

Library of Congress Control Number: 2013944959

This book is available electronically in the ElgarOnline.com
Economics Subject Collection, E-ISBN 978 1 78254 947 5

ISBN 978 1 78254 946 8

Typeset by Servis Filmsetting Ltd, Stockport, Cheshire
Printed and bound in Great Britain by T.J. International Ltd, Padstow

Contents

Contributors

Thiago Caliari is at ICSA – Federal University of Alfenas, Brazil.

Peera Charoenporn is at the Faculty of Economics, Thammasat University, Bangkok, Thailand.

Sudip Chaudhuri is at the Indian Institute of Management Calcutta, Kolkata, India.

Song Hong is at the Institute of World Economics and Politics, Chinese Academy of Social Sciences (CASS), People's Republic of China.

Patarapong Intarakumnerd is at the National Graduate Institute for Policy Studies (GRIPS), Tokyo, Japan.

Sunil Mani is at the Centre for Development Studies, Trivandrum, Kerala, India.

Roberto Mazzoleni is at the Department of Economics, Hofstra University, Hempstead, New York, USA.

Latha Nagarajan is at Rutgers, The State University of New Jersey, New Brunswick, USA.

Richard R. Nelson is at Columbia University, New York, USA.

Luciano Martins Costa Póvoa is Economic Advisor, Federal Senate of Brazil.

Carl Pray is at Rutgers, The State University of New Jersey, New Brunswick, USA.

V.K. Unni is at the Indian Institute of Management Calcutta, Kolkata, India.

Acknowledgements

The authors themselves financed the research underlying the various country studies. However, a research grant received from the Earth Institute by Professor Nelson facilitated the three project meetings that were held at Columbia University, New York. Jennifer Washburn organized these meetings with considerable skill. We are extremely grateful to her for her great logistical support, which enabled the team to have uninterrupted conversations. Research assistance provided by V.S. Sreekanth and K. Kavitha at Trivandrum has also been a great source of support. J. Devika read through some of the chapters and improved their presentation. We are very much thankful to them as well. Caroline Cornish at Edward Elgar supervised the production of the book with remarkable ease. We owe a debt of gratitude to her and her colleagues.

1. Introduction

Sunil Mani and Richard R. Nelson

1. CONTROVERSIES REGARDING TRIPS

This book is a report on the effects of the worldwide adoption of TRIPS on the economic development being experienced in four countries presently behind the technological and economic frontier and struggling to catch up. The countries are Brazil, India, Thailand, and China.

The discussions leading to the establishment in 1995 of the requirement that countries adhere to the principles written down in TRIPS (Trade Related Aspects of Intellectual Property Rights) in order to be members of the WTO (World Trade Organization) often were heated. In particular, a number of economists disputed the argument, put forth by advocates of TRIPS, that less developed countries would develop more rapidly and widely if they had in place the kind of strong intellectual property rights law that TRIPS codified.

The advocates of TRIPS proposed that there were two kinds of gains that would accrue to developing countries that signed on. First of all, the incentives for R&D and invention of their indigenous companies and potential inventors more generally would be strengthened. Second, companies and patent holders more generally, residing in the advanced industrial countries, would be more likely to invest in developing countries, or facilitate technology transfer to them, if those countries respected their intellectual property rights. But many economists who had studied technological advance, and the roles played by intellectual property in the process, questioned both of these proposals.

Partly their argument was based on a series of empirical studies that had explored the importance of patent protection as an incentive for R&D and inventive activity, and found that in most industries patents were not very important. The findings of these studies invariably were that, while patents were essential for inventors to gain significant returns from their inventions in pharmaceuticals and a few other industries, in most industries, including many where technological advance was rapid, the principal mechanisms through which inventors were able to reap profits from the

1

new products their work enabled were the advantages of head start, particularly where learning curves were relatively steep, and through building strong service capabilities to attract and hold buyers to their products. And keeping knowledge of the production process private, rather than patents, was the principal vehicle used by companies to protect their process technologies. The economists studying technological advance also pointed out that the development of a number of important technologies had been stymied for a while by legal action, or the threat of it, by agents who held patents and were trying to make money through this vehicle.

At the time of the discussions that led up to TRIPS, there had been little detailed study of the role of intellectual property rights in the earlier catching up experiences of countries like Japan, Korea, and Taiwan, but scholars of economic development held the general impression that the role had not been significant. The impression was that the prospect of gaining an internal patent had not been an important part of the incentives for the indigenous entrepreneurs who drove the catching up process. And it was believed that only rarely did foreign companies try to use their intellectual property rights to prevent indigenous companies from developing their production capabilities, and indeed in many cases assisted in the process.

These beliefs were largely supported by an empirical study published in 2010, focused on just these issues, titled *Intellectual Property Rights, Development, and Catch-up: An International Comparative Study* (Odagiri et al., 2010). That study examined the catching up experience of a number of different countries, and found that, while there were some exceptional cases, and these seemed to be more frequent in recent years, there was little evidence that intellectual property played an important role in the processes involved. The present study should be regarded as a natural follow up to the earlier one, and looks at experience in recent years as TRIPS came into force.

There are a number of reasons why past experience may not be a good indication of what is going on under TRIPS. An important one is that years ago, for example in the earlier stages of Japan's development as a manufacturing power, the leading companies in countries at the economic frontier did not worry about companies in the developing countries rapidly becoming competitors in world markets, much less in their home markets. In recent years, however, this has become a real concern. Indeed, the study reported above found that in recent years there had been an increase in litigation against companies in developing countries whom the patent holders in frontier countries clearly regarded as potential threats. Second, and more generally, the last quarter century has seen companies in the United States, and to some extent in Europe and Japan, paying more attention to intellectual property rights than they used to, and a noticeable increase in patent litigation. And third, over this same period policy makers in developing countries have become much more oriented to building up the scientific and technological capabilities of their countries, and following the development paths of Korea and Taiwan, than used to be the case.

And of course TRIPS is new. Until recently many less developed countries had intellectual property regimes that were quite loose. TRIPS has resulted in a significant tightening up of IP law in these countries.

Two broad questions are explored in this study. One is whether strengthened indigenous intellectual property rights seem to have drawn forth an increase in indigenous investments in R&D and efforts at innovation more generally. We note, however, that the increased vigor of policies to support innovation that one sees in many developing countries, including all of those reported on here, makes it difficult to sort out the effects of a strengthened IP regime from other factors. The other is whether companies at the technological frontier have responded to stronger IP protection in developing countries by increasing their investments there, and their assistance to indigenous catching up through expanding their licensing and associated technology transfer to domestic companies, or whether they have used stronger IP laws to try to hinder foreign companies from catching up. Again, it is not easy to tease out how much difference TRIPS has made on these fronts, given the increased zeal in protecting their intellectual property that IP holders have shown more generally. The authors of the empirical country studies presented in this book were aware of these analytical difficulties, and have tried to deal with them.

In undertaking their empirical studies, most of the economists contributing to this book were of two different minds, somewhat at odds with each other. One was that it facilitated economic development if the IP regimes in countries aiming to catch up were relatively weak, and that it was particularly important not to give foreign companies a strong legal handle to discourage indigenous companies from acquiring modern technology, or to enable them to require high royalty and other payments from companies they could accuse of using their patented technologies. From this perception, TRIPS could well interfere with the ability of countries behind the frontier to catch up. But the other belief was that in most cases IP didn't matter much, and that in fact TRIPS would not have much of an effect.

However, there was one important sector where there was general agreement that TRIPS could matter significantly. An important particular recent development has been, on the one hand, the efforts of a number of developing countries to establish an indigenous pharmaceuticals industry, and on the other hand the increased aggressiveness of pharmaceuticals companies in the United States and Europe to enforce their intellectual property rights. Prior to TRIPS many third world countries (as some high income countries) did not grant product patents on pharmaceuticals.[1] In many cases the rationale was that patents on pharmaceuticals increased the cost of medical care and, in particular, handicapped public health programs. In some developing countries this policy also was associated with a desire to foster the development of an indigenous pharmaceuticals industry, serving not only domestic but world demands. As we will note later, in India this effort was quite successful; in Brazil less so.

Big pharma was very active in the campaign to establish TRIPS. Lobbyists from a few other high-tech industries, like electronics, also were active, but played a much less powerful role than did those representing pharmaceuticals.[2]

Thus issues of medical care costs are an important part of the debate about whether or not TRIPS is a good policy, and about whether pharmaceuticals ought to be treated as a special case. These arguments and policies play an important role in the developments that have occurred in several of the countries in our sample.

2. TRIPS FLEXIBILITIES

Concerns about the possible detrimental effects of TRIPS, held by participants in the treaty writing process, from both developing and frontier countries, led to the building into the treaty of a number of different kinds of flexibility. These included prominently, (i) a transition period before which a country had to get its IP system to meet TRIPS standards, (ii) provisions that permitted compulsory licensing of patents under certain circumstances, (iii) the ability of governments to use patented technologies for certain public purposes without explicitly licensing them, (iv) ability under certain circumstances to import patented items from other countries, (v) exceptions, and (vi) exemptions, giving some flexibility regarding just what can be patented and what not.

(i) The Compliance Period

TRIPS came into existence in 1995, but most developing countries were given time until 2005 to get their systems aligned with requirements, and especially poor countries until 2016. During the transition period, starting in 1995, countries were required to accept patent applications and keep them in a 'patent pending' mailbox, which would be opened when the country became TRIPS compliant, and evaluated then according to the patent law the country had put in place. This provision was particularly important for pharmaceuticals, because it meant that, for a country that delayed putting a TRIPS compliant patent law in place, generics could be used and produced.

(ii) Compulsory Licensing

A compulsory license (CL) is an authorization which is granted by the government without the permission of the patent holder. This is one of the most frequently encountered flexibilities that has actually been used. It means that the government of a country under certain grounds may issue a compulsory license to a domestic manufacturer for producing the generic version of a patented drug. Most countries have provisions for compulsory licenses, either under their patent law or, as in the US, through anti-trust legislation. There are many different grounds for issuing CLs; these can include public health reasons. Other grounds are, for instance, emergency situations, epidemics, public non-commercial use, to remedy anti-competitive practices or to protect the environment; it is entirely up to the national law to decide which are the grounds and so there is a fair amount of flexibility. A CL limits the rights of the patent holder, but does not take those rights away. TRIPS therefore specifies the conditions that need to be applied when countries want to grant a compulsory license. An important condition is that each case shall be considered individually. Also, in general, efforts should first be made to obtain a license from the patent holder (a so-called voluntary license). One of the important conditions that are attached to the issuance of a compulsory license is that the patent holder is remunerated through the grant of a royalty. The size of the royalty (usually denoted as a percentage of the price of the product manufactured under CL) is decided by the governmental authority that grants the CL in the first place. The other two conditions are that the decision to issue a CL is subject to a review and the CL is predominantly for the supply of the domestic market. It was generally believed that the Doha declaration on public health would precipitate a number of CLs to be issued. However, a recent study by Beall and Kuhn (2012) identified 24 CLs that were issued mostly between 2003 and 2005, involved drugs for HIV/AIDS, and occurred in upper-middle-income countries. Aside from HIV/AIDS, few CL episodes involved communicable disease, and none occurred in least-developed or low-income countries (Table 1.1). It is interesting to note that over a third of the CLs have been issued by two of the four countries in our sample, namely Brazil and Thailand.

Table 1.1   Compulsory licensing episodes by year and country

Year	Nation	Disease	Total products	Outcome
2001 (2007)	Brazil	HIV/AIDS	2	CL/discount
2001	Brazil	HIV/AIDS	1	Discount
2001	Canada	Anthrax	1	Discount
2001–03	South Africa	HIV/AIDS	8	VL/discount/none
2001	United States	Anthrax	1	Discount
2002	Egypt	Erectile dysfunction	1	CL
2003–04	Malaysia	HIV/AIDS	3	CL
2003–07	Brazil	HIV/AIDS	1	Discount
2003	Zimbabwe	HIV/AIDS	All	CL
2004	Mozambique	HIV/AIDS	3	CL
2004	Zambia	HIV/AIDS	3	CL
2005–06	Argentina	Pandemic flu	1	VL
2005–07	Brazil	HIV/AIDS	1	Discount
2005–09	Brazil	HIV/AIDS	1	Discount
2005	Ghana	HIV/AIDS	All	CL
2005	Indonesia	HIV/AIDS	2	CL
2005	Taiwan	Pandemic flu	1	VL
2006–07	India	Cancer	1	None
2006 (2010)	Thailand	HIV/AIDS	1	CL
2007	Rwanda	HIV/AIDS	1	CL
2007 (2010)	Thailand	HIV/AIDS, CVD	2	CL
2007–08	Thailand	Cancer	1	Discount
2007–08	Thailand	Cancer	3	CL
2010	Ecuador	HIV/AIDS	1	CL

Source: Beall and Kuhn (2012).

(iii)   Public, Non-commercial Use of a Patent

The right of the state to use a patent without the consent of the patent holder for public health purposes is recognized to be an important public health safeguard by many countries. Although Article 31 of the TRIPS Agreement sets out the conditions governing both government use of patents and compulsory licenses, one important difference is that government use of patents may be 'fast-tracked' because of the waiver requirement for prior negotiations with patent holders.

(iv) Parallel Importation

Parallel importation refers to the importation, without authorization of the patent holder, into a country of a product from a third country, where this product has been marketed by the patent holder or in another legitimate manner. It is mainly used when the price in the third country is considerably lower than the price the patent holder charges in the country concerned. TRIPS explicitly states that it does not address the issue of parallel import, thereby leaving countries free to determine their own policy in this respect especially if they are currently or potentially producers of generic drugs.

(v) Exceptions to Patent Rights

Article 30 of the TRIPS Agreement does not define the scope or nature of the permissible exceptions and the result is that countries have considerable freedom in this area. One of the exceptions is the so-called Bolar provision. This provision or exemption enables the manufacturer of a generic drug to use a patented invention to obtain marketing approval without the patent owner's permission before the patent expires. The generic drug maker can then market his or her own version of the patented drug as soon as the patent expires. This exemption has important implications for those developing countries that are manufacturers of generic drugs.

(vi) Exemptions from Patentability

The TRIPS agreement requires patents to be granted only for inventions that are new, involve an inventive step and are capable of industrial application. A mere discovery of a new form of a known substance which does not result in the enhancement of the known efficacy of that substance or the mere discovery of any new property or new use for a known substance or of the mere new use of a known process, machine or apparatus unless such known process results in a new product or employs at least one new reactant does not have to be granted a patent. In fact, countries have invoked this flexibility in thwarting attempts by drug companies to seek new patents on existing drugs by simply claiming improvements in their efficacy.

Of these six TRIPS flexibilities, the only one that has attracted much attention is the one on CL. There are no cross-country data on whether and how much of the remaining flexibilities have been inserted into national patent regimes.

In the above, we discussed the notion of TRIPS compliance and the various flexibilities that have been provided in the Agreement. It was believed that all these go toward having a minimum standard for IPR protection across countries. Having this minimum standard of IPR protection is expected to confer two kinds of benefits to firms in developing countries. First, it will encourage them to commit more resources to innovative activity, as a strong IPR regime will reduce considerably, if not plug completely, any possibility of leakages of technology. Second, MNCs will be encouraged to transfer disembodied technologies to unaffiliated firms in the south as these unaffiliated firms, given the existence of a stricter IPR regime, will be discouraged from reverse-engineering the transferred technology and will develop local capabilities. These two 'benefits' were believed to be a product of TRIPS compliance. Although much has been written about TRIPS compliance, its actual effects on spurring these two benefits to developing countries have not attracted any attention. The present study seeks to fill in this gap. And it does so by discussing in detail the cases of four developing countries, Brazil, China, India and Thailand. All these four, as mentioned earlier, have made their IPR regimes TRIPS compliant, have provided for TRIPS flexibilities, and have manufacturing capacities for a range of industries including in pharmaceutical products. Further, moving to a TRIPS compliant regime would have also precipitated a number of changes in a nation's innovation system. We seek to document these changes both at the macro level and at the micro level, at the level of specific industries such as pharmaceuticals, agrochemicals and the automotive industry across the four countries that we have selected for in-depth examination. At this juncture, it is important to raise the fact that the period we consider for our study, the two decades from the beginning of the 1990s, saw extensive economic liberalization and indeed globalization, to which the economies of all the countries were subjected. So some of the changes that we observe, for example an increase in innovative activity, may actually result from the competitive pressures imposed by liberalization measures. Therefore it may be difficult to attribute the observed results to just TRIPS compliance alone. Methodologically, it is almost impossible to separate out the differential impact of various differing measures.

3.   MAIN HYPOTHESES EXAMINED IN THE BOOK

From our discussion it is clear that through a stricter IPR regime, TRIPS is supposed to confer a number of advantages to firms in both developing and developed countries. One of the main advantages is that a stricter IPR regime will encourage firms in general and those in the pharmaceutical industry in particular to commit more resources to innovative activity. This is because of the increased possibility of firms being able to appropriate the full returns to their own innovative efforts emanating from a strong patent regime which has severe legal sanctions against those indulging in copying and imitation. More innovation will pave the way for increasing the availability of a range of drugs, including those dealing with the so called 'neglected tropical diseases' (NTDs) such as malaria, filariasis, leishmaniasis, tuberculosis etc. So the first hypothesis we examine is whether there has been an increase in innovative efforts in general and specifically in the pharmaceutical industry consequent to TRIPS compliance. The second hypothesis, which is actually a corollary of the first, is that TRIPS compliance will increase the attention to research on NTDs. A second advantage that is discussed is that a stricter patent regime will encourage MNCs to license their proprietary technologies of various sorts to unaffiliated firms in developing countries. The increased impetus for this comes from a stricter patent regime reducing considerably the scope of reverse engineering, once again plugging the possibility of technology leaking out. This would be a big boon to firms in emerging economies such as Brazil, China and India, which have traditionally depended on licensing of disembodied technologies as a way of developing their local capability. TRIPS compliance was thought of as a way of encouraging the licensing of technologies by MNCs. So the third hypothesis that we take up for empirical examination is the relationship between TRIPS compliance and technology licensing. In very specific terms, through our country case studies, we seek to find out whether TRIPS compliance is leading to increased technology licensing between MNCs and unaffiliated companies in developing countries. A fourth hypothesis is that TRIPS compliance, by emphasizing the importance of having patents, would bring in some much needed clarity on patenting of traditional knowledge and microorganisms. Wrong issuance of patents for inventions based on traditional knowledge residing with indigenous communities such as tribal peoples was rampant during the pre-TRIPS compliance period. Certain firms were profiting from 'inventing' for the first time curative properties of certain plants and trees, which were already known in traditional knowledge. But patent examiners in far off jurisdictions, being unaware of the existence of such traditional knowledge, more often than not issued patents to companies which claimed to have found this out for the first time. The emphasis on patenting would have encouraged national governments to put in place institutional mechanisms for dealing with such issues. Finally, TRIPS compliance would also have reformed patent offices by increasing both the quality and quantity of patent examiners, by automating them through increased usage of information and communication technologies (ICTs).

All these go towards improving the transparency of patent examination, and effecting significant reductions in the time lag between submission of a patent application and the final decision on whether or not to grant it. We seek to verify these five hypotheses through the country case studies. Within the country cases we also have a verification of these hypotheses across specific industries as well.

4.   ORGANIZATION OF THE BOOK

The book is organized into six chapters, which includes the present one. The next four chapters correspond to the four country cases. In each of the country cases we first discuss the processes through which TRIPS compliance was reached in the respective country. In all the countries this was achieved through amendments to the national patent regime and in some cases, for instance in India, this was preceded by a fierce debate which took place both inside and outside the parliament of the country. Thereafter we survey the more proximate and distant changes to innovative activity in general and the pharmaceutical industry in particular. In the case of India, in addition to the discussion on the pharmaceutical industry, we have a discussion on the agrochemical industry – another important industry that would have been affected by TRIPS. Further, in the case of Thailand we consider the automotive industry, as that industry is very important for the country. So, between the macro and micro discussions, we have a fair idea of the impacts of TRIPS. Before we go on to discuss the details of each of the four country cases, it is important to state that the effects, both positive and negative, of TRIPS are vastly exaggerated. The country case studies have observed that some of the positive benefits that were expected of TRIPS were not forthcoming. For instance, the belief that a stricter patent regime would result in easier licensing of disembodied technologies between MNCs and unaffiliated companies in developing countries does not seem to have been fulfilled. On the other hand, the concern that innovative performance, especially of generic drugs manufacturers, would be negatively affected as a result of TRIPS also does not seem to have been justified.

In the following we attempt a chapter-wide summary of what we have found. For the details, the reader is advised to dip into the specific cases.

In Chapter 2, Caliari, Mazzoleni, and Póvoa discuss the Brazilian case, and present arguments that the TRIPS compliance by the Brazilian patent law in 1996 did not cause significant changes in the innovative behavior of Brazilian industry as a whole. However, it induced some changes that seem to be small today, but have potential to become important in the future.

Since the new patent law there was a significant increase in the share of non-resident patent applications at the Brazilian patent office, the INPI, as well as a change in the profile of patent applications made by non-residents in Brazil. Foreign patents dominate important technological areas, such as chemistry, pharmaceuticals, biotechnology and ICTs. This may represent a strong barrier to the technological development of domestic firms in the future.

The faster and most important changes induced by the TRIPS compliance were related to the new role of universities in the Brazilian system of innovation and to the importance of innovation – and patents as an indicator – in the government policies. First, Brazilian universities are now exploring their potential to generate patentable technologies and become important actors in innovation issues, especially regarding technology transfer. Second, innovation became an essential part of the industrial policy. New laws and plans are designed to enable partnerships between firms and universities and to incentivize innovation in the productive sector. But the government is not yet concerned about the potential barriers patents may represent to technological developments in the future.

Probably one of the sectors that will feel most the impact of TRIPS compliance in the future is the national pharmaceutical industry. So far, it is not possible to say that there has been a negative impact. The start of production of generic medicines in the Brazilian market helped to smooth the expected negative impacts by causing a shift in favor of domestic industry, which has been passing through a period of technological learning and strengthening of its brands. These national companies will enjoy the intense learning acquired with the production of generic products if they try to innovate in a next step. It is then that the negative effects of TRIPS compliance may appear.

In Chapter 3, Mani, Chaudhuri, Unni, Pray and Nagarajan discuss the Indian case. The chapter discusses both the macro implications of TRIPS compliance and its micro implications in the case of two specific industries, pharmaceuticals and agrochemicals.

India's patent regime was made TRIPS compliant in 2005 after a series of three amendments and an intense debate which involved a number of stakeholders. The major facet of the TRIPS compliant patent regime is the recognition of product patents in pharmaceuticals, agrochemicals and food industries. In this chapter the authors analyze in depth the implications of this change in governance rule for innovative activity in India as a whole and the pharmaceutical and agrochemical industries in particular. Of the various flexibilities provided in TRIPS, India has invoked only one, namely the one on compulsory licensing, and that too in the very recent period. The authors find that although patenting has increased from India, most of these patents are secured by foreign firms located in the country. An interesting finding was that the leading information technology firms have started filing for patents at the United States Patent and Trade Mark Office (USPTO) where software patenting is allowed. During this time India has becoming a contracting party to the Patent Cooperation Treaty, thus enabling Indian inventors to patent their inventions in a large number of jurisdictions. The government has also initiated steps to bring utility models within the ambit of its IPR regime so that incremental innovations by small and medium enterprises can be protected. Creation of the Traditional Knowledge Library has enabled India to successfully oppose the granting of patents to inventions based on India's traditional knowledge in other jurisdictions. The expert committee that was appointed to see if microorganisms should be patented has reached the conclusion that they should. There is also some limited evidence to show that research in NTDs has increased in India although this appears to be confined to public research institutes and the research is leading to more publications rather than new drugs. Also, it is less clear whether the domestic pharmaceutical industry is involving itself in this area. Tightening up of the patent regime through TRIPS compliance has not resulted in unaffiliated Indian firms being able to secure foreign technical collaboration agreements on a large scale. However, continued reform of the patent office has made the whole process of patenting more transparent and less time consuming, although the time taken for examination of applications is still high when compared to best practices. TRIPS have allowed pre- and especially post-grant opposition, and patent litigation has shown an increase. More striking are instances of domestic companies litigating against each other and that too in non-pharmaceutical industries.

Their analysis of the post-TRIPS R&D strategies of domestic pharmaceutical firms shows that little has changed to dispute the conventional wisdom that the developing countries should not grant products patent protection. They are already paying the cost of high prices of patent protected products. But the technological benefits claimed have not yet taken place. While R&D activities have diversified, Indian pharmaceutical firms are yet to prove their competence in innovating new products. No 'new chemical entity' (NCE) has yet been developed for marketing. There have been several setbacks and the partnership model has not always worked properly. What Indian companies have really demonstrated is the ability to develop generics – an ability which they acquired and improved during the pre-TRIPS period. Contrary to what was claimed during the TRIPS negotiations, the product patent regime has not prompted Indian companies to devote more resources to developing drugs for neglected diseases that exclusively or predominantly affect developing countries.

There is of course some evidence to show that public agencies in India have started devoting more attention to research on drugs for NTDs. The large Indian pharmaceutical companies, which are the major R&D spenders in the country, have been focusing on the larger and the more lucrative developed-country markets, particularly that of the US. In that regard, the primary incentive to invest in R&D, whether for NCEs, for modifications, or for the development of generics, has not been the new TRIPS-compliant product patent regime in India but the product patent regime in developed countries that was in place well before TRIPS. TRIPS may have accelerated the trend toward such R&D because of the anticipated shrinkage of domestic opportunities. But in the absence of TRIPS, such R&D activities would still have been undertaken. With the larger domestic operations, Indian companies, in fact, would have had access to larger resources and would have been better placed to undertake such R&D.

Another industry considered for in-depth examination is the agrochemicals industry, of which pesticides is an important component. The evidence presented by the authors suggests that compliance with TRIPS has had some positive impact on R&D and innovation in the pesticide industries. Some growth in these indicators would have taken place anyway, driven by liberalization of industrial policy, increased demand for pesticides in India and the increase in pesticide exports, but discussions with industry leaders and the evidence on IPRs, R&D and innovation indicate that stronger IPRs have also had an impact. The impact seems to have been greatest on the MNCs, which have made the most use of pesticide and biotech patents. These companies are investing in major laboratories that are part of their global R&D networks, but they are also building their R&D programs to develop innovations for the Indian market. The changes in patenting and the investments by multinationals also appear to have stimulated more research and innovation by Indian pesticide companies.

Finally, it is seen that most of the alleged positive benefits of TRIPS are exaggerated, while at the same time its negative effects on some fronts are also equally exaggerated. The truth lies in between the two.

In Chapter 4, Intarakumnerd and Charoenporn discuss the Thai case. Their analysis explored the co-evolution of the IPR regime and technological capability of automotive firms in the country. The ensuing analysis showed that there is only a small extent of co-evolution. Other government policies and changes in TNCs' strategies and the market in general are much more important factors shaping technological capability development of firms in the sector. Specifically, they discovered the following. Firstly, there have been some atmospheric changes in terms of an increasing awareness of the importance of patents in the industry after the patent regime became stronger. Secondly, the stronger patent regime has slight impacts on the extent and nature of knowledge transfer between transnational corporations and local part suppliers. It has no obvious impacts on the extent and nature of knowledge transfer between universities and public research institutes on the one hand and firms on the other. Last but not least, the stronger patent regime has impacts on firms climbing up technological ladders from production to more sophisticated activities. To be able to climb up the technological ladders, local latecomer firms need to develop their own 'independent' effort based on active learning in the building up of indigenous technological capabilities and leveraging external sources of knowledge besides their existing production networks, in order to circumvent difficulties partly generated by the stronger patent regime.

In Chapter 5, Song Hong discusses the Chinese case. China made its IPR regime TRIPS compliant in 2000, as it was a precondition for its admittance to the WTO which it joined in 2001. It is interesting to note that China is the only country in our sample that has hardly used any of the TRIPS flexibilities (Table 1.1). By taking the specific case of the Chinese automotive industry, Song Hong shows that TRIPS compliance has actually brought to the fore the importance of patenting among Chinese companies. The result has been a dramatic spurt in patenting, both within China and abroad by Chinese inventors.

Finally, in Chapter 6, we conclude the book by summarizing the main findings from the country case studies. Different facets of TRIPS compliance are drawn from the cases, and they point to the fact that effects of TRIPS are vastly exaggerated. Neither extreme positive nor extreme negative implications of TRIPS have been found. In very specific terms the concluding chapter deals with three issues. The first is how the countries have (or have not) employed the flexibilities in TRIPS, and also other relevant policies they have put in place. This is followed by a discussion of effects on the litigation front. Thereafter we conclude with a section on what has happened to innovation in these countries, and our assessment of the extent to which TRIPS mattered.

NOTES

1. These number about 40.
2. Producers of films, books, and other products protected by copyright, who argued that their work was being copied and sold internationally by infringers in less developed countries, were also active. But in this book we focus on patents and manufacturing.

REFERENCES

Beall, R. and R. Kuhn (2012), 'Trends in compulsory licensing of pharmaceuticals since the Doha Declaration: a database analysis', *PLoS Med*, **9** (1), http://www.plosmedicine.org/article/info:doi/10.1371/journal.pmed.1001154 (accessed March 5, 2013).

Odagiri, Hiroyuki, Akira Goto, Atsushi Sunami and Richard R. Nelson (eds) (2010), *Intellectual Property Rights, Development and Catch-up: An International Comparative Study*, New York: Oxford University Press.

2. Innovation in the pharmaceutical industry in Brazil post-TRIPS

Thiago Caliari, Roberto Mazzoleni and Luciano Martins Costa Póvoa

1. INTRODUCTION

Although intellectual property rights, such as patents, have been recognized in Brazil since the early nineteenth century, they played a very modest role in the economic development of the country. Industrial policies of import substitution between the 1950s and 1980s and high inflation produced a diversified industry, but with little incentive to innovate.

However, IPR may become more important given the new economic context of the country. In the 1990s structural and macroeconomic changes occurred, including the opening of the market, inflation control and institutional reforms such as privatization. In the 2000s there was a significant economic growth associated with reduction in income inequality that has expanded the consumer demand. All these factors contributed to attracting FDI. On the other hand, the increase in the international prices of commodities contributed to the appreciation of the real, leading the country to experience the 'Dutch disease'. This fact contributed to raise the debate on the premature process of de-industrialization which Brazil is going through. Industry, which represented 22 per cent of GDP in the 1970s, represented only 14 per cent in 2011.

It was precisely in the early formation of this new economic context that Brazil passed a TRIPS compliance patent law in 1996. What are the effects of a stronger IPR regime on the innovative behavior in this new context? Our results suggest that it is not possible to state that the TRIPS compliance has hindered innovation in Brazil. But we argue that patents will represent technological barriers to indigenous firms in industrial sectors like pharmaceuticals. For example, before the new patent law, there was an exclusion of patentability for pharmaceutical products and processes, and now more than 90 per cent of patent applications in this sector in the Brazilian Patent Office – INPI – are made by non-residents.

This chapter assesses the effects of TRIPS on patent trends and on innovation, and the prospects for innovation in Brazil, with special attention to the pharmaceutical sector. In Section 2 we present an analysis of the changes in the Brazilian IPR legislation, with special attention to those concerned with drugs. Section 3 describes the main institutional and policy changes involving IPR. Trends in patenting patterns (from residents and non-residents, main technologies affected etc.) as well as in FDI and royalties and licenses payments after TRIPS compliance are the object of Section 4. Sections 5 and 6 present the analysis of a stronger IPR on innovative behavior in the pharmaceutical sector. Section 7 presents the most important patent litigation episodes since TRIPS compliance and Section 8 concludes.

2.   CHANGES IN THE PATENT LAW DUE TO TRIPS

The protection of the rights of inventors has a long history in Brazil. Already in 1809, inventors and adopters of foreign technology could be granted exclusive privileges, and Brazil's first patent law was approved in 1830, shortly after the country's independence from Portugal. In 1882, the law was reformed in order to comply with the principles of the Paris Convention that Brazil signed in 1883. Further reforms followed in 1923, 1945 and 1969. An important aspect of the 1945 changes in the national patent laws was the creation of statutory exclusions of patentability for inventions relating to chemical products, food and pharmaceutical products. Inventions related to pharmaceutical processes were added to this list in 1969.

Key motivations for these reforms were the government's concern for public health needs and its desire to preserve and promote the indigenous production of pharmaceutical drugs. With respect to the latter, we note that Brazil's pharmaceutical industry was struggling to keep pace with the technological advances that occurred abroad since the 1930s and 1940s. Over the following decades, however, the exclusion of patentability for pharmaceutical products proved to be insufficient to promote a robust technological effort by local firms (Mazzoleni and Póvoa, 2010). It is for this reason that the exclusion of patentability was extended to pharmaceutical processes in 1969.

This weakening of intellectual property protection had important repercussions for Brazil's trade relationships, particularly with the US. Already in 1987 the Pharmaceutical Manufacturing Association filed a case with the United States Trade Representative complaining about Brazil's lack of patent protection for pharmaceuticals. Under the provisions of Section

301 of the Trade Act of 1974, the US government imposed retaliatory tariffs equal to 100 per cent of price on a variety of imports from Brazil. While the Brazilian government filed a complaint under GATT rules, the US complaint was withdrawn in 1990 as a result of an agreement between the USTR and representatives of the upcoming administration of President Fernando Collor. According to this agreement, the US would withdraw the sanctions in exchange for Brazil's commitment to reforming its patent laws in such a way as to strengthen the protection offered to inventors, and to provide intellectual property rights protection on pharmaceuticals, biotechnology processes and microorganisms.

The new patent bill sponsored by the Collor administration was submitted to Brazil's Chamber of Deputies in April 1991 (Bill 824/91). Beside doing away with the exclusions of patentability for the classes of inventions mentioned above, the bill proposed other changes, ranging from a longer period of patent validity (20 years rather than 15), to the inversion of the burden of proof in infringement cases (from plaintiff to defendant). The bill included also 'pipeline' provisions according to which patents could be granted for pharmaceutical and other inventions made before the new patent law comes into effect (Hathaway, 1993).

An amended version of the bill was approved by the Chamber of Deputies on June 2, 1993, and introduced in the Senate as Bill 115/93. The examination and revision of the bill dragged on for several years, during which Brazil's Senate approved Brazil's adhesion to the WTO treaty and the TRIPS agreement. The TRIPS agreement came into effect on January 1, 1995. According to the treaty, Brazil had five years to comply with the treaty's general provisions and ten years to begin offering IPRs for pharmaceuticals and other classes of inventions that were previously excluded from patentability under national law (TRIPS, Part VI, Art. 65). However, there was sufficient support for the reform of the country's patent laws that Congress approved a final version of the bill and Brazil's new president, Fernando Henrique Cardoso, signed into Law 9.279 on May 14, 1996.

The reform of Brazil's patent laws was the culmination of a legislative process that began in the context of bilateral trade negotiations with the US government. GATT and WTO rules, and the TRIPS agreement, informed the process and – in the case of TRIPS – influenced some specific aspects of the new patent law (see Table 2.1 for the last major changes in the patent law). We examine these aspects below. First, however, we wish to note that Brazil did not take full advantage of the implementation flexibilities of the TRIPS agreement because a sufficiently broad coalition of political forces emerged – including the administration headed by three presidents (Collor, Franco, and Cardoso) – which considered patent law

Table 2.1   Last major changes in the Brazilian Patent Law

	Patent Law no. 5,772 (1971)	Patent Law no. 9,279 (1996)	Amendment Law 10,196 (2001)
Reasons	1. Government concern for public health needs 2. Desire to preserve and promote the indigenous production of pharmaceutical drugs	1. Agreement with USTR to solve questions related to section 301 of Trade Act of 1974 2. To comply with TRIPS 3. Restore the confidence of international investors	1. Government concern for public health needs
Major changes	Extended the exclusion of patentability to pharmaceutical processes (included in the Decree n. 1,005 of 1969).	1. Extended patent validity from 15 to 20 years 2. Expanded scope of protection 3. Modification of the requisites for compulsory licenses (e.g. included explicitly cases of abuse of economic power and national emergency) 4. Inversion of the burden of proof in infringement cases (from plaintiff to defendant)	1. Included the requirement of previous analysis by ANVISA for patents related to pharmaceutical products and processes 2. Changed some aspects of the pipeline provision 3. Introduced the Bolar Exemption

Source: Authors' elaboration.

reform an essential part of a comprehensive plan of economic reforms whose objective was to control inflation, restore the confidence of international investors and promote greater foreign direct investment into the country.

To be sure, several actors among political parties and civil society organizations (unions, the Church, NGOs, professional and scientific associations, etc.) opposed the reform bill 824/91. Provisions related to the patentability of biotechnologies and living organisms such as plants and animals were especially contentious because of their ambiguity. In fact, while the bill prohibited the granting of patents on natural living beings and biological material found in nature, the exact scope of the restriction was ambiguous as there was no clearly defined standard for determining when a living being is not natural. Moreover, the restriction did not include microorganisms that can be used for a specific process in order to generate a specific product, making it possible – opponents of the bill argued – for the holder of patent rights on a microorganism to establish de facto control over transgenic plants or animals.

While the opposition to the reform bill was not altogether successful, the bill that was signed into Law No.9.272 did contain a variety of provisions that addressed at least some of the concerns expressed by the opponents of the early draft of the reform bill. Many of these provisions exploited the so-called TRIPS flexibilities, opportunities for the signatories of the WTO treaty and the TRIPS agreement to exercise discretion in the design of their domestic patent system. Brazil chose not to benefit from the transition period contemplated in Art. 65 of the TRIPS agreement. However, on many other aspects of the IPR regime, Brazil did in fact exploit such flexibilities, and in a few cases it adopted rules of patent law that might be in conflict with its obligations under TRIPS. We review these features of the new patent law in the following paragraphs.

The law reserves generally to the inventor the right to file for patent protection. The standards of patentability include the requirement of novelty, inventive activity, and industrial application. Practical objects having a new form or shape can receive protection as utility models as long as they represent a functional improvement in the use or manufacture of the object. The law excludes from patentability a well defined set of things that are not inventions (Art. 10) and a set of inventions (Art. 18). The former set includes discoveries, scientific theories, mathematical methods, computer programs as such, business methods, medical and surgical methods, therapeutic and diagnostic methods for use in humans and animals, as well as natural living organisms, biological material (when found in nature or isolated therefrom, including genome and germplasm), and biological processes. The latter set includes: (a) inventions contrary to morals and good customs, as well as to public security, order, and health; (b) inventions that were achieved by manipulating the atomic nucleus; and (c) living organisms in whole or part except for transgenic microorganisms that meet the patentability requirements of novelty, inventiveness, and usefulness, and that are not mere discoveries. Microorganisms are defined as organisms, except for the whole or part of plants and animals, which – because of human intervention on their genetic composition – display characteristics not found in the corresponding species in natural conditions.

According to the TRIPS agreement, pharmaceutical inventions could not be excluded from the definition of patentable subject matter. Developing countries where pharmaceutical inventions could not be patented previously, were given time until January 1, 2005, in order to bring their patent system into line with TRIPS obligations. Moreover, these countries were asked to create a 'mailbox' where patent applications for pharmaceutical inventions could be deposited from January 1, 2000. After January 1, 2005, patents could be granted on these applications as long as they satisfied all other criteria of patentability and had not been already commercialized in the country by the inventor or their licensees. The patents on mailbox applications would be assigned an expiration date corresponding to the end of a twenty-year period since the date of invention.

Brazil did not avail itself of the right to a ten-year transition period, and extended the patent privilege to pharmaceutical inventions since May 15, 1997. Moreover, the patent reform included 'pipeline' provisions (Art. 230 and Art. 231) allowing domestic and foreign inventors of pharmaceutical products and processes to submit patent applications since May 14, 1996, for inventions made at an earlier date that had not yet been commercialized, or for whose commercialization no investments had been made by domestic firms. This pipeline provision was crafted on the assumption that the patentability standards of the new law would only apply to patent applications filed after May 14, 1996. Applications filed before that date were argued to be subject to the patentability standards of the 1971 law.[1]

These transitional arrangements were modified retroactively by executive decrees (Provisional Measures) signed by President Cardoso in 1999 and 2000, and later approved by Brazil's Congress as Law 10.196 of February 14, 2001. Key amendments of the 1996 law concerned the pipeline provisions laid out in Article 229. First, Law 10.196 denied all patent applications on pharmaceutical products and processes filed before January 1, 1995. Second, it denied all patent applications on pharmaceutical processes filed between January 1, 1995, and May 15, 1997. Third, it granted the status of pipeline applications to all patent applications concerned with inventions related to pharmaceutical products and chemical products related to agriculture, filed between January 1, 1995, and May 15, 1997, in accordance with the pipeline provisions of articles 230 and 231. The start date of the pipeline was pushed back to the date when the TRIPS agreement became effective in Brazil. Beside the pipeline provisions, Law 10.196 (Art. 229-C) also introduced a further requirement for patentability of inventions related to pharmaceutical products and processes. Patents on such inventions could only be granted with the prior consent of ANVISA (National Health Surveillance Agency), a regulatory agency of the Department of Health established in 1999.

The law did not clarify the criteria according to which ANVISA would give or withhold its consent, so this provision of the law occasioned a prolonged jurisdictional conflict between INPI and ANVISA regarding the scope of the latter's authority. Since ANVISA has carried out its mandate by evaluating whether or not the inventions fulfill all requirements for patentability, INPI filed a request with the Attorney General in 2007 requesting that the scope of ANVISA's review of patent applications be clarified in order to avoid duplications and conflicts. The opinion rendered by the Attorney General on October 6, 2010, would limit ANVISA's review to public health considerations.

The jurisdictional conflict between the two agencies was complicated further by the fact that INPI and ANVISA clashed over the interpretation of the patentability standards with respect to various classes of pharmaceutical invention. In particular, whereas INPI has endorsed a narrow view of patentability standards, and approved applications for second and subsequent uses of existing drugs, ANVISA has taken the opposite view and denied its 'prior consent' to these applications. The examination of the applications rejected by ANVISA suggests further that prior consent was denied for patent applications that failed to provide adequate disclosures for inventions representing claims from Markush groups and polymorphs (Basso, 2005). In August 2004 ANVISA declared that claims for second and subsequent uses of existing compounds failed patentability standards, and that granting such patents would represent a grave threat for people's access to medicines, and thus a danger for public health.

By denying ANVISA's jurisdiction over the evaluation of patentability standards, the 2010 decision of the Attorney General can be expected to lead to a regime distinctly more favorable to foreign pharmaceutical firms whose innovative record has been dominated of late by the sorts of innovations for which ANVISA was ready to deny protection. As discussed later in the chapter, decisions regarding the patentability of various classes of pharmaceutical inventions (second uses, polymorphs etc.) has important consequences for the development of a domestic industry focusing on generic versions of branded drugs.

While a thorough discussion of this matter is left to a later section of the chapter, we note here that other key legislative developments accompanied the evolution of the patent laws and policy described above. In particular, we note that ANVISA was established in 1999 as a result of Law No. 9.782 of January 26th, 1999. Within a few days, Brazil's Congress modified the regulatory framework within which the commercialization of medicinal drugs takes place. The Generic Medicines Law (No. 9.787 of February

10th, 1999) formally established the class of generic medicines, as distinct from similar ones, and assigned to ANVISA the task of developing the regulatory process designed to establish the efficacy, safety and quality of generic drugs. The creation of a regulatory framework for the development of a generic industry was accompanied by an amendment to the 1996 Patent Law (Art. 43-VII) exempting from the scope of the rights of patent holders the right to prevent non-authorized uses of patented inventions when the objective of such activities is to apply in a timely fashion for regulatory approval of the commercialization of a generic medicinal drug (so called Bolar Exemption).

The creation of a market for generic drugs was enabled not only by the creation of the appropriate regulatory framework, but also by the legislative mandate that the public Unified Health System (Sistema Unico de Saude, or SUS) should procure needed medicines under their generic name, and should acquire generic versions of the drugs when these are available at prices no greater than corresponding branded products. The preference for generics responded to the twin goals of promoting the development of indigenous technological capabilities in the pharmaceutical sector, and of reducing the cost of the public health programs whereby many Brazilians have access to medicinal drugs.

One of the most visible among these programs focuses on the treatment of the population living with HIV/AIDS. While this kind of program was first implemented in the State of Sao Paulo during the 1980s, since 1991 Brazil's federal government began distributing the first anti-retroviral drug (zinovudine, or AZT) to people living with HIV/AIDS. With the approval of Law 9.313 in 1996, Brazil's government launched a program offering free universal Highly Active Anti-Retroviral Treatment (HAART) to all people living with HIV/AIDS. During the early years of the program, the first-line treatment offered to most people consisted of drugs that were not protected by patents in Brazil or in other countries. This made it possible for generic (non-licensed) versions to be used, whether imported or produced domestically. Later on, the need to provide second- and third-line treatment options to a growing number of people interacted with the onset of the new patent regime to produce significant increases in the cost of the treatment program.

The threat of rapidly escalating cost of purchasing the needed anti-retroviral drugs from the patent-holding multinational firms led Brazil's government to exploit the so-called TRIPS flexibilities in order to realize substantial procurement cost savings. Such savings resulted in some cases from the use of generic versions of ARV drugs produced domestically or imported, and in others from discounts agreed to by patent-holding multinational firms and their licensees when confronted by a credible threat that the Brazilian government could grant compulsory licenses on the relevant patents. Indeed, the effectiveness of these threats calls our attention to a few controversial aspects of Brazil's patent law, namely its treatment of compulsory licenses and the continuing enforcement of a working requirement.

Circumstances leading to the issuing of compulsory licenses on a patent are laid out in Art. 68, 70, and 71. They include the exploitation of patents in an abusive manner (Art. 68), the non-exploitation of the subject matter of a patent within the territory of Brazil (Art. 68, §1-I), commercialization that does not meet the needs of the market (Art. 68, §1-II), and cases of national emergency or public interest when the patentee or its licensee does not meet such necessity (Art. 71). The rules for granting compulsory licenses in cases of national emergency or public interest were laid out in a presidential decree issued in 1999 and amended in 2003. The latter version of the decree establishes among other things that the titleholder might be obligated to assist the assignees of the compulsory licenses. The government will resort to imports of the relevant product whenever it will prove impossible to address the emergency or the public interest with products manufactured domestically by private or public sector organizations.

The Brazilian government's threat of granting compulsory licenses on certain pharmaceutical patents has always been supported by the argument that the AIDS pandemic does represent a national emergency that is not adequately addressed by the pharmaceutical companies. This interpretation of the law is consistent with the Doha Declaration. Although Brazil's government has repeatedly brandished the threat of a compulsory license in order to obtain discounts from multinational firms, the threat was ultimately carried out for the first time in 2007 when negotiations with Merck over the price of the drug Efavirenz failed.

3. MAIN INSTITUTIONAL AND POLICY CHANGES RELATED TO IPR AND INNOVATION

Before turning our attention in the following section to the broad patterns of patenting activity and innovation on the eve of Brazil's signing of the TRIPS agreement and of the multifaceted changes in the IPR regime that followed, we think it is important to comment on the radical transformation that has occurred in the country's handling of IPR matters. In fact, whereas the reform of patent law was occasioned by trade frictions and US external pressures, a key characteristic of the reform of Brazil's IPR regime is that it has exceeded TRIPS obligations along many dimensions. It is not so much a question of failing to exploit TRIPS flexibilities in designing specific features of the patents system. Brazil did exploit such flexibilities, and has been perhaps one of the developing countries that most aggressively sought clarifications and changes in the spirit of the TRIPS agreement that appear to benefit the developing countries. But at the same time, Brazil has created other components of the broader IPR system that were not mandated by its adherence to the TRIPS agreement.

These events signal a broad convergence toward the viewpoint that generally speaking IPRs can exert a positive influence on the country's innovative performance, and that promoting innovation is an important (perhaps central) aspect of modern industrial and development policies. We note in particular that after the reform of its patent system, Brazil moved on to design an institutional framework aimed at tying academic and public sector research more closely with industrial innovation.

The building blocks of this infrastructure are Decree No. 2.553 of April 16, 1998, and the Law of Innovation (No. 10.973) of December 2004. The former sanctioned the principle that employees of public sector institutions (thus including researchers in public universities and research institutions) ought to receive a share of the royalty income generated by patents on their inventions. With the latter, the government created the framework for greater support to innovative activities carried out by public and private sector entities, alone or in collaboration with each other. An important aspect of the law consists of the articulation of the framework for various forms of research collaborations between private firms and universities or public research organizations, including the transfer to industry of technologies created by scientists in the academic and public research sectors.

The importance attributed to IPRs as an institution regulating these forms of collaboration is borne out by the legislative mandate that all public institutions involved in scientific and technological research would have to establish an administrative unit (nucleus of technological innovation – NIT) responsible for managing their innovation policy. The creation, management, and licensing of IPRs on inventions for the purpose of facilitating the transfer of technology to industry is the most prominent responsibility of these nuclei.

In addition to the stimulus of university–industry cooperation, the Law of Innovation also created a new instrument allowing the government to use non refundable grants to private R&D called economic subvention. This innovation policy instrument consists in a sharing of the risks between government and firms conducting projects to develop innovative products or processes.

The administration of President Lula (2003–10) recovered the industrial policy by launching the Industrial, Technology, and Foreign Trade Policy (PITCE) in 2004. One of the main focuses of this policy was to increase competitiveness through incentives to improve the innovation capacity of Brazilian firms. The diagnosis of the weak innovative capability by that time was based on the first results of the PINTEC (national survey of technological innovation) indicating a relatively low rate of innovation – discussed in more detail in the next section – and on the small number of Brazilian patents at the USPTO – only 332 in 2002–04. In the last decade, patents became one of the main indicators that policy makers, analysts, scholars and the government used to show the innovative weakness of national firms. Therefore, patents are respected and their increase is considered as a target in government plans.

Innovation became the main point in the policies elaborated by the Ministry of Science, Technology, and Innovation – the word 'innovation' was added at the end of 2011 – and the Ministry of Industry, Development and Foreign Trade.

Another institutional effect of the importance that patents have been achieving is present in the new Antitrust Law (no. 12.529) of 2011, which includes among the infractions of the economic order to 'exercise or abusively exploit industrial and intellectual property rights, technology or brand'. The former antitrust law (from 1994) did not have this concern.

The dissemination to the culture of using IPR is carried out by the Brazilian Patent Office (INPI). Over the last decade, INPI established a strong policy in training on IPR matters with courses and seminars around the country and a Master's degree program on intellectual property and innovation. The administration of INPI was reformulated to gain in efficiency and improved its information systems. All these factors have contributed to make INPI a stronger agency, recognized as an important part of the Brazilian innovation system.

It can be seen that from the viewpoint of the role of IPRs in the process of innovation, the convergence between Brazil's legislative framework and that of the US and other advanced economies has been broader than an exclusive emphasis on TRIPS would suggest. The following section traces the broad characteristics of the changes in Brazil's innovative performance wrought by these legislative changes.

4.   MACRO-TRENDS AFTER TRIPS COMPLIANCE

This section presents the evolution of some important variables, especially FDI, patent applications, royalties and technology licenses, in order to evaluate the effects of a more restrictive IPR law. After the analysis of

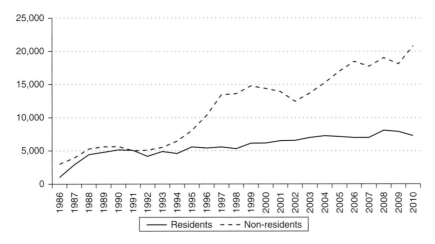

Source: Authors' elaboration based on INPI data.

Figure 2.1   *Patent applications in Brazil by residents and non-residents:*
1986–2010

these macro-trends we present the micro-trends for pharmaceuticals and
seeds industries in the next section.

Two facts limit our analysis. First, the time span of some variables
is restricted and will not allow more than speculation about the trend.
Second, and perhaps more important, it is not possible to separate the
effects of TRIPS from others, like inflation control, economic growth,
and exchange rate fluctuations. Therefore, our analysis intends only to
highlight trends and aspects that should be evaluated in more detail in
future studies.

4.1   Patent Applications at the Brazilian Patent Office – INPI

Figure 2.1 presents the evolution of patent applications in Brazil by residents and non-residents before and after TRIPS compliance. It is possible
to draw two important facts from this data.

First, from 1986 to 1996, the numbers of patent applications by residents
and non-residents were similar. During this period, the means of resident
and non-resident applications were 4,335 and 5,803 respectively. But, from
1997 to 2007, the difference between resident and non-resident applications
increased, reaching a mean of 6,493 and 14,961 respectively. Before TRIPS
compliance, non-resident patent applications accounted for 54 per cent of
total applications at INPI. Immediately after, they rose to 70 per cent.

Clearly, the 1996 Patent Law induced different patterns.[2] It seems to have modified only non-residents' behavior towards protecting inventions in Brazil, while residents' applications continued to present a slow and steady growth. If a stronger IPR regime is supposed to induce innovation, it is not possible to verify this causality for residents, nor for local multinationals' subsidiaries, since most non-resident applications are made via Patent Cooperation Treaty (the share of non-resident PCT patents presents a steady growth, from 63 per cent in 1997 to 86 per cent in 2006).

Second, the boom of non-resident patent applications started a couple of years before the legal effects of the 1996 Patent Law (starting in May 1997), probably due to positive expectations about the approval of the Law, inflation stability and, in minor extension, because of the 'pipeline' provisions, as discussed in the previous section.

On the other hand, it is possible to verify a major shift in the composition of patent applications by residents. The Brazilian Patent Law provides protection for utility models, and over several years residents had a higher proportion of patent applications in utility models. However, as shown in Figure 2.2, there has been a significant drop in participation of this type of invention by residents.

Throughout the 1990s, on average, 52 per cent of patent filings by residents were related to utility models. However, in 2000 this value showed a systematic decline, falling to 40.5 per cent in 2010. That is, patent applications related to priority of invention have grown, which suggests that

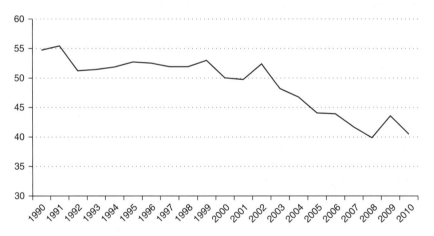

Source: Authors' elaboration based on INPI data.

Figure 2.2   *Utility models in patent applications in Brazil by residents: 1986–2010 (%)*

the inventive content of the patent may be becoming more complex. This changing profile of patent applications by residents is related more to ST&I policies in the first decade of 2000 than to TRIPS.

Most patent applications by residents are made by individuals, which demonstrates the performance fragility of firms in the Brazilian system of innovation. According to Albuquerque et al. (2011), the share of firms in patent applications by residents increased from 34 per cent in 1990–99 to 38 per cent in 2000–05.

Albuquerque et al. (2011) analyzed the patent applications at the INPI conducted between 1980 and 2005. The authors classified the patent applications by residents and non residents in accordance with technological sub domains. According to the authors, there is no significant change in the types of technology from 1980 to 2005. This result shows the Brazilian technological stagnation, concentrated on simpler technologies and with a static structure. Technological areas benefited by the TRIPS agreement, such as biotechnology, pharmaceuticals, agricultural products and food, did not show relevant changes in the period. Therefore, the TRIPS compliance did not change the technological profile of patent applications in the country.

Thus, the hypothesis that a strong IPR regime would promote more inventions by indigenous firms and individuals or by local multinational firms is not confirmed in general terms.

However, the 1996 Patent Law did induce inventions by two important agents of the Brazilian system of innovation: universities and public research institutions. The Law allowed these agents to patent results of research related to chemistry, pharmaceuticals, and biotechnology. As discussed in the previous section, it represented a window of opportunity for universities and public research institutions to try to earn more financial resources by promoting technology transfer offices.

The relevance of patenting activity by these agents in Brazil after TRIPS compliance is remarkable (see Póvoa, 2010 for details). According to INPI (2011), among the top 20 patent applicants resident in Brazil between 2004 and 2008, there are seven universities (UNICAMP, USP, UFMG, UFRJ, UFPR, UFSC and UFRGS), two public research institutions (EMBRAPA and Center of Nuclear Technology Development) and two public agencies for research support (FAPESP and FAPEMIG – in fact they are co-owners with universities).[3] In other words, half of the major patent applications by residents in Brazil are related to teaching and research. This fact places the universities and public research institutions in a prominent position in the Brazilian innovation system, which can hardly be achieved in other developing countries. In addition, the second and third places on the list are occupied by two universities (UNICAMP and USP), just behind the largest Brazilian company, Petrobras.

Albuquerque (2003) argues that if on one hand we can observe the effect of universities and research institutions in patentable knowledge production, on the other hand the good position of Brazilian universities may not represent a virtue of universities, but a weakness of the productive sector. Indeed, the TRIPS compliance placed these institutions in a strategic position in the national innovation system because most researchers in Brazil work at universities and public research institutions and Brazil has a long tradition in research in health sciences, chemistry and agricultural science.

The strength of these institutions is evident for some important technology fields. Brazilian universities and public research institutions made only 3.1 per cent of total patent applications by residents between 2000 and 2005. However, when we classify the applications by technology field[4] we can see that these institutions generated 68 per cent of applications in organic chemistry, 62 per cent in biotechnology, 38 per cent in nuclear techniques, 31 per cent in semiconductors, and 20 per cent in pharmaceuticals-cosmetics. Therefore, Brazil depends heavily on universities and public research institutions in important technology fields that are crucial for the catch-up process. This is the reason why the Innovation Law and the industrial policy emphasize the university–industry cooperation as an important means to promote innovation in Brazil.

Table 2.2 presents patent applications at INPI by residents and non-residents classified according to the Observatoire des Sciences et des Techniques (OST).[5] The data shows that most of the important technology fields (especially science-based ones) are dominated by non-resident applications. This fact represents a potential technological barrier in the future for domestic firms that plan to enter in more sophisticated R&D plans.

Considering patent applications in the pharmaceutical field in Brazil after the 1996 Patent Law, there is an impressive predominance of non-resident applicants. Only 6.3 per cent of patent applications in the area of pharmaceuticals-cosmetics were carried out by residents in the period 2000–05. Furthermore, Suster (2009) points out that it is not possible to verify a growing tendency by domestic firms in this area.

According to Albuquerque et al. (2011), 16.9 per cent of all non-resident applications in Brazil between 2000 and 2005 were related to pharmaceuticals-cosmetics.

4.2   Royalties and Licenses, and Foreign Direct Investments (FDI)

The movements in the Brazilian expenditures in royalties and licenses appear to be more connected to the variations in the exchange rate and economic growth than to stronger IPR.

Table 2.2   *Relative share of patent applications from residents and non-residents at INPI, selected OST technology areas, 2000–05*

OST technology area	Non-residents (%)	Residents (%)	Patent applications (total)
Non-residents' advantage			
Organic fine chemistry	97.7	2.3	14,157
Pharmaceuticals, cosmetics	93.7	6.3	3,730
Macromolecular chemistry, polymers	92.6	7.4	1,882
Biotechnology	91.1	8.9	4,644
Basic materials chemistry	87.4	12.6	5,190
Telecommunications	87.0	13.0	218
Semiconductors	84.6	15.4	3,175
Information technology	84.5	15.5	1,984
Surface technology, coating	84.2	15.8	2,773
Residents' advantage			
Handling, printing	47.4	52.6	1,984
Thermal processes and apparatus	42.9	57.1	2,773
Civil engineering, building, mining	36.8	63.2	814
Agricultural machinery and apparatus	31.7	68.3	4,465
Consumer goods and equipment	25.8	74.2	4,446

Source: Adapted from Albuquerque et al. (2011).

In 1994, the implementation of the Real Plan finished the process of hyperinflation that had lasted nearly two decades. Immediately, the currency – real – appreciated, causing a surge of imports of consumer and capital goods, and facilitated the acquisition of external technologies. Figure 2.3 shows that until 1998 there was an intense growth of payments of royalties and licenses. By the end of 1998 Brazil experienced an international speculative attack that forced the government to adopt a floating exchange rate in early 1999, followed by a large devaluation of the real that followed until 2004. Increased global demand for Brazilian commodities led to a new appreciation of the real. These exchange rate movements and economic growth in the last decade explain most of the fluctuations observed in Figure 2.3.

Figure 2.4 details the Brazilian expenditures on technology transfer agreements. Although the expenditures associated to the use of patents grew between 2000 and 2009, they represented less than 10 per cent of the total of expenditures on technology transfer. The main cause of the growth of spending on technology transfer was the payments related to

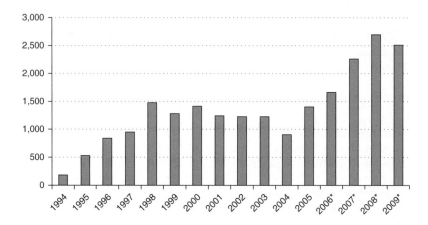

Note: Obs.: (*) Preliminary data.

Source: Brazilian Central Bank.

Figure 2.3 Royalties and licenses expenditures (U$ million): 1994–2009

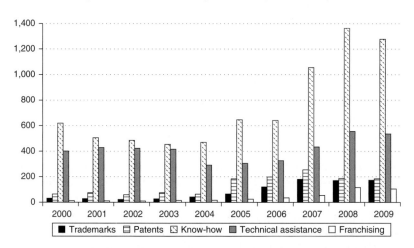

Source: Brazilian Central Bank.

Figure 2.4 Technology transfer expenditures (U$ million): 2000–09

know-how. This reflects the fact that Brazilian industry is in an intermediate stage of technology development.

Advocates of a stronger patent law argue that it would create a better institutional environment and induce more FDI. However, as pointed

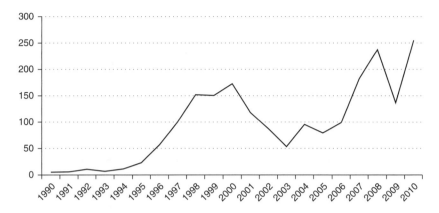

Source: Brazilian Central Bank.

Figure 2.5 Index of foreign direct investments in Brazil: 1990–2010 (1997 = 100)

by Maskus (2005), several factors affect FDI, like political stability and economic growth.

In the Brazilian case, there was a remarkable growth in FDI after the economic stabilization occurred in 1994. The control of inflation after two decades, a stabilized exchange rate, and a massive program of privatizations occurred almost at the same time as the 1996 Patent Law. All these factors contributed to the increase in FDI at the end of the 1990s, but the patrimonial change due to privatizations (telecommunications and mining are representative cases) was the most important for the cycle that ended at the beginning of 2000 (Figure 2.5). The inflow of FDI started again after 2006, mainly due to the good economic performance.

4.3 Innovation

One of the theoretical bases for the existence of patents is that they serve as an incentive for innovation. It is difficult to analyze the relationship between intellectual property and innovation, particularly because of the lack of a historical series of data on rate of innovation. Since 2000, the IBGE – Brazilian Institute of Geography and Statistics – has performed a survey of technological innovation – PINTEC – which provides important data for the study of innovation in Brazil. It is a three-year (except 2005) sample survey (2000, 2003, 2005 and 2008) and is based on the methodology presented in the Oslo Manual. Data from each PINTEC refers to the last three years, including the reference year of the survey. For example,

Table 2.3   Innovation rates in manufacturing industry by type – % of total firms, 1998–2000 through 2006–08

	1998–2000	2001–03	2003–05	2006–08
Innovation rate	31.9	33.5	33.6	38.1
Product innovation	17.9	20.7	19.8	22.9
new to the national market	*4.2*	*2.8*	*3.3*	*4.1*
Process innovation	25.4	27.0	27.0	32.0
new to the national market	*2.8*	*1.2*	*1.7*	*2.4*

Source: PINTEC (several issues). Obs.: CNAE 1.0.

PINTEC 2000 presents data on innovation in firms in the 1998–2000 period.

Thus, Brazil has innovation data only for the period subsequent to TRIPS, which makes impossible a before–after comparison. What is presented below is a brief analysis of the evolution of the rate of innovation – innovative firms as a percentage of total enterprises – and the main innovative activities carried out by Brazilian firms, although without assessing the impact of TRIPS on this variable.

The rate of industrial innovation is presented in Table 2.3. The data shows that the rate of innovation has increased over ten years, from 31.9 per cent in the period 1998–2000 to 38.1 per cent in the 2006–08 period. The rate of innovation of Brazilian firms is similar to those observed in Italy and Spain. According to data from the Community Innovation Survey 2006 (Eurostat, 2010), about one in three firms in these countries is innovative.

However, the type of innovation conducted by Brazilian firms is different from that of more developed countries. For example, only 4.1 per cent of Brazilian companies realized a product innovation that was new for the domestic market between 2006 and 2008, which is less than half the percentage observed in Spain.

The rate of innovation of Brazilian firms reflects the low value of the expenditure in intramural R&D (0.62 per cent of total turnover in 2008). Considering the total expenditures in innovative activities – 2.5 per cent of total turnover in 2008 – we notice that 52 per cent is concentrated in expenditure for acquisition of machinery, equipment and software and only 24.4 per cent in expenditure on intramural R&D. These values have not changed much since 2000. That is, these data reinforce the conclusion that Brazilian industry is characterized by low and medium technology.

Table 2.4 shows data of innovative firms with patent applications in the 2006–08 period by manufacturing sector, as well as the rate of innovation in each sector. On average, only 7.3 per cent of manufacturing companies

Table 2.4   *Innovative firms with patent applications by manufacturing sectors (PINTEC – 2008)*

Manufacturing sectors	Total of firms	Innovators	Innovation rate	Innovators with patent applications	(%)
Motor vehicles, trailers and semi-trailers	36	30	83.3	11	36.7
Beverages	889	308	34.6	85	27.6
Electrical equipment	1,938	900	46.4	196	21.8
Machinery and equipment	5,551	2,831	51.0	600	21.2
Tobacco products	62	16	25.8	3	18.8
Rubber and plastics products	6,461	2,342	36.2	370	15.8
Repair and installation of machinery and equipment	2,343	608	25.9	94	15.5
Coke and biofuels	286	94	32.9	14	14.9
Basic pharmaceutical products and preparations	495	315	63.6	46	14.6
Coke, refined petroleum products, and biofuels	204	131	64.2	19	14.5
Petroleum refining	82	37	45.1	5	13.5
Other	80,073	30,196	37.7	1,340	4.4
Mean			38.4		7.3

Source: Authors' elaboration based on PINTEC 2008. Obs.: CNAE 2.0.

made patent applications in the period. However, there is great variability among the sectors. We highlight firms in the sector of manufacture of motor vehicles, trailers and semi-trailers – dominated by multinationals – with 36.7 per cent of innovative firms with patent applications and the highest rate of innovation (83.3 per cent), followed by manufacture of beverages sector with 27.6 per cent of innovating firms with patent applications, but with an innovation rate below the national average (34.6 per cent). This shows that there is not always a close correlation between innovation and patent.

Another sector that stands out is the manufacture of basic pharmaceutical products and preparations, featuring 315 innovative firms, of which only 46 made patent applications (14.6 per cent). This percentage, despite being twice the mean in Brazil, is low compared to that expected for a sector that gives more importance to patents as a protection to innovations than the average. Paradoxically, it is among the sectors with the highest rate of innovation (63.6 per cent). This data suggests that the pharmaceutical sector in Brazil performs a very simple type of innovation. This fact will be discussed in the next section.

5.   THE PHARMACEUTICAL INDUSTRY

5.1   Industry Structure before and after TRIPS

The Brazilian pharmaceutical structure before TRIPS comes from a historical perspective starting in the 1930s. According to Frenkel et al. (1978), it must be seen as a confluence of three main factors: (i) the lack of sectoral policies of the government to protect the national industry; (ii) the technological innovation introduced in the sector since the 1940s, which created a situation of fragility for national firms; and (iii) the inflows of foreign capital in the 1950s. In other words, Souza Paula (1991) highlights that the Brazilian industrialization process, based on import substitution, was inadequate for the pharmaceutical industry. This policy, according to the author, improved the growth of international firms in the national market with the supply of new goods, internalizing the production of only the final stages of production, which means that the R&D and innovation stage (the first one) were realized outside the country. As pointed out by Queiroz (1993):

> Resuming, the period that remarks the emergence of the modern pharmaceutical industry is also a radical change in the way this industry was inserted in Brazil. The strong presence of multinational firms, on the one hand, improves

the production and trade of drugs (3° and 4° stages), reaching international standards; but on the other hand, it is a limited development, making the development of the other stages (1° and 2° stages) difficult (p. 109).[6]

Instead of promoting the national capital, the association of actions made by the government allowed international firms to enter the national market producing goods with advanced technology and delegating to national firms a fringe activity in the market. According again to Souza Paula (1991), in 1980 the national companies had just a 22 per cent share in the pharmaceutical market, and only one of them was among the top ten companies in the market.

In the 1990s the internationalization of productive capital was intensified, and the macroeconomic conditions must be pointed out as the principal factor of this process. The trade and financial liberalization and, after that, the exchange rate valorization – in the context of price stabilization – led to the scrapping of national productive installation in the pharmochemical sector. Oliveira (2005) points out that 1,096 productive units of fine chemistry were closed before 1994. According to Rebouças (1997), the amount of total investment in pharmochemicals in 1999 was less than the average of 1987–89.

These macroeconomic changes and the new competitive environment in the pharmochemicals industry changed also the pharmaceutical industry. A massive number of drug producers implemented a strategy based on specialization and financial and trade complementarity, increasing the imports of drugs and pharmochemicals inputs, expressing increasing deficits in the sectoral balance of trade. This new competition base created paths of investment where the foreign firms intensified the creation of scale to produce standardized products inside the country, associating this specialization to a production deverticalization and complementation of portfolio by imports from country of origin (Magalhães et al., 2003).

In the relevant papers about the period, the main speculation about these changes credits them to macroeconomic changes. But, how can we understand the impacts of TRIPS compliance in the innovative and productive structure of the pharmaceutical sector in Brazil? It is difficult to evaluate the effects of changes that occurred in the same period and, as there were no R&D and innovation surveys in Brazil before 2000,[7] it is a hard task to separate the changes caused by a stronger IPR and the changes caused by trade liberalization and, mainly, by macroeconomic stabilization post-1994. Magalhães et al. (2003) present proxies that can help us to analyze these changes separately. Table 2.5 presents some information about the industry to support the analysis.

The data shows that there was a movement by foreign firms to improve

Table 2.5   Firms by origin of capital – number of pharmaceutical firms and investment in immobilized assets (US$ thousands 1999)

Firms by number of workers	National firms				Foreign firms				Total
	0–99	100–499	More than 500	Total	0–99	100–499	More than 500	Total	
1985 Number of firms	233	51	7	291	10	17	15	42	333
Total investment	9,455	9,301	15,085	33,841	1,479	11,453	12,711	25,643	59,484
(%)	15.9	15.6	25.4	56.9	2.5	19.3	21.4	43.1	100.0
Average investment	41	182	2,155	116	148	674	847	611	179
1996 Number of firms	271	55	12	338	8	13	25	46	384
Total investment	10,256	45,074	93,787	149,117	2,962	37,797	289,628	330,387	479,504
(%)	2.1	9.4	19.6	31.1	0.6	7.9	60.4	68.9	100.0
Average investment	38	820	7,816	441	370	2,907	11,585	7,182	1,249
1999 Number of firms	292	68	18	378	6	11	23	40	418
Total investment	13,242	19,369	111,155	143,766	588	53,717	317,508	371,813	515,579
(%)	2.6	3.8	21.6	27.9	0.1	10.4	61.6	72.1	100.0
Average investment	45	285	6,175	380	98	4,883	13,805	9,295	1,233

Source: PIA-IBGE in Magalhães et al. (2003).

investments. In 1985, the investments made by foreign firms represented 43.1 per cent of total investment; the percentage increased in 1996 to 68.9 per cent, and it increased again in 1999 to 72.1 per cent. Despite the increase in the number of national firms, foreign firms increased their capacity of production more, which points to the growing importance of the national market. There was, however, a structural break in 1996: comparing the investments made in 1996 with the investments made in 1985, the growth was about 706 per cent. This structural break was caused mainly by the growth of 1288 per cent of the investments realized by foreign firms. The behavioral change of firms in the pharmaceutical industry, notably foreign ones, is thus clear.

But, what was the quality of these investments? In other words, what was the aim of these firms? Table 2.6, extracted from Magalhães et al. (2003), clarifies the understanding of this trend.

The table presents data about pharmaceutical firms located in Sao Paulo state[8] in the year 1996, which represents about 78 per cent of total investments by the entire Brazilian pharmaceutical industry. Despite the small number of foreign firms (41 foreign firms and 123 national firms), they were responsible for 70 per cent of the total invested in 1996. However, the increase of investments made by foreign firms has as one of its main components the acquisition of national machinery and equipment (each big foreign firm invests 285 per cent of national ones). As pointed by Magalhães et al. (2003), this strategy by foreign firms suggests a growth strategy directed by the specialization in products of small technological density.

In the opposite strategy, national firms spent more on foreign machinery and equipment, mainly the big ones (on average, each big national firm invests 165 per cent of foreign ones). Basically, these opposite movements show the different capabilities evolved: while national firms need to worry about the increment of capabilities to produce products of high technological density internally, to compete with foreign ones in the national market, foreign firms can continue to import new brand drugs from their headquarters and can specialize in standardized products (such as OTC drugs and similar drugs) or just improve the capacity of manufacturing the final stages of production (mostly packaging and distribution).

Nevertheless, the difference in acquisition of foreign equipment was tenuous, which suggests that the strategy of foreign firms was stronger than that of national ones. Despite the need of national firms to equalize the technological capability with foreign firms, especially at headquarters level, there is a pecuniary barrier to doing this, and the speed of growth of national big firms increasing their absorption of technology through foreign equipment does not point to a technological approximation.

At this point, a clear connection with TRIPS can be made: as we could

Table 2.6 Investment in pharmaceutical firms in São Paulo in 1996 by type of assets (US$ thousand 1999)

Firms by number of workers	National firms				Foreign firms				Total
	0–99	100–499	More than 500	Total	0–99	100–499	More than 500	Total	
Number of firms	87	23	13	123	7	14	20	41	164
(%)	53.0	14.0	7.9	75.0	4.3	8.5	12.2	25.0	100.0
Total of acquisitions	4,247	11,916	97,201	113,364	2,858	53,729	207,641	264,228	377,592
(%)	1.1	3.2	25.7	30.0	0.8	14.2	55.0	70.0	100.0
Land and buildings	557	1,979	39,216	41,752	1,184	20,655	51,108	72,947	114,699
(%)	0.5	1.7	34.2	36.4	1.0	18.0	44.6	63.6	100.0
National machinery and equipment	1,700	4,756	15,683	22,139	140	15,255	68,895	84,290	106,429
(%)	1.6	4.5	14.7	20.8	0.1	14.3	64.7	79.2	100.0
Foreign machinery and equipment	269	1,743	6,418	8,430	1,788	768	5,979	8,535	16,965
(%)	1.6	10.3	37.8	49.7	10.5	4.5	35.2	50.3	100.0
Transport	1,122	1,392	4,402	6,916	17	4,598	15,052	19,667	26,583
(%)	4.2	5.2	16.6	26.0	0.1	17.3	56.6	74.0	100.0
Other assets	598	2,044	31,481	34,123	1,514	12,450	66,605	80,569	114,692
(%)	0.5	1.8	27.4	29.8	1.3	10.9	58.1	70.2	100.0

Source: PAEP in Magalhães et al (2003).

see in section 3, the number of non-resident patents increased after the 1996 Patent Law. This process is congruent with the foreign firms' strategy: by patenting internally, these firms protect their products, which allows importation without the need of internal production. So, the strategy in national production can be to acquire capacity in standardized products as a way to compete in these markets after the patent expires. Where there clearly exists a competitive advantage in technology in favor of foreign firms, TRIPS thus represented a great barrier to national firms: either these firms reach sufficient scale in production and innovation to enter a market dominated by multinationals, or they have to specialize in less dynamic markets. We will see that the second option, facilitated by generic drugs law, was the choice, given the conditions.

5.2   The Generic Medicines Law and its Consequences

According to the Food and Drugs Administration (FDA), a generic drug is defined as a 'drug product that is comparable to brand/reference listed drug product in dosage form, strength, route of administration, quality and performance characteristics, and intended use'. They are standardized products, usually produced after patent expiration, which means the increase of competition in specific markets.

The Brazilian Generic Medicines Law dates from 1999, which points to a late introduction. In the USA, the legalization of these drugs dates back to 1984, with Hatch Waxman Act (Berndt, 2002). In India, the institution of the Indian Patents Act in 1970 created patent protection just for process – only three years – which permits reverse engineering and technological learning on existing drugs (Fink, 2000; Kremer, 2002; Grace, 2004). Table 2.7 shows market share of generic drugs in selected countries for selected years.

Table 2.7   Market share of generic drugs in selected countries (%)

Country	1980	1985	1993	2009[a]	2011[b]
France	–	32	13	35	42
UK	3	9	50	60	60
Canada	–	21	–	45	45
USA	21	25	30	60	60
Brazil	–	–	–	19	25

Notes:
a. Market share in June, 2009.
b. Market share in December 2011 and April 2012 for Brazil.

Source: Authors' elaboration with data from Bermudez (1994) and Pro-Genericos.

Although late, the growth rate of market share is fast. As informed by Pro-Genericos Association, the growth of market share in 2010 was about 15 per cent in units of drugs (which means that in December of 2010 the generic drugs market represented 22 per cent of the total market of drugs). In April 2012 it increased to 25 per cent.

There is no doubt that the Generic Medicines Law generated a structural change in the Brazilian pharmaceutical industry. Despite being mainly a policy focused on social aspects (such as minimization of price for final consumer),[9] the institution of generic drugs in the national market caused a significant change in the structure of the industry in favor of domestic firms. As pointed out before, national firms had problems competing with foreign ones, mainly in innovation: the production scale did not allow national firms to create enough innovative scale to enter more sophisticated markets. So, given the previous specialization in standardized products, the generic drugs law opened a comparative advantage guaranteed by law in favor of these firms.

6.   INNOVATION IN THE PHARMACEUTICAL INDUSTRY

The central focus of this section is to analyze the innovative behavior of the Brazilian pharmaceutical sector. First, we present general data on innovation. Then, we proceed to an analysis of disaggregated data comparing national and foreign firms in this sector.

6.1   General Aspects

Table 2.8 presents data on the rate of innovation for the manufacturing industry as a whole and for the pharmaceutical sector. Innovations are divided by product and process, which may be new only to the firm or new to the market. We compare two periods: 1998–2000 and 2006–08. Despite the short period, it is possible to notice some changes that differentiate the behavior of the pharmaceutical sector from the rest.

As expected, pharmaceutical firms are more innovative than the manufacturing industry as a whole, in both product and process new to the market. The analysis of innovation in the Brazilian pharmaceutical sector must take into account the introduction of generic drugs.

In 1998 there was only one national company (Aché) among the top 10. With the entry of generic drugs in the market there was a rapid restructuring of the pharmaceutical sector in favor of national companies, with five in the top 10 in 2012. National manufacturers of generic drugs had to go

Table 2.8   *Innovation rate in manufacturing and in the pharmaceutical sector by product and process: 1998–2000 and 2006–08 (%)*

	Type of innovation	Degree of innovation	Manufacturing (all sectors)	Pharmaceutical sector
1998–2000	Product	New to the firm	14.6	27.8
		New to the market	4.2	12.7
	Process	New to the firm	23.5	30.3
		New to the market	2.8	9.7
2006–08	Product	New to the firm	20.1	34.5
		New to the market	4.1	16.7
	Process	New to the firm	31.0	42.8
		New to the market	2.3	3.8

Source: Authors' elaboration based on PINTEC 2000 and 2008.

through a quick learning process, which is reflected in the process innovation rate. In addition, each generic drug for which the company is authorized to begin production reflects a product innovation for the company or the national market in some cases.

With respect to product innovations, 12.7 per cent of firms in the pharmaceutical sector made innovations new to the market between 1998 and 2000, and this rate increased to 16.7 per cent between 2006 and 2008. The rate of innovation of new products to the market grew faster for the pharmaceutical sector than for manufacturing as a whole. This performance is due almost exclusively to the increasing introduction of generic drugs in the domestic market, since only 2.8 per cent of pharmaceutical companies in Brazil innovated a new product to the world market between 2006 and 2008.

With respect to process innovations, it is noted that in the period 1998–2000 the pharmaceutical sector had a rate of new-to-the-market process innovation of 9.7 per cent, which fell to 3.8 per cent in 2006–2008. This can be explained by the restructuring of the pharmaceutical market due to the entry of generic drugs. Domestic companies had to make an effort to dominate the production of generic drugs, which has resulted in an enormous gain in learning and upgrading their production processes. After this stage of restructuring, the rate of innovation of new processes for the domestic market fell to a level close to the average in the manufacturing industry as a whole.

With regard to the forms of protection of innovation, the pharmaceutical sector uses them more intensely than the manufacturing industry as a whole. The introduction of generic drugs also caused an interesting shift in how firms protect their innovations in a short time (Table 2.9).

Table 2.9   Alternative forms to protect innovation, used by firms as percentage of total of innovative firms in manufacturing (all sectors) and in pharmaceutical sector

Protection form	2001–03		2003–05		2006–08	
	Manufac-turing	Pharma	Manufac-turing	Pharma	Manufac-turing	Pharma
Patent	7.5	13.7	6.8	8.3	9.2	17.5
Trademark	21.9	44.1	23.6	46.0	24.1	71.7
Design complexity	1.4	0.0	1.6	1.2	1.6	5.7
Trade secret	8.4	13.1	8.3	13.8	8.7	31.1
Time leading	1.9	3.5	8.7	8.9	2.1	16.8
Others	3.5	7.0	4.8	8.3	5.0	15.6

Note: Data for 1998–2000 are not available.

Source: Authors' elaboration based on PINTEC 20003 and 2008.

The percentage of firms in the pharmaceutical industry that use patents as a way to protect their innovations increased from 13.7 per cent in 2001–03 to 17.5 per cent in 2006–08. However, the most commonly used form of protection has been the trademark, which was used by 44.1 per cent of the pharmaceutical firms in 2000–03 and increased to 71 per cent in 2006–08. Time leadership has grown substantially. That is, with the entry of generic drugs in the Brazilian market, firms are increasingly seeking to differentiate their products through marketing and strengthening their brands. There was a substantial leap in the use of all means of protection of innovation by the pharmaceutical sector between 2003–05 and 2006–08. This movement is a result of increasing competition in the sector.

Among the pharmaceutical companies that did not innovate in the period 2006–08, only 14.7 per cent said this was due to the existence of previous innovations. This suggests that previous patents have not hindered drug companies in Brazil. Among the factors hampering innovation activities, the most important is the high cost of innovation. The lack of skilled personnel is also among the most important factors hampering innovation activities.

6.2   Industry Structure (Scale, Sales, Profit)

In order to analyze the innovative behavior of national and foreign firms in the pharmaceutical sector, we use a classification of firms by technological capability, as done by De Negri and Salerno (2005), regarding the specificities of the pharmaceutical industry.[10] Among others, a special weight was given for patenting, since patent protection is the main way of appropriating the gains from innovation. The following analysis is limited by the fact that it was not possible to use disaggregated data for PINTEC 2008. So, comparisons are related to the years of 2000, 2003, and 2005.

We decided to set up a classification which emphasizes patent applications, by defining a list of innovation indicators in which a unit value is given for the presence of each item, namely:

1. Product innovator (Source: Technological Innovation Survey – PINTEC);
2. Process innovator (Source: PINTEC);
3. Registration of patents in the National Institute of Industrial Property (INPI) (Source: PINTEC);
4. Continuous R&D (Source: PINTEC);
5. Average schooling of workers above the sectoral average (Source: Annual Relation of Social Information – RAIS);
6. Firm exports (Source: Secretary of Foreign Trade – SECEX);
7. The firm exports and gets a premium price (Source: SECEX).

Based on these elements, firms were classified in three groups:

1. Innovative: firms which appear in at least six of the items above, provided patent application is one of them (i.e. total items 6 or 7);
2. Imitative: firms which include 3 to 5 of the items above, provided patent application is not one of them;
3. Competitive: firms which appear in 0 to 2 items, provided patent application is not one of them.

This classification assures that innovative firms are the only ones presenting patents of products or processes, which is reasonable given the innovative dynamics of the sector. We are going to analyze the Brazilian sectoral classification named Drugs Production, because it is the least aggregated information from PINTEC. For further information on the database, see De Negri and Salerno (2005). The years of analysis are 2000, 2003, and 2005, for which there is information available on the technological capability of firms. The results are presented in the next subsections.

Table 2.10 presents economic characteristics for a representative sample of firms in the pharmaceutical sector.[11]

Some relevant characteristics can be highlighted. First, the correlation between scale (employees and NSR) and innovation is confirmed: larger

Table 2.10 Characteristics of the main firms in the pharmaceutical sector in Brazil – selected years

Year	Variables	National firms			Foreign firms		
		Innovative	Imitative	Competitive	Innovative	Imitative	Competitive
2000	Number of firms	6	45	58	13	13	7
	Aver. NSR (R$ million)	312.65	73.95	28.26	595.02	345.66	69.97
	Aver. profit (R$ millions)	−4.33	6.61	3.51	46.40	−10.39	−1.12
	Average employees	986.14	296.54	218.64	908.57	671.49	282.18
	NSR/Cost	0.99	1.10	1.14	1.08	0.97	0.98
2003	Number of firms	18	60	15	14	16	—
	Aver. NSR (R$ million)	265.06	38.20	13.47	584.50	286.64	—
	Aver. profit (R$ million)	2.57	−1.50	−0.14	−8.01	−1.88	—
	Average employees	1073.35	187.25	119.57	959.13	617.89	—
	NSR/cost	1.01	0.96	0.99	0.88	0.94	—
2005	Number of firms	12	38	59	10	27	—
	Aver. NSR (R$ million)	285.15	74.93	15.41	668.09	245.71	—
	Aver. profit (R$ million)	18.694	7.900	−1.050	32.074	1.608	—
	Average employees	1005.25	449.13	161.85	1088.4	551.44	—
	NSR/cost	1.07	1.12	0.94	1.05	1.01	—

Note: NSR – net sales revenues.

Source: Authors' elaboration using data from PIA/IBGE.

firms are more innovative, no matter what the origin of capital. Second, there was an increase in the number of national innovative firms, and a decrease of foreign innovative firms. As discussed before, this result is consistent: Table 2.5 showed a movement of foreign firms in the direction of the production of standardized products for the national market, and an opposite direction for national firms. This movement persisted in the last decade.

And third, there is a significant increase in the profits of domestic innovative firms: from negative values in 2000 to over R$18 million in 2005. Since profits are important for financing innovation, this increase in profitability of indigenous innovative firms may bring about positive impacts in innovation. But, the analysis of the results regarding the increase in profitability should also consider the macroeconomic scenario during the period. The pharmaceutical sector presents a high dependence on imports, and thus it is strongly affected by changes in the exchange rate. The period after 2002 is characterized by a strong appreciation of the Brazilian currency, which decreases import costs in the sector. So, the increase in profitability may be more closely associated with exchange rate changes than with the TRIPS or policy of generic drugs.

The analysis of the profit rate (NSR/cost) points to a recovery of profit margins for innovative domestic firms and to a stable result for the other firms, except for the competitive domestic firms, which presented declining profit rates. However, we should also consider in this case the positive effect of currency appreciation on production costs, particularly because the data shows that revenues have barely changed for Brazilian firms between 2000 and 2005.

6.3   R&D Investment and Innovation Rate

This section discusses some innovation indicators from PINTEC's questionnaires. The variable associated with total innovation corresponds to the total amount of expenses on innovative activities, according to PINTEC's questionnaire, and all these variables are related to the firms' revenues. We begin by analyzing expenses on marketing (Table 2.11).

The inclusion of this variable in the analysis of technology is justified by the fact that one of the main strategies in the pharmaceutical industry is product differentiation via marketing efforts (Angell, 2004; Bastos, 2005; Gagnon and Lexchin, 2008; PhRMA, 2009; among others).

Thus, it is likely that the increase in the market share of generic drugs would modify such expenses due to a decline in product differentiation. The result is interesting and shows the difference in strategies between

Table 2.11 Marketing and technological effort in relation to net sales revenues

Year	Variable	National firms			Foreign firms		
		Innovative	Imitative	Competitive	Innovative	Imitative	Competitive
2000	Marketing	6.63	3.63	2.24	8.31	7.90	4.89
	Internal R&D	0.63	1.17	0.11	0.95	0.11	0.00
	Total of innovation	4.89	5.68	2.75	6.60	6.05	1.59
2003	Marketing	3.98	1.89	0.99	7.06	6.27	–
	Internal R&D	1.41	0.92	0.90	0.37	1.21	–
	Total of innovation	5.74	4.34	1.98	3.78	14.96	–
2005	Marketing	3.66	1.87	1.26	10.02	5.95	–
	Internal R&D	1.47	0.98	1.48	0.71	0.71	–
	Total of innovation	6.40	2.65	1.52	6.99	1.84	–

Source: Authors' elaboration using data from PIA and PINTEC/IBGE.

domestic and foreign firms. Brazilian companies reduced expenses on marketing between 2000 and 2005 for all types of firms. For foreign companies, however, the evolution of such expenses was different: an increase of 21 per cent for innovative firms and a decline of 25 per cent for imitative firms. Thus, there is a clear decline in marketing expenses by domestic firms, but the same pattern is not detected for foreign firms.

The result is not the same for R&D expenses internal to the firm. For the initial period of analysis, domestic firms spent less than foreign firms. Innovative domestic firms spent only 66 per cent of the amount spent by multinationals. The result is inverted in 2005, when domestic firms spent 107 per cent of the amount spent by foreign firms. The expenses of domestic firms increased whereas those of foreign firms declined. However, the analysis of these variables should also consider the specificities of multinational firms, again highlighting the analysis in the last section. It was a strategy of multinational firms, at least since the 1996 Patent Law: it is more profitable to keep large research and development centers in their countries of origin, the so-called in-house R&D. For national companies, it is necessary to improve these R&D investments; as can be seen, this happened, but comparing the national pattern on R&D expenses (about 1.47 per cent of NSR for innovative firms) with R&D expenses of companies from the Phrma group in the USA (which reaches 15.6 per cent of the NSR (Phrma, 2009)), indigenous firms are still operating at a small innovative scale.

This pattern is confirmed by the increase in the number of qualified workers. The number of qualified workers reflects the technological capacity of industry, and therefore it is expected that innovative firms hire those workers in larger numbers. In addition, it is important to notice that the number of qualified workers has increased in the innovative domestic firms, which confirms the previous results regarding increasing technological effort.

Despite this increment, the number of qualified workers is still low. On average, there was only one PhD worker and less than three Master's scientists in innovative national firms in 2005. So, the innovative scale in Brazilian firms points to an improvement, but at a slow pace. The same is verified for foreign firms.

7. PATENT LITIGATION

In the 1990s, the Brazilian government created one of the most important anti-AIDS programs in the world, recognized as a model by the WHO in 2003. Since 1996 it '. . . has established a consistent legal framework to

Table 2.12 Average number of workers in R&D in the pharmaceutical industry

Year	Qualification level	National firms			Foreign firms		
		Innovative	Imitative	Competitive	Innovative	Imitative	Competitive
2000	PhD scientists	0.78	0.24	0.02	0.33	0	0
	Master's scientists	1.02	0.33	0.02	1.02	0	0
	Graduates	5.67	3.33	0.24	8.33	1.08	0
2003	PhD scientists	1.11	0.03	0	0.21	0	—
	Master's scientists	2.78	0.17	0	1.29	0	—
	Graduates	12.83	0.73	0.06	7.36	1.25	—
2005	PhD scientists	1.08	0.32	0.02	1.00	0.04	—
	Master's scientists	2.58	0.24	0	2.20	0.11	—
	Graduates	19.33	3.89	0.19	17.80	0.96	—

Source: Authors' elaboration using data from PINTEC/IBGE.

provide free and universal access to diagnosis, prevention and treatment for patients with HIV/AIDS' (Orsi et al. 2007, p. 2000). Most drugs of the antiretroviral therapy (ART) were produced by international laboratories. In January 1999, Brazil had an exchange rate crisis which affected the cost of imported drugs. The government, facing the high prices of the ARTs and resource constraints, decided to incentivize 'public pharmaceutical laboratories and national pharmochemical companies, aiming at the local manufacturing of generic versions of ART. This collaboration resulted in the national production of ten low-cost generic versions of the non-patented ART drugs listed in the national therapeutic guidelines' (Orsi et al., 2007, p. 2000).

This was the scenario when the patent battles started between the Brazilian government and some important pharmaceutical laboratories. In 2000 the government threatened the Swiss pharmaceutical laboratory Roche with compulsory licensing of the anti-AIDS drug Nelfinavir, arguing that it was a national emergency case (because of the effect of the exchange rate crisis on the costs). An agreement was reached that there was no need of compulsory licensing.

From 2000 to 2007 there were several price agreements between the Brazilian government and pharmaceutical laboratories such as Bristol, Abbot and Merck. But the sustainability of the program was questioned because in 1998–99, about 50 per cent of anti-AIDS drugs were imported, increasing to 80 per cent in 2004. After this, the government started to consider local production.

In June 2005 the Brazilian government made another threat of compulsory licensing, for the anti-AIDS drug Kaletra owned by Abbott. This drug accounted for 30 per cent of the share of the anti-AIDS program. Abbot agreed to reduce its price from US$ 1.17 to US$ 0.70. Although Farmanguinhos, the laboratory of Fundação Oswaldo Cruz (Fiocruz), was technically capable of producing this drug, the Brazilian government decided to make an agreement with Abbot. But the anti-AIDS budget rose from R$592 million in 2004 to R$945 million in 2005.

In April 2007, the government made its most serious threat of compulsory licensing an anti-AIDS drug. This time the company was the US Laboratory Merck, and the drug was Efavirenz, the most used imported anti-AIDS drug in Brazil. The Health Minister, José Gomes Temporão, gave assurance that the government's concern was just the anti-AIDS program, and was not to incentivize local laboratories. For a critique of the compulsory licensing, see Pessoa et al. (2007).

The failure of the negotiations led the Brazilian government to decide on compulsory licensing Efavirenz in May 2007, and a generic of Efavirenz is now produced by Farmanguinhos.

What are the international laboratories doing? In 2010, for example, 12 drugs patents fell into the public domain in Brazil. In order to keep their profits, some laboratories tried to extend the life of their patents.

The Brazilian Superior Court has ruled against the extension of several patents in recent years. The main problem is with patents granted by the mechanism of 'pipeline' (patents retroactive to 1996). Multinationals argue based on latest international application, but the Supreme Court interprets that the earlier application should be taken into account (see Barbosa, 2010). In 2010, for example, the extension of the Pfizer patent on Viagra was denied. Immediately after the patent expiration, the domestic company EMS started to market a generic version. INPI has worked to hasten the trial of non-extension of several other patents based on this argument. Each patent extended means an additional cost to the Health budget.

8.   CONCLUSIONS

This chapter presented arguments which show that the TRIPS compliance by the Brazilian Patent Law in 1996 did not cause significant changes in the innovative behavior of Brazilian industry as a whole. However, it induced some changes that seem to be small today, but have potential to become important in the future.

Since the new patent law there was a significant increase in the share of non-resident patent applications at INPI, as well as a change in the profile of patent applications made by non-residents in Brazil. Important technological areas, such as chemistry, pharmaceuticals, biotechnology and ICTs are dominated by foreign patents. This may represent a strong barrier to the technological development of domestic firms in the future.

The most important and fast changes induced by the TRIPS compliance are related to the new role of universities in the Brazilian system of innovation and to the importance of innovation – and patents as an indicator – in government policies. First, Brazilian universities are now exploring their potential to generate patentable technologies and became important actors in innovation issues, especially regarding technology transfer. Second, innovation became an essential part of the industrial policy. New laws and plans are designed to enable partnerships between firms and universities and to incentivize innovation in the productive sector. But the government is not yet concerned about the potential barriers patents may represent to technological developments in the future.

Probably one of the sectors that will feel the impact of TRIPS compliance in the future is the national pharmaceutical industry. So far it is not possible to say that there was a negative impact. However, the start of production of generic drugs in the Brazilian market has caused a shift in favor of domestic industry, which passes through a period of technological learning and strengthening of brands. These national firms will enjoy the intense learning acquired with the production of generic products to try to innovate in a next step. It will be then that the negative effects of TRIPS compliance will appear.

NOTES

1. The pipeline was a controversial provision at the time. First, it had legal effects before the other articles of the law – the law started to have its full legal effects only a year later. Second, according to the law, inventions must be new to be patentable, and the pipeline provision allowed inventions already patented abroad – with information disclosed and, therefore, not new – to have a different treatment for a year. Barbosa (2006) argues that it was an unconstitutional provision since patents granted through the pipeline provision were not analyzed according to the patentability requisites of the new law (art. 8), and national applications were. Pipeline provision was applied to 1,182 patents and at least 340 drugs were introduced in the Brazilian market, according to http://www.deolhonaspatentes.org.br/media/file/Publica%C3%A7%C3%B5es/ PergResp_PIPELINE_PT.pdf (accessed May 2012).
2. The same conclusion is reached by Laforgia et al. (2007).
3. The number of universities among the top 20 is growing. Between 1999 and 2003 there were only three (UNICAMP, UFMG and USP).
4. Patent applications were classified according to the Observatoire des Sciences et des Techniques (OST). For example, pharmaceuticals-cosmetics are related to the IPC A61K and A61P.
5. See http://www.obs-ost.fr/en.html.
6. Authors' translation.
7. The Industrial Survey of Technological Innovation (PINTEC) started only in 2000.
8. Brazil's richest state (33.1% of national GDP in 2008).
9. The studies concerning price aspects of generic drugs involve a wide and ambiguous literature. As it is not our focus in this chapter, we suggest in the international literature Statman (1981), Grabowski and Vernon (1992), Franck and Salkever (1997), Caves et al. (1991) and Griliches and Cockburn (1993), and in the Brazilian case Fiúza and Lisboa (2001), Hasenclever (2002), Nishijima (2008) and Caliari et al. (2009).
10. A previous analysis of the pharmaceutical sector with this same methodology is presented in Caliari and Ruiz (2010).
11. As defined by PINTEC's methodology.

REFERENCES

Albuquerque, E. (2003), 'Patentes e atividades inovativas: uma avaliação preliminar do caso brasileiro', in E.B.E. Viotti and M.M. Macedo (eds), *Indicadores de ciência, tecnologia e inovação no Brasil*, Campinas, São Paulo: Editora da UNICAMP, pp. 329–76.
Albuquerque, E., L. Silva, A. Baessa and L. Ribeiro (2011), 'Atividades de

patenteamento em São Paulo e no Brasil', in *Indicadores de Ciência, Tecnologia e Inovação em São Paulo 2010*, vol. 1, São Paolo: FAPESP, Chapter 5.

Angell, M. (2004), 'Excess in the pharmaceutical industry', *Canadian Medical Association*, **171** (12), 1451–3.

Barbosa, D.B. (2006), 'Inconstitucionalidade das patentes pipeline', available at http://denisbarbosa.addr.com/pipeline.pdf (accessed May 2012).

Barbosa, P. (2010), 'Revoluções e patentes', *Abifina Informa*, **25**, available at http://www.abifina.org.br/informaNoticia.asp?cod=375 (accessed July 26, 2013).

Basso, M. (2005), 'Preliminary background paper on prior consent for pharmaceutical products by ANVISA in Brazil', April, available at http://www.wissensgesellschaft.org/themen/publicdomain/priorconsent.pdf (accessed July 26, 2013).

Bastos, V.D. (2005), 'Inovação farmacêutica: padrão setorial e perspectivas para o caso brasileiro', *BNDES Setorial*, Rio de Janeiro, **22**, 271–96.

Bermudez, J. (1994), 'Medicamentos genéricos: uma alternativa para o mercado Brasileiro', *Cadernos de Saúde Pública*, **10** (3), 363–78.

Berndt, E.R. (2002), 'Pharmaceuticals in US health care: determinants of quantity and price', *Journal of Economic Perspectives*, **16** (4), Fall, 45–66.

Caliari, T. and R.M. Ruiz (2010), 'A indústria farmacêutica e os medicamentos genéricos: as intenções políticas e os impactos não planejados', in Mario Jorge Salerno, João Alberto De Negri, Lenita Maria Turchi and José Mauro Morais (eds), *Inovação: Estudos de Jovens Pesquisadores Brasileiros*, vol. 2, São Paulo: Papagaio, pp. 392–428.

Caliari, T., R.M. Ruiz and A.M.H.C. Oliveira (2009), 'Uma década de medicamentos genéricos: Sucesso relativo e progressiva perda de eficácia?', paper presente at the conference 'XXXVII Encontro Nacional de Economia', Foz do Iguaçu.

Caves, R.E., M.D. Whiston and M.A. Hurwitz (1991), 'Patent expiration, entry, and competition in the U.S. pharmaceutical industry', *Brookings Papers: Microeconomics*.

De Negri, J.A. and M. Salerno (eds) (2005), *Inovações, Padrões Tecnológicos e Desempenho das Firmas Industriais Brasileiras*, Brasília: IPEA.

EUROSTAT (2010), *Science, Technology, and Innovation in Europe*, Luxembourg: EUROSTAT Statistical Books.

Fink, C. (2000), 'How stronger patent protection in India might affect the behavior of transnational pharmaceutical industries', World Bank Policy Research Working Paper No. 2352, May.

Fiúza, E.P.S. and M.B. Lisboa (2001), 'Bens credenciais e poder de mercado: um estudo econométrico da indústria farmacêutica Brasileira', technical report, Texto para Discussão do IPEA, Rio de Janeiro.

Franck, R.G. and D.S. Salkever (1997), 'Generic entry and the pricing of pharmaceuticals', *Journal of Economics & Management Strategy*, **6** (1), 75–90.

Frenkel, J., J.A. Reis, J.T. Araujo Jr and L.C. Naidin (1978), 'Tecnologia e competição na indústria farmacêutica Brasileira', mimeo, November, Rio de Janeiro: FINEP.

Gagnon, M.A. and J. Lexchin (2008), 'The cost of pushing pills: a new estimate of pharmaceutical promotion expenditures in the United States', *PLoS Med*, **5** (1).

Grabowski, H. and J. Vernon (1992), 'Brand loyalty, entry and price competition in pharmaceutical after the 1984', *Journal of Law and Economics*, **XXXV** (2), October, 331–50.

Grace, C. (2004), 'The effect of changing intellectual property on pharmaceutical industry prospects in India and China: consideration for access to medicines', London: DFID Health Systems Resource Centre, June.

Griliches, Z. and I. Cockburn (1993), 'Generics and new goods in pharmaceutical price index', Technical Report 4272, National Bureau of Economic Research.

Hasenclever, L. (2002), *Diagnóstico da indústria farmacêutica brasileira*, Brasília/Rio de Janeiro: Unesco/FUJB/IE-UFRJ.

Hathaway, D. (1993), 'Brazil about to patent life?', *Seedling* (October), available at http://www.grain.org/article/entries/504-brazil-about-to-patent-life (accessed July 26, 2013).

INPI (2011), 'Principais Titulares de Pedidos de Patente no Brasil, com Prioridade Brasileira: Depositados no Período de 2004 a 2008', available at www.inpi.gov.br.

Kremer, M. (2002), 'Pharmaceuticals and the developing world', *Journal of Economic Perspectives*, **16** (4), 67–90.

Laforgia, F., F. Montobbio and L. Orsenigo (2007), 'IPRs, technological and industrial development and growth: the case of the pharmaceutical industry', Centre for Research on Innovation and Internationalization, available at ftp://ftp.unibocconi.it/pub/RePEc/cri/papers/WP206LaforgiaMontobbioOrsenigo.pdf.

Magalhães, L.C.G. et al. (2003), 'Estratégias empresariais de crescimento na indústria farmacêutica Brasileira: Investimentos, fusões e aquisições, 1988–2002', Discussion Paper 995, IPEA/Brasília, Brasília.

Maskus, K. (2005), 'The role of intellectual property rights in encouraging foreign direct investment and technology transfer', in C. Fink and K. Maskus (eds), *Intellectual Property and Development: Lessons from Recent Economic Research*, Washington, DC and New York: World Bank and Oxford University Press, pp. 41–74.

Mazzoleni, R. and L.M.C. Póvoa (2010), 'Accumulation of technological capabilities and economic development: did Brazil's regime of intellectual property rights matter?', in H. Odagiri, A. Goto, A. Sunami, and R.R. Nelson (eds), *Intellectual Property Rights, Development, and Catch-Up: An International Comparative Study*, New York: Oxford University Press.

Nishijima, M. (2008), 'Os preços dos medicamentos de referência após a entrada dos medicamentos genéricos no mercado farmacêutico brasileiro', *Revista Brasileira de Economia*, **62** (2), April–June, 189–206.

Oliveira, N.B. (2005), 'Os fármacos e a saúde pública no Brasil – uma visão da cadeia produtiva', *Parcerias Estratégicas*, no. 20.

Orsi, F., D'Almeida, C., Hasenclever, L., Camara, M., Tigre, P. and Coriat, B. (2007), 'TRIPS post-2005 and access to new antiretroviral treatments in southern countries: issues and challenges', *AIDS*, **21** (15), 1997–2003.

OST (Observatoire des Sciences et des Techniques) (2006), *Science & Technologie: Indicateurs 2006*, Paris: Economica, available at http://www.obs-ost.fr/le-savoir-faire/etudes-en-ligne/etudes-2006/rapport-2006.html.

Pessoa, S., C. Considera and M. Ribeiro (2007), 'O papel do instituto da patente no desempenho da indústria farmacêutica', in *Proceedings of the 35th Brazilian Economics Meeting*, available at http://www.anpec.org.br/encontro2007/artigos/A07A073.pdf (accessed July 26, 2013).

Pharmaceutical Research and Manufacturers of America (PhRMA) (2009), *Pharmaceutical Industry Profile 2008*, Washington, DC: PhRMA.

Póvoa, L.M.C. (2010), 'A universidade deve patentear suas invenções?', *Revista Brasileira de Inovação*, **9** (2).

Queiroz, S.R.R. (1993), 'Os determinantes da capacitação tecnológica no setor químico-farmacêutico Brasileiro', PhD thesis, Instituto de Economia/Unicamp, Campinas.

Rebouças, M.M. (1997), 'A indústria de química fina: um estudo de política industrial', PhD thesis, Instituto de Economia/Unicamp, Campinas.

Ryan, M. (2010), 'Patent incentives, technology markets, and public–private biomedical innovation networks in Brazil', *World Development*, **38** (8), 1082–2010.

Schmoch, U. (2008), 'Concept of a technology classification for country comparisons', Final report to the World Intellectual Property Organization (WIPO).

Souza Paula, M.C. (1991), 'Oportunidades e entraves ao desenvolvimento tecnológico no Brasil: a experiência da indústria aeronáutica e indústria farmacêutica', PhD thesis, FFLCH/USP, São Paulo.

Statman, M. (1981), 'The effect of patent expiration on the market position of drugs', in E.B. Helmes (ed.), *Drugs and Health: Economic Issues and Policy Objectives*, Washington, DC: American Enterprise Institute for Public Policy Research, pp. 140–50.

Suster, R. (2009), 'A Lei n° 9.279/96 – Lei da Propriedade Industrial, sua influência no panorama nacional de patenteamento de fármacos', Master's dissertation, Instituto Nacional da Propriedade Industrial (INPI).

3. TRIPS compliance of national patent regimes and domestic innovative activity: the Indian experience

Sunil Mani, Sudip Chaudhuri, V.K. Unni, Carl Pray and Latha Nagarajan

1. INTRODUCTION

An important aspect of changes in international governance rules with respect to intellectual property regimes is the passage of the Agreement on Trade Related Aspects of Intellectual Property Rights (TRIPS). The TRIPS Agreement has been in force since 1995 and is to date the most comprehensive multilateral agreement on intellectual property (IP). The Agreement introduced global minimum standards for protecting and enforcing nearly all forms of intellectual property rights (IPR), including those for patents. International conventions prior to TRIPS did not specify minimum standards for patents. At the time that negotiations began, over 40 countries in the world did not grant patent protection for pharmaceutical products. The TRIPS Agreement now requires all WTO members, with few exceptions, to adapt their laws to the minimum standards of IPR protection. In addition, the TRIPS Agreement also introduced detailed obligations for the enforcement of intellectual property rights. However, TRIPS also contains provisions that allow a degree of flexibility and sufficient room for countries to accommodate their own patent and intellectual property systems and developmental needs. This means countries have a certain amount of freedom in modifying their regulations, and various options exist for them in formulating their national legislation to ensure a proper balance between the goal of providing incentives for future inventions of new drugs and the goal of affordable access to existing medicines. The protection and enforcement of intellectual property rights should contribute to the promotion of technological innovation and to the transfer and dissemination of technology, to the mutual advantage of producers and users of technological knowledge and in a manner conducive to social and economic welfare, and to a balance of rights and obligations.

Although TRIPS came into being in 1995, developing countries were given time until 2005 to have their respective IPR regimes aligned to the varied provisions of TRIPS. After a series of three amendments, the Indian Patents Act, 1970 was made TRIPS compliant with effect from January 1, 2005. In the context, the purpose of the present study is to analyse the potential and actual effects of the TRIPS compliant patent regime on innovative activity in the country not only at the macro level but also on those industries such as pharmaceuticals and agrochemicals, the two industries that are most likely to be affected as a result of some major changes which the TRIPS compliance has brought about.

The study is structured into six sections following this introduction. Section 2 traces the evolution of the patent regimes in India over time. The emphasis here is to distil in very specific terms the precise connotations of TRIPS compliance. Section 3 discusses the macro implications of TRIPS compliance in as much as it affects innovative activity. We divide these macro changes into proximate and distant changes. Section 4 maps out the increasing cases of patent litigation which TRIPS compliance seems to have precipitated. Section 5 analyses its effects on the R&D strategies of the domestic pharmaceutical industry and Section 6 its effects on the agrochemicals industry. Finally, Section 7 summarizes the main findings of our study.

2.   THE LONG ROAD TO TRIPS COMPLIANCE OF INDIA'S PATENT REGIME[1]

The Indian patent system, dating as far back as 1856, has undergone several modifications at different times that have strengthened or relaxed patent rights. The Patents Act, 1970 that came into force on April 20, 1972 was a response to the growing national debate on how to best strike a balance between patent rights as incentives to innovation and the need to protect the public interest and to boost industrial development. Up until the 1960s foreign multinational pharmaceutical companies supplied almost 85 per cent of medicines in India, and prices were among the highest in the world. To redress this problem and with a view to make the patent law compatible with Indian developmental objectives, in the post-independence period from 1947 to 1970, the Indian Parliament vehemently debated amendments to the Patents Act. One of the main changes of the Patents Act, 1970 was that it allowed process patents in pharmaceutical and agrochemical based products, but not product patents. This allowed the national pharmaceutical industry to develop technical expertise in the manufacturing process – and thus to become an efficient producer of generic medicines (Chaudhuri, 2005; Sampat, 2010).

- The establishment of IPR in India commenced in 1856 with the enactment of an Act of Protection of Inventions, based on the British Patent Law of 1852, when certain privileges were granted to the inventor for new methods of manufacture.
- The Patent Act of India, 1911 was fairly liberal as patenting of products related to foods, pharmaceuticals, chemicals, etc. was available with a full term of 16 years. This was directly in line with the British Patent Act of 1907. India follows the 'first-to-file' system as in most countries.
- The Indian Patents Act, 1970 brought in significant changes with restrictions related to patenting of inventions in the areas of chemicals, pharmaceuticals, agrochemicals, foods, in which product patents had been discontinued and patenting of processes with a restricted life of seven years from the date of filing of the complete specification (or five years from the date of sealing the patent, whichever is shorter) was introduced.

The Three Amendments

India did not come out with a new Patents Act in 2005, but merely amended its Patents Act, 1970 three times in 1999, 2002 and finally in 2005 to make it TRIPS compliant. In the following we undertake a quick survey of these three amendments with a view to understanding the specific changes that were made.

The Amendment in 1999

Being a developing country, India was given a 10 year transition time from 1995 through 2005 to make its 1970 IPR regime TRIPS compliant. The most important requirement for TRIPS compliance is the granting of both product and process patents for all inventions including those in pharmaceuticals, agrochemicals and food on which the 1970 Act had a different position.[2] There are two important substantive obligations that have been effective from the entry into force of the TRIPS Agreement on January 1, 1995. One is the so-called 'non-backsliding' clause in Article 65.5, which concerns changes made during the transitional period, and the other the so-called 'mailbox' provision in Article 70.8 for filing patent applications for pharmaceutical and agricultural chemical products during the transitional period. So the 1999 amendment also put in place this mailbox provision under which from January 1, 1995 till January 1, 2005, an application could be filed for a product patent (in pharmaceuticals and agrochemicals) under the provision of this mailbox clause and after January 1, 2005 the applications would get examined and only those that complied would be granted product patents.

However, the applicants in the mailbox could apply to be granted exclusive marketing rights to pharmaceutical products as an alternative to product patent protection during this period. This led to the amendment in 1999 which introduced Chapter IVA in the 1970 Act: under Chapter IVA, Exclusive Marketing Rights (EMRs) to sell and distribute a pharmaceutical product were granted to applicants on satisfaction of a set of five conditions:

1. A patent application covering the new drug or agrochemical should have been filed in any of the WTO member countries after January 1, 1995;
2. A patent on the product should have been obtained in any of the member countries (which provide for product patents in drugs and agrochemical) after January 1, 1995;
3. Marketing approvals for the product should have been obtained in any of the member countries;
4. A patent application covering the product should have been filed after January 1, 1995 in the country where the EMR is sought;
5. The applicant should apply seeking an EMR by making use of the prescribed form and paying the requisite fee.

Once granted, these exclusive marketing rights were valid for a period of five years and would come to an end earlier on grant or rejection of the patent. Although about 8500 applications were received under this facility, only about 12 were actually granted (Table 3.1). Four of these were from domestic companies (although one of them, Ranbaxy, has become an affiliate of a Japanese MNC since 2008). The important point is that these numbers show that the worst fears expressed by a variety of commentators that a large number of EMRs would be awarded have been proved wrong.

An analysis of the mailbox applications in 2005 showed that the majority of them referred to minor changes to the structure of molecules and not to patenting new chemical entities. Thus, according to Abbott et al. (2005), MNCs, which accounted for the majority of these applications, were actually using the mailbox provision to erect a barrier of sorts to the Indian generic manufacturers who were making drugs invented before 1995. The

Table 3.1 Profile of applicants who were granted exclusive marketing rights in India: post-1999 amendment

EMR no.	EMR applicant	Title	Nature of ownership
1. EMR/1/2000	Hoffman-La Roche Inc.	Pharmaceutical composition (details not available)	MNC
2. EMR/2/2000	Schering-Plough Corporation of USA	Formulation for protection of PEG-Interferon Alpha Conjugate	MNC
3. EMR/4/2001	Ranbaxy Laboratories Limited	Pharmaceutical composition in the form of oral controlled release tablets or capsules	Domestic
4. EMR/2/2001	United Phosphorus Limited	A synergistic composition of Carbendazim and Mancozeb	Domestic
5. EMR/3/2003	Novartis AG of Schwarzwaldallee	Crystal modification of N phenyl-2-phenyl-2-pyrimidineamine derivative, process for its manufacture and use	MNC
6. EMR/3/2003	Eli Lilly & Co.	On Teteractadic derivative process	MNC
7. EMR/1/2003	Nichola Piramal India Limited	Combination of kit for Malaria	Domestic
8. EMR/2/2003	United Phosphorus Limited	Insecticidal composition of Carbendazim and Mancozeb	Domestic
9. EMR/3/2003	Eli Lilly & Co.	Tetracyclic derivative preparation and use	MNC
10. EMR/3/2004	Panacea Bio Tec. Limited	Pharmaceutical composition (details not available)	Domestic
11. EMR/2/2004	Eli Lilly & Co.	Tadalafil and its dosage forms	MNC
12. EMR/1/2004	Hoffman-La Roche Inc.	Interferon conjugates	MNC

Source: Adapted from Kankanala et al. (2010), p.3.

fear of a protracted and costly patent litigation would have loomed large for them.

The Amendment of 2002

The amendment effected in 2002 was a major step towards aligning the Patents Act, 1970 more closely with all the provisions of TRIPS. Further, it incorporated safeguards for protection of public interest, national security, biodiversity, traditional knowledge, etc. Patent granting procedures were harmonized with international practices so that the system became more user friendly. Some of the important changes made are as follows:

- The definition of the term 'invention' has been modified in consonance with international practices and consistent with the TRIPS Agreement.
- Section 3 of the 1970 Act has been modified to include exclusions permitted by the TRIPS Agreement and also subject matters like discovery of any living or non-living substances occurring in nature in the list of exclusions, which in general do not constitute patentable inventions and also to specifically exclude inventions which in effect are traditional knowledge.
- The rights of patentees have been aligned as per Article 28 of the TRIPS Agreement.
- A provision for reversal of burden of proof in the case of an infringement suit on a process patent, in accordance with Article 34 of the TRIPS Agreement, has been added.
- A uniform term of patent protection of 20 years for all categories of invention as per Article 33 of the TRIPS Agreement has been prescribed.
- Three flexibilities are provided for: (i) the provisions relating to *compulsory licensing* have been modified to suit the public interest requirements and also to comply with the TRIPS Agreement; (ii) a provision has been incorporated for enabling *parallel import* of patented products at lowest international prices; (iii) to ensure smooth transition of a product from the monopoly status created by the patent to the public domain, a provision has been incorporated for obtaining marketing approval from the appropriate regulatory authorities before the expiration of the patent term. This 'Bolar provision' then allows the generic producer to market and manufacture their goods as soon as the patent expires. Bolar Provisions have been upheld as conforming to the TRIPS agreement.
- The provisions relating to national security have been strengthened.

- A provision has been incorporated for hearing of appeals, which at present lie before the High Court, by the Intellectual Property Appellate Board, for speedy disposal of such appeals.
- A science background was made compulsory for a person seeking to be registered as a patent agent under the Act. Earlier, lawyers without scientific backgrounds could become patent agents.

In our view, the two most significant changes that the 2002 amendments have brought about are in lengthening the term of patent protection and in reversing the burden of proof. For the former, the term has been raised to 20 years from the date of filing: the original Act allowed only 5 years for process patents in pharmaceuticals and that too from the date of grant (sealing) or 7 years from the date of application. For all non-pharmaceutical products and processes, the term was 14 years. In other words, TRIPS has increased, considerably, the monopoly protection for a new invention. In the case of pharmaceuticals this can mean very high prices being charged. Reversal of the burden of proof being the responsibility of patent infringers imposes considerable costs on those infringers of the small and medium category, given the high costs of patent litigation.

The Amendment of 2005

The last step in India's implementation of the changes required to make its patent law TRIPS compliant happened by way of the 2005 amendment. By this amendment Indian law, for the first time since 1970, allowed product and process patent protection to substances capable of being used as pharmaceuticals, food and agrochemicals. The 2005 amendment was preceded by a presidential ordinance in 2004.[3] After its promulgation there were intense debates about the scope of various provisions and finally the Indian Parliament enacted the 2005 amendment after making certain changes in the ordinance.

The 2005 amendment contains many controversial features which have led to many disputes post-2005. They cover elaborate provisions mentioning what is and is not considered patentable subject matter, a new definition of the 'inventive step' criterion of patentability, procedures governing both pre- and post-grant opposition, and a more liberal framework for compulsory licensing. Since most of the disputes that have arisen after 2005 involve interpreting various provisions of the said amendment, it will be covered in detail in the section dealing with patent litigation.

These amendments have virtually closed the option of reverse engineering that largely contributed to the growth of the Indian pharmaceutical industry. It will now not be possible to produce the patented product by adopting a different process. Some safeguard measures and flexibilities contained in the TRIPS Agreement were introduced in the patent system to protect public health, such as the provision for compulsory licensing to support access to sources of generic medicines, restricting pharmaceutical patents to new chemical and medical entities, and the introduction of pre-grant opposition to patent applications.

In sum, TRIPS compliance means the following:

- Introduction of product patents in chemicals, pharmaceuticals, agrochemicals and food products.
- Harmonization of patent term to 20 years irrespective of the field of technology.
- Publication of the patent application 18 months after filing.
- Further definition of non-patentable inventions.
- Definition of requirements for biological materials.
- Faster prosecution of patent application and transparency in the whole process.
- Reversal of the burden of proof of process when there is an infringement of process patents. As per the TRIPS requirement the alleged infringer will have to prove that he is not infringing the process patent.
- Effective framework for enforcement.
- Conditions for 'working of patents', 'compulsory licensing', 'opposition' and 'revocation'.
- Introduction of Bolar provisions. This exemption allows generic manufacturers to prepare generic drugs in advance of the patent expiration without any time restrictions.

India provides an example of the flexibilities under TRIPS which can effectively be used by developing countries. Instead of rejecting TRIPS, India has engaged in creative acts of legal interpretation that take full advantage of known TRIPS flexibilities, and has also generated new grounds. As our brief survey has shown, India's new patents regime is at an evolutionary stage and the jury is still out on the issue whether India will be in a position to successfully exploit the TRIPS flexibilities. Undoubtedly India got a good beginning with its patent amendments; however, it needs to be seen whether this can be converted into a successful model where the interests of all stakeholders can be safeguarded.

Of the three flexibilities provided under TRIPS, hitherto the country has invoked only one of them, dealing with compulsory licensing for the manufacturing of an anti-cancer drug by an Indian pharmaceutical manufacturer (Box 3.1). The domestic generic manufacturer was able to make a

BOX 3.1   COMPULSORY LICENSING: CASE OF *BAYER* VS *NATCO PHARMA*

Department of Industrial Policy and Promotion (Government of India) states that so far one compulsory license has been granted by the Controller General of Patents, Designs and Trade Marks to a drug manufacturing company since the amendment of the Patents Act in 2005 for an application filed under Section 84 of the Patents Act (as amended in 2005). The details are as follows:

● The compulsory license has been granted by the Controller General of Patents, Designs and Trade Marks for the anti-cancer drug in which the compound is 'Sorafenib Tosylate' (Patent No. 215758). The patent was granted to M/s Bayer Corporation, USA on 03.03.2008 by India Patent Office, consequent to their filing a national phase application in India.

● Bayer Corporation, USA developed the drug under the trade name 'NEXAVAR'. They received regulatory approval for importing and marketing the drug in India, and launched it in India in the year 2008.

● The compulsory license for the drug has been granted to Natco Pharma Ltd, Hyderabad, Andhra Pradesh.

● As per the orders of the Controller of Patents, Mumbai compulsory license has been granted to Natco for manufacture of 'NEXAVAR'. Natco Pharma Ltd are required to sell this drug at a price not exceeding Rs. 8880/- for a pack of 120 tablets, required for one month's treatment, which was earlier being sold by M/s Bayer Corporation at Rs. 2,80,428/- for one month's treatment.

● The patent office stipulated that Natco pay 6% of net sales as royalty to Bayer.

Source: Lok Sabha Unstarred Question No. 6851, answered on 17 May 2012, http://164.100.47.132/LssNew/psearch/QResult15.aspx?qref=124620 (accessed July 24, 2012).

generic version of a patented anti-cancer drug at 3 per cent of the cost of the original drug. This decision to use TRIPS flexibility is likely to send an important signal that despite the rigidities under TRIPS, it is still possible to have beneficial rulings in favour of domestic manufacturers.

3.   MACRO IMPLICATIONS OF TRIPS COMPLIANCE

The entire process of TRIPS compliance of India's patent regime, covering a period of over ten years, has had many potential and actual effects on innovative activity in the country. It must, however, be stated at the beginning that it is not at all easy to separate out the TRIPS effects from the effects of economic liberalization in general which was also happening during exactly the same period. In fact, one may argue that TRIPS compliance itself was part of the larger liberalization efforts that had gripped the world's economy. Given the inexorable link between the two, one has to be cautious in attributing some of the changes that we observe merely to TRIPS compliance.

Proximate and Distant Implications of TRIPS Compliance

Notwithstanding this caveat, the larger atmospheric changes brought about by TRIPS compliance may broadly be divided into proximate and distant changes. Under the former, we may add the following: (i) increased emphasis placed on the importance of patenting in various national and sub-national authorities (defining work done in government research institutes in terms of number of patents granted, setting up of patent facilitation centres, becoming a contracting party in the UN Patent Cooperation Treaty etc. are tangible manifestations of this); (ii) as a corollary of this, attempts made by those national IPR regimes that did not hitherto recognize 'utility models' to have them included as a way of recognizing incremental innovations in especially SMEs; (iii) more research on neglected tropical diseases; (iv) more clarity on patenting of medicinal plants and traditional knowledge; (v) reforms of national patent offices etc. and facilitating patents by domestic inventors; (vi) relationship between TRIPS compliance and licensing of disembodied technologies. This is because it was generally argued that a tighter IPR regime would encourage MNCs to transfer technologies to local firms, as technology suppliers need no longer worry about the possibility of licensees trying to learn the technology and developing local capabilities through reverse engineering.

Under distant changes we may list all those changes to instruments and institutions that support local development of technology (introduction or elaboration of tax incentives of various types, introduction of research grants, establishment of new technology funding institutions etc., schemes for improving the quality and quantity of science and engineering workforce). The very first initiative of the government was to come out with an explicit policy on innovation, the Science and Technology Policy, 2003.[4]

Incidentally it was the first time in twenty years that a new policy on innovation was stated and above all it was the very first time that a policy on science and technology had some explicit references to the term 'innovation'. It had also some specific pronouncements on strengthening the IPR regime. This will be seen in more detail when we discuss the proximate changes. Further, these measures include successive increases in plan allocations for scientific departments, setting up of new institutions for science education and research, creation of centres of excellence and facilities in emerging and frontline areas in academic and national institutes, introduction of new and attractive fellowships, strengthening infrastructure for research and development (R&D), encouraging public-private R&D partnerships, and the launching of programmes like Innovation in Science Pursuit for Inspired Research (INSPIRE), Nano Mission, Mega Facilities, Open Source Drug Discovery, Network Projects, National Biotechnology Development Strategy. The government has established a Science and Engineering Research Board (SERB) in the country as an autonomous body through an Act of Parliament. The creation of SERB, apart from significantly enhancing the level of basic research funding, should also impart the necessary autonomy, flexibility and speed in shaping the research programmes and delivery of funds to researchers. For experimenting and opening new areas of research and entering into novel territories, programmes such as Encouraging and Motivating Pursuit of World Class Exploratory Research (EMPOWER), Research Initiative to Scale New Knowledge (RISK) and CSIR.WWW have been launched. The outlay proposed for the 12th Plan for Science and Technology is Rs. 1700 billion. Apart from expanding the scope of investigator-centric extra mural research support programmes in terms of quantity and quality, multifaceted programmes like the Start-up Research Grant for Indian Diaspora undertaking faculty assignments in Indian academia, overseas doctoral scholarships and post-doctoral fellowships, Building Educators for Science Teaching, PAN India Mission, Public Private Partnerships for R&D, Disha Programme for Women in Science, Platforms for Technology Solution, Challenge Award for Global Positioning etc. are proposed for the 12th five year plan to take R&D to higher levels. To this one may also add a number of new institutions such as the National Knowledge Commission and its successor the National Innovation Council. Further, a number of technology policies have been announced in areas such as telecommunications, information technology, automotives, semiconductors, and electronics. The policies have several instruments to promote innovations in these specific areas.

Proximate Changes

As argued earlier, it is not easy to attribute the distant changes to TRIPS compliance per se as some of these changes have been precipitated by liberalization policies. On the contrary, the proximate changes are more the result of TRIPS compliance. We believe that six of these changes merit attention. They are:

(i) Increased emphasis on patenting
Before TRIPS compliance of the IPR regime, Indian scientists and inventors, whether based in industry, academia or research institutes, barely patented their inventions. But with so much discussion on the need for and importance of taking ownership of intellectual property rights on new inventions, one could see a change in the attitude towards patenting inventions. A clearer articulation of this new emphasis on patenting could be seen in the then new Science and Technology Policy, 2003 (Box 3.2). Three indicators of this increased propensity to patenting are considered: (a) increase in the number of patents secured by Indians in the India Patent Office[5] and at the US Patent and Trademark Office (USPTO; Figures 3.1 and 3.2); (b) emergence of the CSIR, the government research institute, as a major patenter of its inventions. CSIR accounts for a large proportion of domestic patents; and (c) participation of India as a contracting party in the Patent Cooperation Treaty (PCT).

Traditionally, most of the patents granted by the India Patent Office have been secured by MNCs. This continues to be so, although one can see that there has been a distinct upturn in patenting by both Indian and foreign inventors since 2005 or so. Figure 3.1 also shows that the number of US patents granted to Indian inventors is also showing an increasing trend, especially after TRIPS compliance. But Mani (2010) has shown that over two-thirds of the US patents are secured by foreign firms located in India. This implies that the tightening up of the patent regime in India has led to a number of MNCs locating at least a portion of their R&D activities in India. In other words, the period of TRIPS compliance is also accompanied by an increase in R&D outsourcing to India.[6]

Another issue to be examined is the technology-wide distribution of patenting. We did an exercise with the data on patenting in India by both Indian and foreign inventors (Figure 3.2).[7] The results show that the share of pharmaceuticals in total patents granted, after reaching its zenith in 2003, has started declining and currently accounts for just about 9 per cent of the total number of patents granted. This shows that, although TRIPS compliance led to an increase in the number of patents initially, the growth was not sustained. The numbers of patents granted for pharmaceuticals

BOX 3.2   REFERENCES TO GENERATION AND
          MANAGEMENT OF INTELLECTUAL
          PROPERTY AS CONTAINED IN SCIENCE
          AND TECHNOLOGY POLICY, 2003

● Intellectual Property Rights (IPR) have to be viewed, not
  as a self-contained and distinct domain, but rather as an
  effective policy instrument that would be relevant to wide
  ranging socio-economic, technological and political concepts. The generation and fullest protection of competitive
  intellectual property from Indian R&D programmes will be
  encouraged and promoted.
● The process of globalization is leading to situations where
  the collective knowledge of societies normally used for
  common good is converted to proprietary knowledge for
  commercial profit of a few. Action will be taken to protect
  our indigenous knowledge systems, primarily through
  national policies, supplemented by supportive international
  action. For this purpose, IPR systems, which specially
  protect scientific discoveries and technological innovations
  arising out of such traditional knowledge, will be designed
  and effectively implemented.Our legislation with regard to
  Patents, Copyrights and other forms of Intellectual Property
  will ensure that maximum incentives are provided for individual inventors, and to our scientific and technological
  community, to undertake large scale and rapid commercialization, at home and abroad.
● The development of skills and competence to manage
  IPR and leverage its influence will be given a major thrust.
  This is an area calling for significant technological insights
  and legal expertise and will be handled differently from the
  present, and with high priority.

Source: Department of Science and Technology (2003), http://www.dst.gov.in/
stsysindia/stp2003.htm#c7 (last accessed July 24, 2012).

and food items have been showing considerable year to year variations
(Figure 3.2). It is interesting to note that the numbers of patents granted in
both have spiked since TRIPS compliance in 2005, but declined from 2010
for pharmaceuticals and 2008 in the case of food.

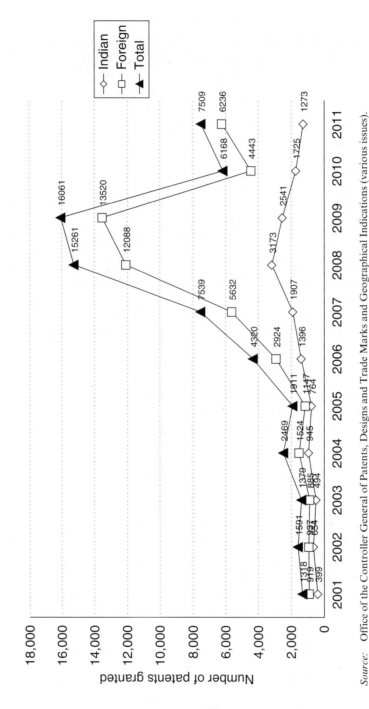

Source: Office of the Controller General of Patents, Designs and Trade Marks and Geographical Indications (various issues).

Figure 3.1 *Trends in the number of patents granted to Indian and foreign inventors by the India Patent Office, and to Indian inventors by the USPTO*

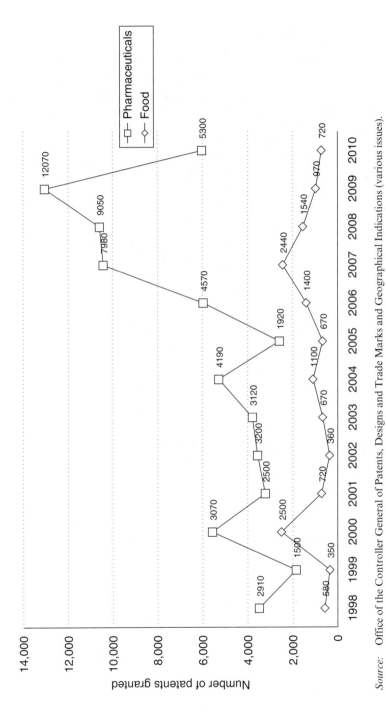

Source: Office of the Controller General of Patents, Designs and Trade Marks and Geographical Indications (various issues).

Figure 3.2   Trends in the number of patent grants in India for pharmaceuticals and food

71

The India Patent Office does not provide us with a breakdown of industry-wide patents applied for and granted. So we are unable to find out the figures for Indian and foreign patentees in this case, although given the overall distribution between foreigners and domestic patentees, it is highly probable that even in the case of pharmaceuticals most of the patentees are foreign companies. One thing that is clear is that TRIPS compliance has led to a sort of surge in patenting in India, although most of the patentees are foreign companies rather than Indian ones.

For a brief period in 2004–05, software patents were allowed in India for embedded software. According to press reports,[8] about 150 patents on technical effects of software were granted by the India Patent Office in areas such as video imaging systems in mobile handsets and data transmission systems as well as methods for controlling speeds of devices. However, software patents are allowed by the USPTO. Given India's expertise in software, a number of MNCs have established software development centres in India and these have been increasingly securing a number of patents granted at the USPTO (Figure 3.3). What is important is that software patents now account for about a quarter of all patents granted to Indian inventors at the USPTO. Of late, Indian IT companies too have been securing software patents at the USPTO: their share has increased from just about 2 per cent of software patents from India to about 5 per cent in 2011. Indian IT companies have been a bit slow in patenting their inventions, but with growing awareness of patenting they too have been following the pharma firms in taking IPRs over their new inventions.

Another interesting finding is that the number of Indian inventors patenting at USPTO has increased significantly in a number of high-technology areas such as those of telecommunications, medical devices and semiconductor devices – two fast growing industries in India (Figure 3.4).

The most prolific Indian inventor is the Council for Scientific and Industrial Research (CSIR),[9] an important civilian scientific research establishment in the country. The CSIR in 1996 announced a reform strategy[10] wherein it set a target to hold a patent bank comprising 50 Indian and 1000 foreign patents by 2001, as against 80 Indian and 436 foreign patents in its portfolio in 1996. Thus it actively encouraged its scientists to file patents, in both India and abroad (Figure 3.5).

As against this target, the CSIR, by March 31, 2010, has in its portfolio 2349 Indian patents and 3054 patents abroad.[11] This increased patenting has certainly improved its stature in the scientific landscape. It has now published a new vision document[12] which extends to the year 2022 and this has IP generation as an important measurement of work done. But there is very little information on whether these patents are yielding any royalties to the research network,[13] although the CSIR apparently spent to date

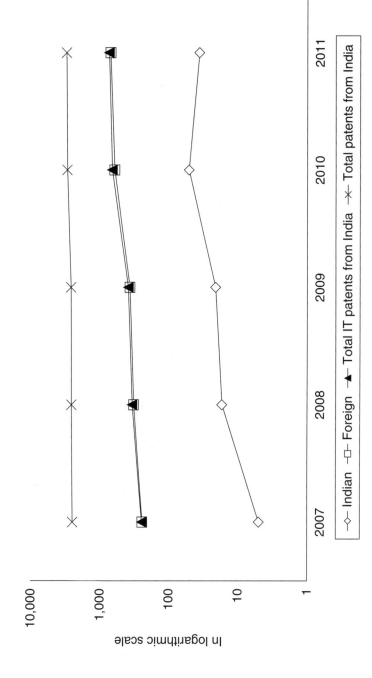

10,000

1,000

100

10

1

In logarithmic scale

2007   2008   2009   2010   2011

—◇— Indian   —□— Foreign   —◣— Total IT patents from India   —✕— Total patents from India

Source: Computed from USPTO.

Figure 3.3   Trends in IT patenting from India at USPTO, 2007–11

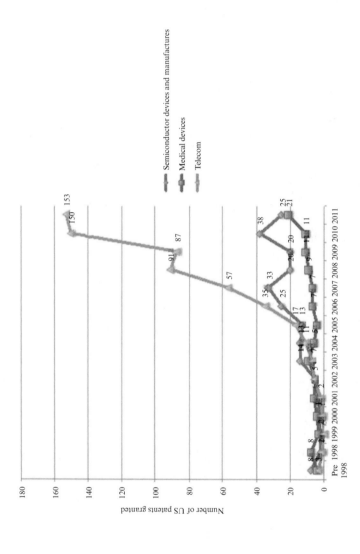

Source: Computed from USPTO.

Figure 3.4 Trends in the number of US patents granted in three high-technology industries post-TRIPS

74

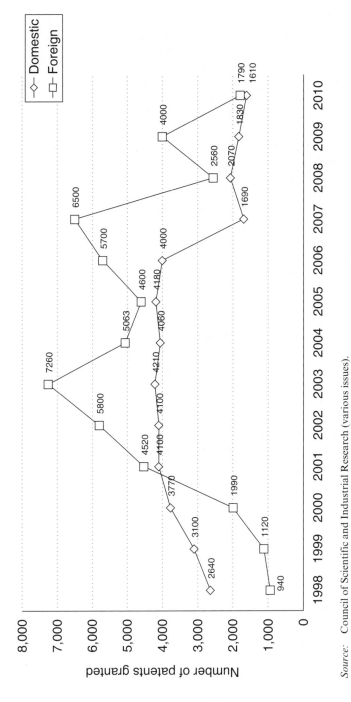

Source: Council of Scientific and Industrial Research (various issues).

Figure 3.5 Trends in foreign and domestic patent applications by CSIR, 1998–2010

a sum of Rs. 742 million on securing these patents, of which only Rs. 18 million or so was spent in securing patents from the IPO.[14] The remaining Rs. 724 million was spent on securing patents around the world, in jurisdictions such as the US, Japan and the EU.

In order to encourage the generation of innovations in universities and government research institutes, the government has tabled the Protection and Utilisation of Public Funded Intellectual Property (PUPFIP) Bill, 2008 before the upper house of India's parliament, the Rajya Sabha.[15] The bill stresses the creation of intellectual property rights (IPR) as a form of accountability – inspired by the American Bayh–Dole Act of 1980. The Parliamentary Standing Committee[16] found that the PUPFIP bill is likely to take away creativity from universities and research institutions, and instead promote crass competition. This is also echoed in other writings on the bill that say it erroneously assumes that protection of intellectual property is the best and only way to promote creativity and innovation (Basheer, 2008; Kochupillai, 2010; Centre for Internet and Society[17]). However, the bill itself is yet to be passed by the parliament and has therefore not come into being as a law.

An important development that merits mention here is that India became a contracting party to the PCT in 1999. This enabled Indian inventors to file applications in over 150 jurisdictions with one PCT application. Consequently, the number of PCT applications has shown a steady increase (Mani, 2010), thereby allowing Indian inventors the chance of their inventions being protected in a larger number of jurisdictions.

The Patent Facilitating Centre (PFC, set up in 1995) at the Technology Information Forecasting and Assessment Council (TIFAC) has also had various schemes of support (technical, legal, and financial) for enabling patenting of innovations emanating from research funded by the Department of Science and Technology, any of the Indian universities or government research institutes. It will also aid private and public sector enterprises for a nominal fee. Further, it has set up state-level Patent Information Centres across 17 states in the country. Together, these centres have been attempting to raise awareness on patenting among inventors and potential inventors. However, to date there has not been any comprehensive evaluation of the activities of the PFC and therefore we are unable to draw any inferences about its efficacy in creating and sustaining a patent culture.

The private sector too has been emphasizing the need for patenting new inventions. In order to sensitize its members, the major industry association in the country, the Confederation of Indian Industry (CII), in association with George Washington University Law School and US India Business Council, has been organizing a series of summits on intellectual property annually since 2004. According to CII, the objective of the summit was, inter alia, to build partnerships between overseas and Indian industries for collaborative R&D projects and to disseminate information about international best practices in IP protection.

Thus our detailed survey has shown that one of the more proximate implications of TRIPS has been to create a great awareness of the importance of patenting their new inventions among researchers of various hues. But foreign companies operating from India seem to have taken advantage of this emphasis rather than Indian inventors, and have vastly improved their patent portfolios, especially in the field of IT.

(ii) Patenting of incremental innovations, especially by small and medium enterprises

India's patent law does not provide for utility models. Utility models are ideal IPRs for incremental innovations. India's industrial structure is characterized by a large number of small and medium firms. These firms do not make new inventions but incremental changes in known products and processes for which a utility model is the most appropriate form of IPR. TRIPS does not specifically mention utility models. However, Part I of this Agreement (Articles 2,3 and 4) refers to the provisions of the Paris Convention. Further, Article 1 mentions 'Members may, but shall not be obliged to, implement in their law more extensive protection than is required by this Agreement, provided that such protection does not contravene the provisions of this Agreement.'Given this, policy makers in India are favourably disposed to including utility models in India's IPR regime. Towards this end, the Department of Industrial Policy and Performance (DIPP) has floated a discussion paper on utility models.[18] Several reactions from a variety of stakeholders to the inclusion of utility models have been received.[19]

(iii) More research on neglected tropical diseases

India is home to a number of 'neglected tropical diseases' (NTDs), the incidence of which has been growing (Table 3.2). It is often the very poor whom these diseases afflict. Given that the market for the drugs for these diseases is small, even the domestic companies were not interested in R&D to find new drugs for their treatment. TRIPS compliance with product and process patent protection was expected to improve the investment climate for R&D in these NTDs. A recently released report (Adams, Gurney and Pendlebury, 2012) measured NTD coverage in scientific publications across the world between 1992 and 2011, using data from *Web of Science*, an online database that covers 11,500 journals worldwide. During the time period (1992–2011) analysed, more than 73,000 papers on NTDs were published. Most of these focused on a single disease, and articles covered diverse aspects of NTDs,

Table 3.2   Incidence of NTDs in India (number of cases)

	Dengue	Rabies	Leprosy	Kala-Azhar	Active trachoma	Trichiasis	Lymphatic Filariasis
2008	12,581	259		33,598			1,130,016
2009	15,535	263	134,184	24,212			1,179,051
2010	28,292	162	133,717	28,941			1,210,108
2011	10,344		126,800		15,289	3,436	

Source: Compiled from Lok Sabha, Annexure referred to in reply to Unstarred Question No. 813, http://164.100.47.132/Annexure/Isq15/9/au813.htm (last accessed July 30, 2012).

ranging from the biology of disease vectors to healthcare solutions. The number of papers doubled from around 2,500 in 1992 to more than 5,000 in 2011, the report states. As a share of world research output, the papers on these diseases accounted for around 0.4 per cent of total global articles and reviews for much of the period, but that share began to rise in 2005, around the time that the general term for this disease group also started to come into use. Most papers included at least one author from developed countries, but the presence of authors from Brazil and India is particularly noteworthy. In 2011, more papers on NTDs had an author or co-author from Brazil than from the United Kingdom, and India's participation is higher than Germany's, for example.

In terms of R&D investments, public resources devoted to research on NTDs in India, though rising, is still only a paltry sum compared to what is invested in pharmaceutical R&D in general by both domestic and foreign enterprises (Figures 3.6 and 3.7). According to G-Finder,[20] the government (through either the Indian Council of Medical Research or the Department of Biotechnology) funded $57 million worth of R&D projects in five NTDs during the period 2008–10. All these R&D projects were performed by either the government research institutes or the universities and not a single project was funded with any of the numerous pharmaceutical enterprises in either the public or private sector.

Domestic pharmaceutical firms are continuing to concentrate their research on products for the export market and are therefore not spending much on R&D for NTDs. This will be discussed in detail in the section on R&D strategies.

(iv)   Clarity in patenting of traditional knowledge, medicinal plants and microorganisms

India is the only country in the world to have set up in 2001 an institutional mechanism – the Traditional Knowledge Library (TKDKL)[21] –

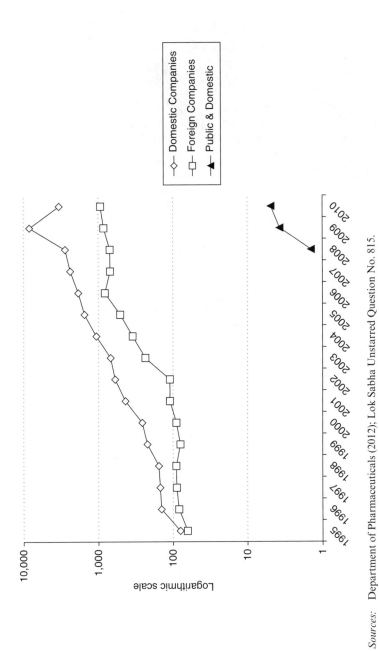

Sources: Department of Pharmaceuticals (2012); Lok Sabha Unstarred Question No. 815.

Figure 3.6 Public R&D investments in NTDs compared to R&D investments by domestic and foreign pharmaceutical firms

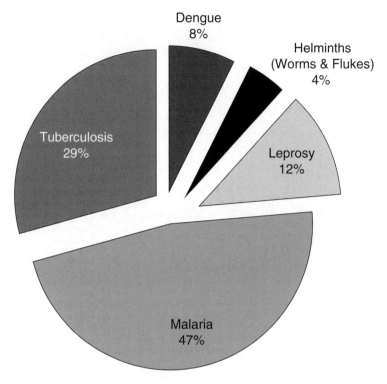

Source: Computed from data provided in G-Finder (Global Funding of Innovation for Neglected Tropical Diseases), http://g-finder.policycures.org/gfinder_report/search.jsp (last accessed August 13, 2012).

Figure 3.7   Disease-wide distribution of public R&D on NTDs, 2008–10

to protect its Traditional Knowledge (TK). The TKDL enables prompt and almost cost-free cancellation or withdrawal of patent applications relating to India's TK. The TKDL is a unique, proprietary database that integrates diverse knowledge systems and languages. It is based on 148 books of prior art relating to Indian systems of medicine. The TKDL connects patent examiners around the world with these books of knowledge and it is available to all patent offices that have signed a TKDL Access Agreement. This has built-in, non-disclosure mechanisms to safeguard India's interests and counter any possible misuse. Under such an agreement, patent examiners may use the TKDL for search and examination purposes only and its contents may only be revealed to third parties for the purposes of citation. So far, India has signed TKDL Access Agreements with the EPO and the patent offices of Australia, Canada, Germany, the United Kingdom and the United States. Negotiations are also ongoing with the patent offices of New Zealand and Japan where agreement in principle has already been reached.

Around the time the TKDL was established, the TKDL expert group estimated that, annually, some 2,000 patents relating to Indian medicinal systems were being erroneously granted by patent offices around the world. Hitherto the TKDL has enabled the cancellation or withdrawal of a large number of patent applications attempting to claim rights over the use of various medicinal plants. It is generally opined that India's TKDL is a unique tool that plays a critical role in protecting the country's traditional knowledge.

The establishment of the TKDL has helped India to resolve patents that were issued abroad for technologies that were based on traditional knowledge. The case of a patent for a method of treatment or management of stress is a good illustration of this (Box 3.3).

Medicinal plants as well as the products derived from them which are part of traditional knowledge or which are an aggregation or duplication of known properties of a traditionally known component or components are not patentable under Section 3(j) and Section 3(p) of the Patents Act, 1970 respectively. However, substantial improvement in products derived from medicinal plants, which fulfils the criteria prescribed for patentability in the Patents Act, 1970, can be granted patents. So far, 18 such patents have been granted to foreign companies. Of these, five are derived from medicinal plants which are indigenous to India. See Table 3.3 for details of patents granted for medicinal plants. As far as Ayurvedic medicines are concerned, since 1995, the India Patent Office has granted four such patents to foreign companies, while Indian companies and institutions have secured 117 patents.[22]

The Biodiversity Act, 2002 takes into account the impact of awarding an intellectual property to a product derived from medicinal plants on the conservation of the medicinal plant. This process is carried out in consultation with state level biodiversity authorities. Section 6 (i) of the Biological Diversity Act states that 'No person shall apply for any intellectual property right by whatever name called, in or outside India for any invention based on any research or information on a biological resource obtained from India without obtaining the previous approval of the National Biodiversity Authority before making such application'. However, this provision is subject to Section 40 of the Biodiversity Act, 2002, which states that the Central Government may, in consultation with the National Biodiversity Authority, by notification in the Official Gazette, declare that the provisions of this Act shall not apply to any items, including biological

---

BOX 3.3   PATENT FOR ASHWAGANDHA EXTRACT

Natreon Inc., a US pharmaceutical company specializing in developing novel compounds extracted from the traditional botanicals of Ayurvedic medicine, had filed a patent application titled 'Method of Treatment or Management of Stress' on July 27, 2006 through a composition comprising *Withania somnifera* plant extract; and a pharmaceutically, veterinary or nutritionally acceptable carrier(s) before the European Patent Office (EPO). The TDKL has submitted evidences to EPO along with references of various texts of the three Indian systems of medicine, namely Ayurveda, Siddha and Unani. These evidences established that Ashwagandha (*Withania somnifera*) is frequently and effectively used through oral administration in the treatment of depression, insomnia, gastritis, gastric ulcer and convulsions which are defined as the causative factors of stress in the patent application. TKDL evidences also mention the use of Ashwagandha in the treatment of palpitation, excessive perspiration, diabetes mellitus and anemia, which have been stated as conditions resulting from stress by the applicant. After examination of the evidence presented before it, the EPO has observed that, in the light of this document, the subject-matter of claims cannot be considered as novel. Accordingly, the applicant Natreon Inc. withdrew its application on March 25, 2010.

Source: Lok Sabha Unstarred Question no. 6818, http://164.100.47.132/LssNew/psearch/QResult15.aspx?qref=87568(accessed July 31, 2012.

---

resources normally traded as commodities. The Ministry of Environment and Forests (see their Notification dated October 26, 2009) has declared that the provisions of the Act would not apply to 190 biological resources which are normally traded as commodities.

Another related but important issue that has been brought to the fore is the patenting of microorganisms. Under Section 3(j) of the Patents Act, 1970 (as amended in 2005), a patent cannot be granted to plants and animals in whole or any part thereof other than microorganisms but including seeds, varieties and species and essentially biological processes for production or propagation of plants and animals. During the debate on TRIPS compliance in the Indian parliament (which took place in 2005),

Table 3.3 Number of patents granted to medical plants by the IPO: post-TRIPS

	Patent no.	Title	Patentee	Nationality	Indian medical plant
1	248562	An antioxidant-promoting composition	Lifeline Nutraceuticals Corporation	USA	Turmeric, which is of Indian origin
2	231692	Compositions for preventing or treating pollenosis, allergic nephritis, atopic dermatitis, asthma or urticaria	Matsuura Yankugyo Co., Ltd	Japan	Cucurbita moschata, originating from either Central America or northern South America, but widely cultivated in India; also Carthamus tinctorius, which is grown/cultivated in India
3	213308	Nutritional supplement	The Quigley Corporation	USA	Turmeric, which is of Indian origin
4	190850	Process for the preparation of herbal pharmaceutical composition for the management of menopausal syndrome	United Global Ventures Limited	Hong Kong (China)	Tinospora cordifolia, known by the common name Guduchi, an herbaceous vine of the family Menispermaceae indigenous to the tropical areas of India
5	243564	Process for the preparation of a herbal composition for the treatment of viral infections	Sage R&D	USA	Composition derived from Chinese herbal medicines. Aeginetia indica is the active ingredient found in India too.
6	211690	Process for preparation of a composition for both human and veterinary application	Ropapharm B.V.	Netherlands	Origanum vulgare, a common species of Origanum, a genus of the mint family (Lamiaceae). It is native to warm-temperate western and southwestern Eurasia and the Mediterranean region.
7	242831	An anti-microbial composition	The Quigley Corporation	USA	Ginger, which is consumed as a delicacy, medicine, or spice. Ginger cultivation began in South Asia and has since spread to East Africa and the Caribbean

Table 3.3 (continued)

	Patent no.	Title	Patentee	Nationality	Indian medical plant
8	219874	Composition useful for the treatment of viral infections in an animal	Sage R&D	USA	Composition derived from Chinese herbal medicines, medical plants and extracts thereof. Aeginetia indica is the active ingredient, found in India too
9	221614	Herbal injection and a method to produce the same	Maoxiang Wang	China	Plant material from the genus Ixeris, which is a flowering plant in the daisy family. The active ingredient is used Chinese traditional medicine. Ixeris Sonchifolia is found in India too
10	200879	Composition for heart disease, method to prepare same	Tianjin Tasly Pharmaceutical Co., Ltd	China	Salvia miltiorrhiza, which is also known as red sage, Chinese sage, tan shen, or danshen. It is a perennial plant in the genus Salvia, highly valued for its roots in traditional Chinese medicine. Native to China and Japan
11	209391	Negatively charged polysaccharide derivable from aloe vera and a process for preparing the same	2Qr Research B.V.	Netherlands	Aloe vera: large scale agricultural production undertaken in Pakistan, Australia, Bangladesh, Cuba, the Dominican Republic, China, Mexico, India, Jamaica, Kenya, South Africa and USA
12	214166	Herbal composition for angina pectoris, method to prepare same and uses thereof	Tianjin Tasly Pharmaceutical Co., Ltd	China	Medicinal plant native to Japan and China

13	219566	Nutraceutical for the prevention and treatment of cancers and diseases affecting the liver	Bui, Cuong, Q.	USA	Aloe vera and Brassica oleracea, which are grown widely in India and other countries
14	238006	Pharmaceutical composition for the treatment of prostatic hyperplasia and prostatitis	Bright Future Pharmaceutical Laboratories Limited	Hong Kong	Medicinal plants endemic to southern China, with further outposts in Europe, and central, southern and eastern Asia
15	221711	Process for preparing a novel medicament mixture	Suleiman Dado	Austria	The process involves mixing honey, olive oil and optionally one or more of: beeswax, propolis, chamomile, sage, aloe vera, thyme, lavender and/or various oils
16	244699	An improved composition of a drug	Malireddy S. Reddy	USA	The drug is selected from the group consisting of herbal drugs, allopathic drugs, periodontal drugs, and combinations thereof
17	206049	Method of producing a herbal composition for angina pectoris, method to prepare same and uses thereof	Tianjin Tasly Pharmaceutical Co., Ltd	China	Medicinal plant native to Japan and China
18	216577	Herbal composition for angina pectoris	Tianjin Tasly Pharmaceutical Co., Ltd	China	Medicinal plant native to Japan and China

Source: Annexure to Starred Question No. 248 answered on December 12, 2011 at: http://164.100.47.132/Annexture/lsq15/9/as248.htm (last accessed July 31, 2012).

patentability of microorganisms were raised. In order to have clarity on this issue, the government established a committee under the chairmanship of Dr R.A. Mashelkar, known as the Technical Expert Group on Patent Law Issues. The final report[23] of the committee, submitted in 2009, concluded that excluding microorganisms *per se* from patent protection would be violative of TRIPS. However, it is not immediately clear if patenting of microorganisms is allowed in India.

(v)   Relationship between TRIPS compliance and technology licensing

One of the most important assertions made during the discussions on TRIPS compliance was that it would cause IPR regimes in developing countries such as India to tighten up to an extent that reverse engineering would be virtually impossible. This state of affairs would prompt MNCs to transfer technology to unaffiliated companies located in developing countries much more freely than before. Due to tighter IPR regimes under TRIPS compliance, one should now be seeing an increase in the number of technical collaboration agreements signed between MNCs and unaffiliated Indian companies.

The period of TRIPS compliance coincides with a period of economic liberalization when the government had already relaxed the conditions under which technical collaboration agreements are contracted between foreign and Indian firms. Specifically, unlike before, these collaboration agreements do not go through a formal approval process. Further, the upper limit that was fixed on royalty payments and technical know-how fees was considerably raised. All these factors would have contributed to a large number of licensing agreements – the traditional model adopted by Indian companies towards technology importation from developed country firms. In order to check this we have compiled data on two different ways of looking at the volume of licensing contracts signed between MNCs and Indian companies. At the aggregate level, we have first put together the fragmentary data that are now available on the total number of collaboration agreements, and the share of those collaboration agreements in the total that does not involve any equity payments (Table 3.4). The share of pure technical collaboration agreements has been steadily coming down over time.

This shows that MNCs are willing to transfer technologies to companies in India only if their own affiliates are allowed in India. In fact, this data from India can be counter-checked with the source of royalty receipts received by US MNCs from abroad: over two-thirds emanate from their own affiliates abroad (National Science Board, 2012).

The argument here is that, while the total number of collaboration agreements may have increased (as do royalty payments per unit of GDP),

Table 3.4   Declining share of foreign technology licensing agreements in total foreign collaborations

Year	FDI cases	Foreign technology licensing agreement	Ratio of licensing agreements to FDI
1991	289	661	2.29
1992	692	828	1.20
1993	785	691	0.88
1994	1,062	792	0.75
1995	1,355	982	0.72
1996	1,559	744	0.48
1997	1,655	660	0.40
1998	1,191	595	0.50
1999	1,726	498	0.29
2000	1,726	418	0.24
2001	1,982	288	0.15
2002	1,986	307	0.16
2003			
2004			
2005		90	
2006		86	
2007		81	

Source: Department of Industrial Policy and Performance, Government of India.

an overwhelming majority of these transactions are intra firm transfers, namely between MNCs and their affiliates in India and not between MNCs and unaffiliated companies.

The number of cases of collaboration agreements may not always give us the full picture, as agreements may differ in scope. So in order to overcome this limitation, and also to have a disaggregated picture, we analysed the direct cost of technology importation (as revealed through a sum of royalty and technical know-how fees) by firms in two of the fast growing industries in India which are most likely to have been affected by TRIPS compliance. These are the chemicals (including pharmaceuticals) and the automotive industries (Figure 3.8).

One caveat is in order. The data on direct costs contained in Figure 3.8 refers to both types of transactions, namely those between MNCs and their own affiliates in India and those between MNCs and unaffiliated companies. Ideally speaking we should have had the two series. Nevertheless, the majority of the firms in the chemicals industry are Indian while in the case of the automotive industry, the industry is divided (in terms of share in sales turnover) more or less equally between the two. It

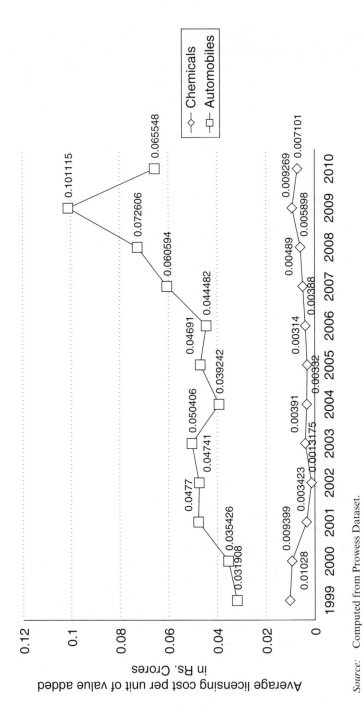

Source: Computed from Prowess Dataset.

Figure 3.8 Trends in average cost of licensing foreign technology: automotive vs chemicals

is interesting to note (from Figure 3.8) that the technology importation of the chemicals industry has increased very slowly, while that of the automotive industry has shot up during the TRIPS compliance period. These two sets of evidence, given their limitations, show us that TRIPS compliance does not appear to have increased technology transfer agreements on a large scale as was predicted. This could be attributed to the imperfections in the market for disembodied technology: the market is highly oligopolistic (Mani, 2002).

(vi) Reform of the Patent Office

The India Patent Office has undergone considerable modernization since TRIPS compliance: a sum of Rs. 1.5 billion was spent during 1998–2007. In very specific terms this resulted in the commissioning of state-of-the-art offices in Delhi, Kolkata, Chennai and Mumbai, creation of additional posts in the Patent Office, and the introduction of E-filing of patent applications. Further, an Intellectual Property Training Institute (IPTI) was set up to impart training to patent examiners. As a result of these initiatives, timelines for patent and trade mark processing have come down considerably, and a backlog of over 44,000 patent applications and 375,000 trade mark applications was done away with in the three years ending 2006–07. The initiatives for creation of awareness have triggered IP activity in the country in terms of increased filing of the applications for grant of IPRs. The impact of these initiatives is as follows:

1. The filing of patent applications increased more than sevenfold, from 4,824 in 1999–2000 to 34,287 in 2009–10, and the patents granted during the period increased more than threefold, from 1881 to 6168;
2. The average time taken for grant of patents reduced from about 6–10 years to about 2–3 years; and
3. An institute for training fresh examiners as well as controllers and registrars in the IPOs was established.

However, even at the time of writing (March 31, 2010), India had a total of only 80 patent examiners to deal with around 34,000 applications, implying that each examiner had to potentially examine 425 applications although only about 75 applications were actually examined during that year (2009–10). Compare this figure with what an average USPTO examiner does: only 88 applications per examiner (Kapczynski, 2010).

4. TRENDS IN OPPOSITION AND PATENT LITIGATION

The amended Patents Act, 1970 allows for pre- and post-grant opposition of patents. Pre-grant opposition can be filed by any person by representation in the IPO within six months from the date of publication of the patent application or in case the six months duration is not available then the representation can be filed until the grant of the patent, whichever expires later. The grounds of opposition are provided under section 25 (1) of the Indian Patents Act, 1970 as amended in 2005. Some important grounds are wrongful obtainment, anticipation by prior publication or use or already being claimed in any other patent, obviousness, or non-patentability under section 3 of the said Act. The applicant or any party considers pre-grant opposition only after the filing of an examination. On receiving the pre-grant opposition the Controller issues a notice to the patentee. The patentee is to submit her statement and evidence against the opposition within three months from the date of notification by the Controller of patent. The Controller may offer a hearing on request by the patentee as well as by the opponent to settle the pre-grant opposition. A pre-grant opposition has to be disposed of by the Controller within one month by rejecting the opposition and granting the patent, or by accepting the opposition and rejecting the application, or by amending the application and granting the patent. As can be seen from Figure 3.9, the number of pre-grant oppositions has always been a very small share of the total number of published cases, and it has decreased over time.

Post-grant opposition can be filed by any interested persons who are engaged in or promoting research in the field of technology. Post-grant opposition can be filed within a period twelve months after the grant of a patent. The grounds of opposition are provided under section 25 (2) of the Patents Act, 1970. Some of the grounds are wrongful obtaining of the invention by the inventor, anticipation by prior publications, use, traditional knowledge, the invention is obvious to a person in the field, non-patentable inventions, disclosure of false information to the patent office, non-disclosure or wrongful disclosure of the biological source etc. An opposition board is formed by the Controller and consists of three members. The examiner who has dealt with the patent application during the procedure for grant is not eligible to become a board member. The opposition board is given three months to conduct an examination and submit a recommendation with reasons on each ground of opposition. The Controller can fix a date for a hearing by giving at least ten days' notice to the parties on receiving the recommendation from the opposition board. After hearing the parties and analysing the recommendation of the

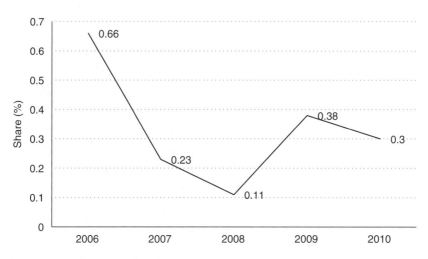

Source: Computed from The Office of the Controller General of Patents, Designs, Trade Marks and Geographical Indications (2010), p. 12.

Figure 3.9   Trends in the share of pre-grant opposition cases in total number of published cases

board the Controller decides the matter and informs the parties about her decision, giving reasons thereof. The Controller can order for the patent to be maintained, or amended, or revoked. As Figure 3.10 indicates, the post-grant oppositions are a small percentage of the total number of patents granted, but their share has been increasing.

Further to these, there has also been an increase in the number of patent litigations in India. Although traditionally these litigations have been between MNC patent holders and domestic companies which have infringed these patents, in the post-TRIPS period, one also sees increasing cases of litigation between rival Indian companies. There are no reliable data on patent litigations. We have been able to piece together some data from a private source (Bhola, 2012) but we have not been able to verify whether these are reliable figures (Figure 3.11). It indicates a significant increase in cases, from just 7 in 2006 to 29 in 2011. There have been a number of high profile cases, the most discussed being the *Bajaj* vs *TVS* (Box 3.4) and the 'Novartis Glivec' cases.

The 'Novartis Glivec' case[24] also brings to our attention a very contentious section in India's IPR regime, namely section 3 (d): under this flexibility certain inventions are not patentable in India. The basic rationale behind the section is to prevent or limit 'evergreening' of existing molecules and patent portfolios as variants of existing compounds that do not show

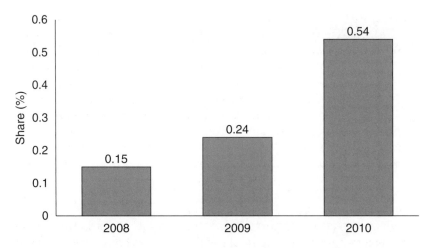

Source: Data on post-grant opposition are compiled from Lok Sabha Unstarred Question No. 5018, http://164.100.47.132/LssNew/psearch/QResult15.aspx?qref=86005 (last accessed on August 2, 2012).

Figure 3.10   Post-grant opposition intensity as a per cent of total number of patents granted

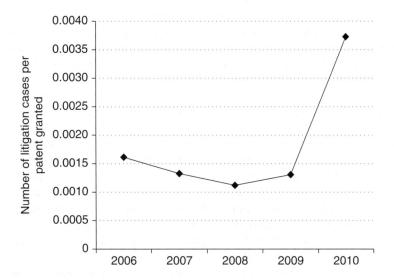

Source: Based on estimated number of litigation cases filed from Bhola (2012).

Figure 3.11   Number of cases of patent litigation per patent granted by IPO: post-TRIPS

BOX 3.4   *BAJAJ* VS *TVS* PATENT LITIGATION CASE

In 2005, Bajaj was granted a patent related to twin spark plugs, and it was called DTS-Itechnology. In 2007, TVS announced the launch of its motorbike Flame. Bajaj alleged infringement at Madras High Court and TVS initiated revocation proceedings against Bajaj's patent. According to TVS Bajaj's invention was prior art and the concept of twin spark plugs was in public knowledge through an expired US patent of Honda. It thus deceptively obtained an Indian patent. But Bajaj has contested this argument and claimed that its invention was directed to improve the combustion of lean fuel mixture in the small bore engine for improved fuel efficiency. The court granted an interim injunction against TVS, but the company filed an appeal against the injunction order. After hearing both the parties, the injunction was lifted by a division bench of the high court and the appeal is still pending in the Supreme Court of India.

Source: Bhola (2012) and other sources.

---

enhanced efficacy and are not considered to satisfy the first criterion of patenting, namely novelty. Invoking this provision, the India Patent Office has rejected the patent application of Novartis and the matter is now before the Supreme Court. Sampat et al. (2012) discuss the implications of this case for patent policy in an emerging economy in the post-TRIPS phase.

5.   R&D STRATEGIES IN THE PHARMACEUTICAL INDUSTRY IN INDIA

In this section our focus is on the impact of re-introduction of product patent protection in pharmaceuticals on R&D for innovation. The other important impact of product patents relates to competition and market prices. As Chaudhuri (2012) finds, the days of product monopolies and high prices are back in India. The MNCs have started marketing new patented drugs at exorbitant prices, particularly for life threatening diseases such as cancer. A 50 ml injection of Roche's anti cancer drug Herceptin (generic name: trastumuzab) costs Rs. 135,200. Among the other high priced drugs are Merck's Erbitux (cetuximab) (Rs. 87,920),

Bristol-Myers-Squibb's Ixempra (ixabepilone) (Rs. 66,430), Pfizer's Macugen (pegaptanib) (Rs. 45,350), Sanofi-Aventis' Fasturtec (rasburicase) (Rs. 45,000), and Roche's Avastin (bevicizumab) (Rs. 37,180). It is important to note that these prices are for a single injection/tablet etc. The cost of treatment per person per year would be much higher. For example, for Dasatinib, used for the treatment of chronic myeloid leukaemia, the price of a 70 mg tablet is Rs. 3,905. But the cost of treatment per person per year exceeds Rs. 2 million.

In the underdeveloped Indian pharmaceutical industry before 1972, the capacity to conduct R&D was limited. But has the situation changed following the rapid growth of the industry since the 1970s to justify stronger patent protection in India? Is it true that product patent protection may have an adverse impact on access by making prices dearer, but can be good for the R&D based pharmaceutical industry in India? What has been the nature of R&D activities and innovation in the Indian pharmaceutical industry? Does India's experience support the claims of MNCs and their advocates that strong patent protection is needed in India for R&D and innovation?

Traditionally, the Indian pharmaceutical industry spent very little on R&D. In the early 1990s, its R&D expenditure amounted to only about 1.5 per cent of sales (Grace, 2004, p. 37). Even larger companies such as Ranbaxy and Dr Reddy's Laboratories spent only 2–3 per cent of their sales on R&D in 1992–93.[25] Since then, however, and particularly since the early 2000s, there has been a substantial increase in research spending in a segment of the industry. While most of the Indian companies continue to be minor R&D spenders, for 38 companies each with R&D expenditure of more than Rs. 100 million in 2010–11, R&D expenditure has increased steadily from 1.7 per cent of sales in 1992–93 to 4.3 per cent in 2001–02, and then sharply to 8.1 per cent in 2004–05 and 9.1 per cent in 2005–06. Thereafter, however, a decline is observed to 7.2 in 2010–11.[26] Here we focus on the more dynamic segment of the Indian pharmaceutical industry for which R&D expenditures have substantially increased (Table 3.5).

The objectives of R&D conducted by Indian companies can be broadly classified as follows:

- Development of new chemical entities (NCEs)
- Modifications of existing chemical entities to develop new formulations, compositions and combinations (also known as incrementally modified drugs)
- Development of generics (that is, development of processes for manufacturing active pharmaceutical ingredients (APIs) and development of formulations to satisfy quality and regulatory requirements for marketing patent-expired drugs).

Table 3.5   *R&D expenditure of major Indian pharmaceutical companies,*
2010–11

Company	R&D expenditure Rs. million	Research intensity (%)	R&D expenditure US $ million
Dr Reddy's Laboratories	6,247	11.1	138.85
Lupin	5,475.6	12.3	121.7
Ranbaxy Laboratories	4,978.9	9.3	110.26
Cadila Healthcare	3,017	13.0	67.06
Matrix Laboratories	2,936.9	10.3	65.28
Cipla	2,848.5	4.5	63.31
Aurobindo Pharma	1,732.4	4.2	38.51
Sun Pharmaceutical Inds	1,592	8.2	35.38
Torrent Pharmaceuticals	1,336.5	7.6	29.71
Wockhardt	1,102.2	6.3	24.5
Ind-Swift Laboratories	9,73.5	9.5	21.64
Fresenius Kabi Oncology	850.7	20.7	18.91
Panacea Biotec	849.7	7.4	18.89
Ipca Laboratories	712.7	3.7	15.84
Sun Pharma Advanced Research Co.	701.3	120.3	15.59
Parabolic Drugs	689.7	10.9	15.33
Venus Remedies	685.6	19.2	15.24
Unichem Laboratories	663.5	8.7	14.75
Glenmark Pharmaceuticals	659.2	5.7	14.65
Biocon	520.1	3.4	11.56
Agila Specialties	504.7	17.3	11.18
Alembic Pharmaceuticals	489.8	4.3	10.89
Ajanta Pharma	478.8	10.5	10.64
Piramal Healthcare	413.2	2.6	9.18
Orchid Chemicals & Pharmaceuticals	397	2.4	8.82
Suven Life Sciences	333.8	22.2	7.42
Arch Pharmalabs	314.6	2.5	6.99
Divi's Laboratories	216.6	1.7	4.81
FDC	208.1	3.0	4.63
Surya Pharmaceutical Ltd	158	1.0	3.51
Strides Arcolab	152.5	3.1	3.38
Shasun Pharmaceuticals	142.7	2.5	3.17
Plethico Pharmaceuticals	134.8	3.0	2.99
Vivimed Labs	132.3	4.3	2.94
Neuland Laboratories	118.8	3.0	2.64
J B Chemicals & Pharmaceuticals	113.6	1.4	2.52
Indoco Remedies	113.3	2.3	2.52
Natco Pharma	110.5	3.2	2.46
Total 38 companies above	43,106.1	7.2	957.65
Total 13 NCE R&D companies	26,032.5	9.4	578.21

Source: Calculated from CMIE Prowess database.

The development of NCEs is not yet a significant part of the R&D activities of Indian companies, constituting less than a quarter of the total R&D expenditure by the major companies (Chaudhuri 2010, p. 47). Nor are all the large R&D spenders involved in NCE development; Cipla, for example, is the third largest spender on R&D but has no NCE portfolio.

The Indian pharmaceutical industry is now highly export oriented. The growth in exports has been one of the most outstanding features of the pharmaceutical industry in India. Exports were negligible in the product patent regime before the 1970s. Exports started picking up in the 1970s after the amendment of the Patents Act. Initially the growth was modest. It accelerated in the 1980s. Exports have grown particularly rapidly since the mid-1990s. Exports have been increasing annually at more than 20 per cent in most of the recent years.[27] The export market is larger than the domestic market not only for large companies such as Ranbaxy (63 per cent of net sales in 2010–11), Dr Reddy's (65.1 per cent), Cipla (53.2 per cent), but also for smaller companies such as Granules (77.8 per cent), Shilpa Medicare (76.7 per cent), and Kopran (58.6 per cent).[28]

Significant R&D efforts are directed towards developing processes and products to get regulatory approvals for entry and growth in patent-expired generic markets in developed countries. Development of processes for manufacturing APIs and product development of formulations, process validation, bio-equivalence testing and generation of other data required for getting international regulatory approvals are specifically highlighted as areas where R&D is undertaken by companies active in the regulated markets.[29] Thus much of R&D by Indian pharmaceutical companies has nothing to do with TRIPS. It is the result of the increasing export orientation of Indian pharmaceutical companies and diversification to the regulated markets, particularly to the US.

R&D for New Chemical Entities

But a remarkable feature of pharmaceutical R&D in India is that, though relatively smaller, the Indian private sector has started investing in R&D for NCEs. This began around the time TRIPS came into effect in the mid-1990s.[30] R&D investments were initiated by Dr Reddy's Laboratories followed by Ranbaxy Laboratories. Since then 11 other companies – Sun, Cadila Healthcare, Lupin, Nicholas Piramal, Dabur Pharma, Torrent, Wockhardt, Orchid, Glenmark, Biocon and Seven Lifesciences – have also joined in. These companies are among the major pharmaceutical R&D spenders. Together they invested Rs. 26,032.5 million ($578.2 million) (9.4 per cent of net sales) on R&D in 2010–11 (Table 3.5).

It is important to note that none of these companies is engaged in the entire process of drug development. The reason is simple: Indian pharmaceutical companies are not yet ready for a start-to-finish model in NCE research because of the lack of the skills and funds necessary to develop a drug and put it to the market.[31] Whereas the 13 Indian companies together spent $578.2 million in 2010–11, Pfizer, the largest MNC, alone spent $7.8 billion in 2009 (*Pharmaceutical Executive*, May, 2010). The model that the Indian companies have adopted, rather, is to develop new molecules up to a certain stage and then license them out to partners from developed countries, primarily MNCs. There has been a marriage of interests. It is the development of biotechnology companies which has encouraged specialization according to stages of the drug development process. The MNCs seek and contract out specific activities. As the NCE pipeline of the MNCs started drying up, they in fact have intensified efforts to license promising compounds developed by others and most of the major MNCs have opened compound acquisition departments in their companies. There are also specialized companies which keep track of promising compounds, maintain libraries, catalogue them and offer them for sale to prospective clients.

Even at the pre-clinical stage, Indian companies are not engaged with all the elements of the R&D process. Indian companies are not involved in basic research of target identification for new drugs. They rely on the basic research of others and adopt an approach called 'analogue research.' This entails working on certain pre-identified targets for specific diseases to develop molecules that alter the target's mechanism in the diseased person.[32] But even this requires medicinal chemistry and biology skills that are still scarce in the Indian pharmaceutical industry. In the pre-TRIPS era, Indian pharmaceutical industry scientists primarily acquired and developed organic chemistry skills required for process development. Indian companies are now filling up this gap primarily by hiring Indian scientists who worked in MNC laboratories in India and abroad and in the Indian public sector laboratories.[33]

The entry of Indian companies into new drug R&D was associated with tremendous optimism. The licensing deals of Dr Reddy's, Ranbaxy and others became major news and aroused the expectation that Indian companies would be recognized not only as successful manufacturers but also as successful innovators of new drugs. About 30 NCEs developed by Indian companies are at various stages of clinical trials. But drug development did not progress as anticipated and the prospect of huge licensing revenue through milestone and other payments has failed to materialize.[34] Indian companies, particularly Ranbaxy and Dr Reddy's, the two Indian companies that have invested most heavily in R&D (Table 3.5) and served as prime advocates for new drug R&D in India, have each suffered several setbacks. MNCs such as Novo Nordisk and Novartis discontinued further development of the compounds in-licensed from them.

What the Indian companies initially did not understand was that while their objectives are to earn license fees and royalties from successful commercialization, the MNCs do not necessarily aim to develop the in-licensed compounds for commercialization. In fact, where the compound may compete with the MNC's existing or planned products, the MNC's objective may actually be to 'kill' the compound.

Indian companies are now aware of this potential conflict. In some cases they are attempting to develop drugs further despite the lack of interest on the part of the MNCs who initially licensed them. Torrent, for example, entered into an agreement with Novartis in 2002 for the development of the Advanced Glycation Endproduct or AGE breaker compound for the treatment of heart disease and diabetes. In 2004 the compound was out-licensed to Novartis. The agreement was terminated in 2005 when Novartis decided not to proceed further with the compound. Torrent is now trying to develop it on its own and explore other options. Torrent received only $0.5 million initially and then $3 million from Novartis.[35] This was too small an amount for a large MNC such as Novartis to have any stake in the project. Dr Reddy's has suffered several similar setbacks.

The later the stage at which a compound is licensed out, the higher the license revenues. The licensor is also in a better position to select a licensee who is actually interested in developing the drug for commercializing and may therefore provide a genuine possibility of earning royalties. But Indian companies face the predicament that the unilateral development of a drug to such a later stage entails considerable cost and risk.

The rising R&D expenditure but lack of adequate returns has put strains on the profitability of these companies. Several companies – Ranbaxy, Dr Reddy's, Sun Pharmaceuticals, Piramal Healthcare – cut their R&D budget around 2005–06/2006–07. Ranbaxy, Sun and Piramal have de-merged their NCE business. Such de-risking and reduction of R&D expenditure is an indirect admittance that NCE R&D has not been working as expected. Significantly enough, Ranbaxy and the domestic formulations business of Piramal have been taken over by MNCs as noted above. Dr Reddy's has also changed its R&D strategy. It is experimenting with alternative business models including setting up a separate drug development company to reduce the risk and the dependence on MNCs.

No NCE developed by Indian companies has yet been approved for marketing in any country. But as Table 3.6 shows, 30 NCEs developed by Indian companies are at various stages of clinical trials. Dr Reddy's and Ranbaxy, which are the largest R&D spenders and which have been very active in NCE R&D, have only two NCEs each under clinical trials. Some

Table 3.6   NCEs under clinical trials, Indian pharmaceutical companies

Company	NCE	Indication	Development stage
Cadila Healthcare	ZY11	Pain	Phase II
Cadila Healthcare	ZYH2	Diabetes	Phase I
Cadila Healthcare	ZYH1	Dyslipidemia	Phase II
Cadila Healthcare	ZYH7	Dyslipidemia	Phase I
Cadila Healthcare	ZYO1	Obesity/diabetes	Phase I
Dabur	DRF 7295	Cancer	Phase II
Dr Reddy's Labs	DRF2593	Diabetes	Phase III (partner Rheoscience, Denmark)
Dr Reddy's Labs	DRF1042	Cancer	Phase I (partner Clintec International, UK)
Glenmark	GRC8200	Diabetes	Phase II
Glenmark	GRC6211	Osteoarthritis, pain	Phase II
Glenmark	GRC3886	Asthma/COPD	Phase II
Glenmark	GRC10693	Neuropathic pain	Phase I completed
Glenmark	GRC 4039	Rheumatoid arthritis	Phase I
Lupin	LL3348	Psoriasis	Phase II
Lupin	LL3858	TB	Phase I
Lupin	LL2011	Migraine	Phase III
Lupin	LL4218	Psoriasis	Phase II
Nicholas Piramal	P276	Cancer	Phase II
Nicholas Piramal	P 1448	Cancer	Phase I
Nicholas Piramal	P 1736	Diabetes	Phase I
Nicholas Piramal	P 1201	Diabetes	Phase I
Orchid	BLX1002	Diabetes	Phase II
Ranbaxy Labs (jointly with MMV)	RBx11160	Malaria	Phase II
Ranbaxy	RBx10558	Cholesterol	Phase I
Sun Pharmaceutical Industries	SUN 1334H	Allergy	Phase II
Wockhardt	WCK771	MRSA, resistant infection	Phase II
Wockhardt	WCK1152	Respiratory infections	Phase I
Biocon	IN-105	Diabetes (oral insulin)	Phase II
Biocon	T1h	Oncology inflammation	Phase II
Suven	SUVN 502	Neurodegenerative	Phase I

Source: Company annual reports and websites, accessed April 2009.

smaller companies have a larger NCE pipeline. Glenmark and Cadila Healthcare have five molecules under clinical trials followed by Lupin and Piramal Healthcare with four each. As Table 3.6 further shows, the NCEs being developed by the Indian companies are related primarily to 'global diseases' such as diabetes, cancer, heart diseases, asthma, and obesity. These are the diseases that offer much larger and more lucrative markets in developed countries (though they are also prevalent in developing countries). The 'neglected diseases' which primarily or exclusively affect the developing countries and promise much lower financial returns are absent from the list except for malaria and TB. In both these cases, public sector or philanthropic funding is involved. Ranbaxy is participating in an international project sponsored and funded by the Medicines for Malaria Venture (MMV), a public-private partnership to develop a synthetic anti-malarial drug. Lupin is involved in developing an anti-TB drug in partnership with some publicly funded research institutions in India (Commission on Intellectual Property Rights, Innovation and Public Health, 2006).

Production of Generic Drugs

It is generally held that the earlier Indian Patents Act, 1970 which did not recognize product patents was instrumental in the Indian pharmaceutical industry developing a fair amount of technological capability in designing and indeed manufacturing generic versions of already known drugs which were off patents. TRIPS compliance and along with it the recognition of product patents may have placed the industry in a difficult position. So it is instructive to analyse the performance of the industry post-TRIPS. This is attempted in terms of four sets of indicators: (i) employment in the pharmaceutical industry; (ii) exports; and two indicators of the technological capability – (iii) trends in Abbreviated New Drug Applications (ANDAs)[36] issued by the US Food and Drug Administration (FDA); and (iv) India's share in Drug Master File (DMF)[37] by the USFDA (Table 3.7).

All the four indicators show an improvement. Of particular interest is the number of ANDA approvals and India's share in DMFs. The improvements in these two since TRIPS shows that the Indian generics industry has continued to maintain its capability in the production and marketing of generic drugs in the all-important US market but also has managed to improve its share. This shows that India's technological capability in the manufacture and marketing of generics has been unaffected by the TRIPS regime.

Table 3.7   Indicators of growth of India's generic drug industry

Year	Employment (in numbers)	Exports (millions of US $)	Number of ANDAs approved by USFDA	Percentage of Indian DMF to total
1995	181,497	724.2		
1996	204,609	814		
1997	211,614	947.2		
1998	189,295	933.7		
1999	213,999	1,068.2		
2000	243,410	1,147	9	
2001	233,704	1,322.4	21	
2002	226,416	1,608.7	23	
2003	223,556	1,971.9	17	
2004	240,791	2,271.6	33	
2005	265,396	2,761.8	52	40
2006	290,021	3,416.1	77	46
2007	336,211	4,476.7	135	43
2008	353,692	5,822.7	155	45
2009		5,921.5	152	62
2010			139	50
2011			162	

Source: Department of Pharmaceuticals (2012); Joseph (2012); Kuhrt (2011); Bakhru and Kerai (2011).

6.   R&D IN THE AGROCHEMICALS INDUSTRY

India's patent law since 1972 excluded chemicals and all foods from eligibility for utility patents. However, it did allow process patents for seven years after filing or five years after granting the patent on chemicals. There was no legal protection for plant varieties. All this changed to bring the law in compliance with TRIPS. Chemicals, food, and agricultural products and processes and novel microorganisms could be patented for 20 years starting in 2005. A *sui generis* system of plant breeders' rights was passed and started accepting applications in 2007. Plant varieties and seed are protected by the plant variety protection law and are excluded from coverage in the patent act.

Table 3.8   Private-sector patenting in India, 2000–10

Sector	Firm type	Granted (2000–10)	Published (2004–10)
Plant biotechnology	Indian	1	8
	MNC	78	245
Pesticides	Indian	58	89
	MNC	373[a]	1,199[a]
Fertilizers	Indian	5	46
	MNC	16	25
Agricultural machinery	Indian	31	39
	MNC	52	109
Total	Indian	95	182
	MNC	519	1,573

Note: [a] These numbers may include some chemicals that are not used for agricultural pest control.

Source: Compiled from Intellectual Property India, 2011. This table is from Pray and Nagarajan (2012).

Who Uses Strengthened IPRs?

Table 3.8 provides data by major agricultural input industries on number of patents granted and applications for patents that are published but not yet granted as of 2011. The public sector plays virtually no role in patenting pesticides, biotechnology, food products or agricultural machinery. Data are not available from before 2000 in most agriculture-related industries because product patents were not allowed. The largest numbers of patents granted and of published applications are in the pesticide industry, followed by plant biotechnology. Agricultural machinery has the third-largest amount of patenting. MNCs dominate patenting in most industries except agricultural machinery. This may be due to the fact that much of the intellectual property in the agricultural machinery could already be protected as components of cars, trucks or construction equipment. However, patenting by Indian enterprises is also growing (compare granted with published patents), especially in pesticides, fertilizers, and agricultural machinery. Patents by MNCs primarily reflect research conducted outside India and brought in through local subsidiaries and partners.

Impact on R&D

Although pesticide research worldwide has declined since the 1990s (Fuglie 2012), pesticide research in India has grown – particularly in the

Table 3.9   Sectoral private agricultural investment in R&D (millions of 2005 US$)

Industry	1984–85	1994–95	2008/09		
			Total	Indian firms	MNCs
Seed and biotechnology	1.3	4.9	88.6	49.3	39.3
Pesticides	9	17	35.7	24.4	11.3
Fertilizers	6.8	6.7	7.9	4.9	0.0
Agricultural machinery	3.7	6.5	40.5	20.5	20.0
Biofertilizers and biopesticides	0	0	1.3	1.3	0.0
Poultry and feeds	–	3.5	7.8	7.8	0.0
Animal health	0.9	2.7	18.6	3.7	14.9
Sugar	0.9	2.5	10.8	10.8	0.0
Biofuels	0	0	13.1	13.1	0.0
Food, beverage, and plantations	1.3	10.3	27	16.2	10.7
Total	23.9	54.1	251.3	155.0	96.2

Source: Pray and Nagarajan (2012).

last decade. Growth of Indian private sector R&D on food and agriculture by industry is shown in Table 3.9. It contains our best estimates of the levels of private R&D expenditure in 2008–09 plus data from two previous studies of R&D that were conducted in the mid 1980s and the mid 1990s. Total agribusiness R&D almost doubled between the 1980s and 1990s and then more than tripled in real dollars from the mid 1990s to 2008. The seed/biotech industry registered the most rapid growth – R&D expenditure went up almost fourfold between 1985 and 1995 and then grew by a factor of 10 from the mid 1990s to the present. Pesticide R&D grew rapidly – doubling in the first period and then doubling again in the latest period. Relative to agribusiness as a whole, seeds grew more rapidly and pesticides less rapidly.

Interviews with multinationals suggest that stronger IPRs have been influential in their decisions to increase their R&D in biotech, seed, and pesticides in India. The location of major pesticide discovery labs in India by Syngenta was due to a combination of factors, one of which was stronger IPRs. However, they still take precautions against losing control over new technology by spreading out the different components of the research process around the globe so that no one group in India or China would have all the parts to be able to copy a product that was in the pipeline.[38] The other factors which were also extremely important were relatively low costs of highly skilled scientists both in India and in the Indian community abroad who were interested in returning to India. Other agribusiness multinationals that have made major investments in basic biological and chemical research in India are Monsanto and DuPont.

Pesticide R&D of MNCs listed on the Indian stock exchange (Bayer Crop Science, Monsanto India, Syngenta and BASF) tripled their R&D expenditures between 2003 and 2008.[39] Increases in sales, which doubled during this period, account for much research increase. However, research intensity also increased, which is consistent with the argument that IPRs may also have influenced their decision to conduct R&D. In the 1990s, most pesticide companies were spending about 0.8 per cent or 0.9 per cent of sales annually on R&D. This increased to 1.5 per cent in 2009 (Pray and Nagarajan 2012).

For Indian companies' biotech and pesticide research, stronger IPRs seem to have had some limited impact on R&D. As shown in Table 3.8, Indian pesticide firms and seed firms are just starting to patent pesticides or genes and are far behind their multinational competitors in using these IPR tools. R&D data for large Indian pesticide firms listed on stock markets show a different pattern than the data for MNCs, with slower and less uniform growth among firms. Rallis, the clear leader in 2000, declined in research investment from Rs. 179 million rupees in 2000 to Rs. 23 million in 2008. Gharda, on the other hand, continued to spend about the same amount each year on research and its research intensity is high. In contrast, UPL R&D has increased from about Rs. 100 million in 2000 to Rs. 6.7 billion in 2008,[40] and it has become the leading Indian pesticide research firm. Research intensity of domestic firms, which account for about two-thirds of pesticide industry research, has increased somewhat – from just less than 1 per cent of sales to slightly more than 1 per cent (Pray and Nagarajan 2012).

Indian companies tend to focus research on process innovation, such as finding inexpensive ways of making active ingredients (AIs) developed elsewhere, and on developing new formulations and combinations of AIs. In addition, firms are developing crop management practices to enable farmers to use pesticides more safely, more efficiently, and with less environmental impact. Excel and Rallis focus research on the manufacturing process to develop efficient processes to produce off-patent AIs that have available regulatory dossiers containing efficacy, toxicity and environmental impact data and therefore can easily move through the Indian regulatory approval process. United Phosphorus reports research activities extending from more efficient manufacturing processes to developing safer, easier, and more effective spraying methods. Some firms are also involved in extension demonstrations, regulatory affairs and product stewardship. Gharda Chemicals pioneered pesticide manufacturing technology.

Multinationals are also improving pesticide production and formulation as well as the safety, efficacy and environmental impact of pesticides in India, but they are investing in basic research as well to develop new molecules for pesticides in India. Syngenta established a research and technology centre in Goa in 2006 that has grown to more than 100 scientists working on new chemical products for crop protection (Syngenta, 2010). Bayer is also developing active ingredients in India, where it is working specifically on developing new synthetic pyrethroids through its joint venture with Mitsui called Bilag. Isagro (an Italian firm) has an Indian division with a large research programme developing pesticide production processes. Its new AIs are identified in Italy, and then the India branch develops the least expensive production process. In 2007, DuPont built a basic sciences centre for chemical and biological research in Hyderabad, and BASF announced in 2010 that it will establish a research centre in India to develop new agricultural chemicals.

Both Indian and foreign firms in India conduct significant research on biopesticides. These include the Indian firms TERI, Coromandel and Excel Industries, which together have been granted 25 patents on biopesticides between 1991 and 2009. Camson Bio Technologies entered the biopesticides market in 2001 and spends 20 per cent of its revenues annually on research, having developed 22 biopesticides and 7 biofertilizers, capturing 20 per cent of the Indian bioproducts market (Camson Bio Technologies 2010). Research investment in this area totals about Rs. 68.7 million ($1.4 million), nearly 3 per cent of sales, and investment is increasing as new firms enter the market (Pray and Nagarajan 2012).

Impact on Innovation

While the previous section shows that the impacts of TRIPS compliance on R&D seem to have been positive but limited, what we are really interested in is innovations. They can come from local R&D but also may come into India through licensing, trade and foreign investment. The seed, biotech, and pesticide industries have data on innovation in addition to the data on patents and plant variety protection (PVP) which are used in many studies as measures of innovation. Because the introduction of new technology in all of these industries is regulated, regulators have information on new plant varieties, new pesticides and new genetically engineered genes and plants. The fact that companies or research organizations took the time and invested money to move these products through the

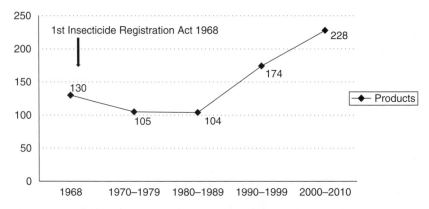

Source: Compiled from Central Insecticide Board and Registration Committee, Ministry of Agriculture, Government of India, New Delhi, http://www.cibrc.nic.in/cibrc.htm.

Figure 3.12   Pesticide registration in India (1968–2010)

regulatory system means that they are expected to be commercially successful and valuable to society.

The numbers and trends of new Indian pesticide registrations (active ingredients not different formulations) are shown in Figure 3.12. The decline in pesticide registrations took place in the 1970s when the product patents were eliminated. There has been a clear upward trend in the number of registrations since the 1980s. However, this acceleration of registrations took place in the 1990s before product patents were put back in place. Part of this could have been in anticipation of TRIPS. Registrations continued to grow in the first decade of the twenty-first century when product patents were implemented again. Careful modelling and more interviews with the industry would be required to show that TRIPS had an important impact.

Our evidence suggests that compliance with TRIPS has had some positive impact on R&D and innovation in the pesticide industries. Some growth in these indicators would have taken place anyway, driven by liberalization of industrial policy, increased demand for pesticides in India and the increase in pesticide exports, but discussions with industry leaders and the evidence on IPRs, R&D and innovation indicate that stronger IPRs have also had an impact. The impact seems to have been greatest on the MNCs which have made the most use of pesticide and biotech patents. These companies are investing in major laboratories that are parts of their global R&D networks but they are also building their R&D programmes to develop innovations for the Indian market. The changes in patenting and the investments by multinationals also appear to have stimulated more research and innovation by Indian pesticide companies.

7.   CONCLUSIONS

India's patent regime was made TRIPS compliant in 2005 after a series of three amendments and an intense debate which involved a number of stakeholders. The major facet of the TRIPS compliant patent regime is the recognition of product patents in pharmaceuticals, agrochemicals and food industries. In this study we analysed in depth the implications of this change in governance rule for innovative activity in India as a whole and the pharmaceutical industry in particular. Of the flexibilities provided in TRIPS, India has invoked only one, namely the one on compulsory licensing and that too very recently. We find that although patenting has increased from India, most of the patents are secured by foreign firms located in the country. An interesting finding was that the leading IT firms have started filing for patents at the USPTO where software patenting is allowed. During this time India has becoming a contracting party to the PCT, thus enabling Indian inventors to patent their inventions in a large number of jurisdictions. The government has also initiated steps to bring utility models within the ambit of its IPR regime so that incremental innovations by small and medium enterprises can be protected. Creation of the Traditional Knowledge Library has enabled India to successfully oppose the granting of patents to inventions based on India's traditional knowledge in other jurisdictions. The expert committee that was appointed to see if microorganisms should be patented has reached the conclusion that they should. There is also some limited evidence to show that research in NTDs has increased in India, although this appears to be confined to public research institutes and the research is leading to more publications rather than any new drugs. Also, it is unclear whether the domestic pharmaceutical industry is involving itself in this area. Tightening up of the patent regime through TRIPS compliance has not resulted in unaffiliated Indian firms being able to secure foreign technical collaboration agreements on a large scale. However, continued reform of the patent office has made the whole process of patenting more transparent and less time consuming, although the time taken for examination of applications is still high when compared to best practices. TRIPS has allowed pre- and post-grant oppositions, and there has been an increase especially in post-grant oppositions and patent litigation. More striking still are instances of domestic companies litigating against each other, and that too in non-pharmaceutical industries.

Our analysis of the post-TRIPS R&D strategies of domestic pharmaceutical firms shows that little has changed to dispute the conventional wisdom that the developing countries should not grant product patent protection. They are already paying the cost of high prices of patent protected products. But the technological benefits claimed have not yet taken place. While R&D activities have diversified, Indian pharmaceutical firms are yet to prove their competence in innovating new products. No NCE has yet been developed for marketing. There have been several setbacks and the partnership model has not always worked properly. What Indian companies have really demonstrated is the ability to develop generics – an ability which they acquired and improved during the pre-TRIPS period. Contrary to what was claimed during the TRIPS negotiations, the product patent regime has not prompted Indian companies to devote more resources to developing drugs for neglected diseases that exclusively or predominantly affect developing countries. There is of course some evidence to show that public agencies in India have started devoting more attention to research on drugs for NTDs. The large Indian pharmaceutical companies, who are the major R&D spenders in the country, have been focusing on the larger and more lucrative developed-country markets, particularly that of the US. In that regard, the primary incentive to invest in R&D, whether for NCEs, for modifications, or for the development of generics, has not been the new TRIPS-compliant product patent regime in India but the product patent regime in developed countries that was in place well before TRIPS. TRIPS may have accelerated the trend toward such R&D because of the anticipated shrinkage of domestic opportunities. But in the absence of TRIPS, such R&D activities would still have been undertaken. With the larger domestic operations, Indian companies, in fact, would have had access to larger resources and would have been better placed to undertake such R&D.

Finally, we see that most of the alleged positive benefits of TRIPS are exaggerated while at the same time its negative effects on some fronts are also exaggerated. The truth lies in between the two.

NOTES

1. For a history of India's patent laws, see Ganguly (2003), Kankanala et al. (2010) and Sampat (2010).
2. Only process patents were granted and not product.
3. Patents (Amendment) Ordinance, 2004, full text available at http://lawmin.nic.in/Patents%20Amendment%20Ordinance%202004.pdf (last accessed July 22, 2012).
4. See Department of Science and Technology, Government of India, http://www.dst.gov.in/stsysindia/stp2003.htm (accessed July 24, 2012).

5.   The official name of the India Patent Office is Controller General of Patents Designs and Trademarks.
6.   See Basant and Mani (2012) for the details.
7.   If one repeats this with the USPTO data on patent grants one gets exactly the same type of results.
8.   'Software patents under ordinance face reversal', *Financial Express*, March 29, 2005, http://www.financialexpress.com/news/software-patents-under-ordinance-face-reversal/82155/ (last accessed July 28, 2012).
9.   CSIR is a network of 37 laboratories spread throughout the country and focusing on a range of technologies from aerospace, biotechnology, chemicals, drugs and pharmaceuticals, energy, food and food processing, information dissemination, leather, metal, minerals, manufacturing etc.
10. CSIR (1996), *CSIR 2000: Vision and Strategy*. In this document, it states: 'The maximization of the benefits to CSIR from its intellectual property by stimulating higher levels of innovation through a judicious system of rewards, ensuring timely and effective legal protection for its IP and leveraging and forging strategies alliances for enhancing the value of its IP.'
11. CSIR, Annual Report 2009–10, http://www.csir.res.in/External/Utilities/Frames/about csir/main_page.asp?a=topframe.htm&b=leftcon.htm&c=../../../Heads/aboutcsir/abo ut_us.htm (last accessed July 29, 2012).
12. *CSIR@80: Vision and Strategy* at http://rdpp.csir.res.in/csir_acsir/PDF/CSIR80-final. pdf (last accessed July 29, 2012).
13. Although very important, data on royalties received through licensing of its patent portfolio is apparently not compiled and available centrally at the CSIR headquarters. Mr T. Prashant Reddy has revealed this to us through an RTI inquiry by him. For details of this communication, see https://docs.google.com/file/ d/0Bxi2TzVXul5ZVDQ5YzFYZzYtNTA/edit?pli=1 (accessed July 29, 2012).
14. This data on costs incurred for securing patents was obtained by Mr Prashant Reddy through a Right to Information application. For details see blog SPICY IP http:// spicyipindia.blogspot.in/2012/03/csir-spends-whopping-rs-7424-crores-on.html   (last accessed July 27, 2012).
15. http://164.100.24.167/newcommittee/press_release/Bill/Committee%20on%20S%20and %20T,%20Env.%20and%20Forests/protection_utlisation.pdf (last accessed July 29, 2012).
16. See the report of the standing committee at: http://164.100.47.5/newcommittee/reports/ EnglishCommittees/Committee%20on%20S%20and%20T,%20Env.%20and%20Fores ts/211%20IPR%20Bill.pdf (last accessed July 30, 2012).
17. http://cis-india.org/a2k/publications/pupfip/why-no-pupfip/ (last accessed July 29, 2012).
18. http://dipp.nic.in/english/Discuss_paper/Utility_Models_13May2011.pdf (last accessed July 29, 2012).
19. These reactions can be seen at http://dipp.nic.in/English/Discuss_paper/FeedBack_ UtilityModels.htm (last accessed July 30, 2012).
20. http://g-finder.policycures.org/gfinder_report/search.jsp (last accessed August 13, 2012).
21. The CSIR and the Department of Indian Systems of Medicine (AYUSH) maintain the TDKL. The idea to establish a TKDL came to the fore amid India's efforts to revoke the patent granted by the United States Patent and Trademark Office (USPTO) on the wound healing properties of turmeric, and the patent granted by the European Patent Office (EPO) on the antifungal properties of neem. These endeavours, while successful, proved extremely costly and time-consuming. For a patent to be granted, an applicant must satisfy certain criteria as defined by national patent law; in particular, an applicant must prove that a claimed invention is novel and not previously known. Why then had patents been granted for so many applications relating to Indian medicinal systems? When patent examiners assessed these applications for patentability, the claimed

inventions did not feature in the prior art searches carried out. They were, therefore, deemed patentable. At that time, however, much of India's traditional medicinal knowledge only existed in Sanskrit, Hindi, Arabic, Urdu and Tamil. These languages were neither accessible to nor understood by patent examiners working in the major patent offices to which the applications had been submitted.

22. During the period 79 applications were received from foreign companies. See Lok Sabha starred question, http://164.100.47.132/LssNew/psearch/QResult15.aspx?qref= 115211(accessed August 14, 2012).

23. This report can be found at the website of Department of Industrial Policy and Performance, http://dipp.nic.in/English/Publications/Report.aspx (last accessed July 31, 2012).

24. For a succinct write up on the implications of the case, see Sampat et al. (2012). For a more detailed discussion on the issue, see James (2009).

25. Calculated from the CMIE Prowess database.

26. Calculated from the CMIE Prowess database.

27. Calculated from DGCI&S data obtained from CMIE India Trades database.

28. CMIE Prowess database.

29. See, for example, Dr Reddy's Laboratories, *Annual Report, 2005–06*, p. 85; Ranbaxy, *Annual Report, 2005*, p. 46.

30. In the Indian private sector, Sarabhai Research Centre was the first one to be set up in the 1960s for developing new drugs. But it was wound up in the 1980s.

31. Chaudhuri (2005), Chapter 5.

32. Glenmark Pharmaceuticals Ltd, *Annual Report, 2003–04*.

33. In the pre-TRIPS regime too some R&D for new drug development was undertaken in India primarily by the Central Drug Research Institute (CDRI) (public sector), Ciba Geigy, Hoechst and Boots (all MNCs). Not many drugs have come to the market as a result of this effort, but it generated specialized skills – see Chaudhuri 2005.

34. There are exceptions: Glenmark earned a total of $117 million as licensing revenue during 2004–07. But Glenmark too has been facing problems (corporate presentation, August, 2009, www.glenmarkpharma.com).

35. 'Novartis acquires rights in Torrent's AGE compound', press release, October 31, 2002, and 'Torrent licenses AGE compound to Novartis', press release, July 29, 2004, Torrent Pharmaceuticals Ltd (accessed from website: www.torrent-india.com).

36. An Abbreviated New Drug Application (ANDA) contains data which when submitted to FDA's Center for Drug Evaluation and Research, Office of Generic Drugs, provides for the review and ultimate approval of a generic drug product. Once approved, an applicant may manufacture and market the generic drug product to provide a safe, effective, low cost alternative to the American public.

37. DMFs are essentially approvals to supply complex raw materials to all generic manufacturers servicing the US market.

38. This is based on personal communication with Syngenta officials, Mumbai, January 2009.

39. The increase would have been even greater if data from Dow and DuPont had been available because both of them are making substantial investments in pesticide research, but they do not make data on their R&D expenditures in India public.

40. A large share of this growth appears to be due to the acquisition of foreign pesticide firms and Advanta.

REFERENCES

Abbott, F.M., Amy Kapczynski and T.N. Srinivasan (2005), 'The draft patent law', *The Hindu*, March 12, 2005.

Adams, Jonathan, Karen Gurney and David Pendlebury (2012), 'Neglected tropical diseases', Global Research Report, Thomson Reuters, http://researchanalytics. thomsonreuters.com/grr/ (last accessed August 3, 2012).

Basant, Rakesh and Sunil Mani (2012), 'Foreign R&D centres in India: an analysis of their size, structure and implications', Working Paper No. 2012–01–06, Ahmedabad: Indian Institute of Management.

Basheer, S. (2008), 'Mysterious Indian Bayh–Dole Bill', http://spicyipindia.blog-spot.in/2008/07/mysterious-indian-bayh-dole-bill.html (last accessed August 2, 2012).

Bakhru, Girish and Damayanti Kerai (2011), 'India pharmaceuticals', *Flash Note*, HSBC Global Research.

Bhola, R. (2012), 'Patent procurement and enforcement in India', Bangalore: K&S Partners, http://www.bcic.org.in/recentevents/7Feb2012/MR._RAVI_BHOLA_PRESENTATION.pdf (last accessed August 2, 2012).

Chaudhuri, Sudip (2005), *The WTO and India's Pharmaceuticals Industry: Patent Protection, TRIPS, and Developing Countries*, Delhi: Oxford University Press.

Chaudhuri, Sudip (2010), 'The industry response', in Sudip Chaudhuri, Chan Park and K.M. Gopakumar, *Five Years into the Product Patent Regime: India's Response*, New York: United Nations Development Programme.

Chaudhuri, Sudip (2012), 'Multinationals and monopolies: pharmaceutical industry in India after TRIPS', *Economic and Political Weekly*, **47** (12), 46–54.

Commission on Intellectual Property Rights, Innovation and Public Health (2006), *Public Health, Innovation and Intellectual Property Rights*, Geneva: WHO, http://www.who.int/intellectualproperty/documents/thereport/ENPublicHealth Report.pdf (last accessed August 2, 2012).

Council of Scientific and Industrial Research (various issues), *Annual Report*, Delhi: Government of India.

Department of Pharmaceuticals (2012), *Annual Report 2011–12*, Delhi: Ministry of Chemicals and Fertilizers, Government of India.

Fuglie, Keith O. (2012), 'Productivity growth and technology capital in the global agricultural economy', in K.O. Fuglie, E. Ball and S.L. Wang (eds), *Productivity Growth in Agriculture: An International Perspective*, Wallingford: CABI.

Ganguly, Prabhuddha (2003), 'Indian path towards TRIPS compliance', *World Patent Information*, **25** (2), 143–9.

Grace, Cheri (2004), 'The effect of changing intellectual property in pharmaceutical industry. Prospects in India and China: consideration for access to medicines', Issue Paper – Access to Medicines, London: DFID Health Systems Resources Centre.

James, T.C. (2009), *Patent Protection and Innovation, Section 3(d) of the Patents Act and Indian Pharmaceutical Industry*, Department of Industrial Policy and Performance.

Joseph, Reji (2012), 'Policy reforms in the Indian pharmaceutical sector since 1994: impact on exports and imports', *Economic and Political Weekly*, **XLVII** (18), 62–72.

Kankanala, K.C., A.K. Narasani and V. Radhakrishnan (2010), *Indian Patent Law and Practice*, Delhi: Oxford University Press.

Kapczynski, Amy (2010), 'The institutional structure of patent offices in developing countries: what India can teach us', presentation slides at the TRIPS@10 conference, Columbia University, http://earth.columbia.edu/tripsat10/sitefiles/file/Panel4_Kapczynski_Amy_PowerPoint.pdf(last accessed July 31, 2012).

Kochupillai, Mrinalini (2009), 'The protection and utilisation of public funded Intellectual Property Bill 2008: a critique in the light of India's innovation environment', *Journal of Intellectual Property Rights*, **15** (1), 19–34.

Kuhrt, Kate (2011), 'India and China forge ahead while Europe plays catch-up', *Generics Bulletin*, February, 20–22.

Mani, Sunil (2002), *Government, Innovation and Technology Policy: An International Comparative Analysis*, Cheltenham, UK and Northampton, MA, USA: Edward Elgar.

Mani, Sunil (2010), 'Are innovations on the rise in India since the onset of reforms of 1991? An analysis of its evidence and some disquieting features', *International Journal of Technology and Globalization*, **5** (1 & 2), 5–42.

National Science Board (2012), *Science and Engineering Indicators 2012*, Arlington, VA: National Science Foundation (NSB 12–01).

Office of the Controller General of Patents, Designs, Trademarks and Geographical Indications (various issues), *Annual Report*, Mumbai: Department of Industrial Policy and Performance, Ministry of Commerce and Industry, Government of India.

Pray, Carl and Latha Nagarajan (2012), 'Innovation and research by private agribusiness in India', IFPRI Discussion Paper 01181, Washington, DC: International Food Policy Research Institute.

Sampat, Bhaven (2010), 'The accumulation of capabilities in Indian pharmaceuticals and software: the roles that patents did (and did not) play', in Hiroyuki Odagiri, Akira Goto, Atsushi Sunami, and Richard R. Nelson (eds), *Intellectual Property Rights, Development, and Catch-Up*, New York: Oxford University Press, pp. 361–77.

Sampat, Bhaven, Kenneth C. Shadlen and Tahir M. Amin (2012), 'Challenge to India's pharmaceutical patent laws', *Science*, **337**, 414–15.

Syngenta (2010), *Annual Report 2010*, http://annualreport2010.syngenta.com/en/Overview.aspx (accessed July 26, 2013).

4. Knowledge transfer in the Thai automotive industry and impacts from changing patent regimes

Patarapong Intarakumnerd and Peera Charoenporn

1. INTRODUCTION

Thailand is not only a latecomer in industrialization but recently the country has also changed from a weak to a stronger patent regime since the first amendment of the Patent Act in 1992. Nonetheless, unlike East Asian newly industrialized economies (NIEs) (Korea, Taiwan, Singapore), firms in Thailand have generally failed to catch up. They have been slow and passive in technological learning. Government policies and institutions like public research institutes and universities have not strongly encouraged and assisted firms to enhance their indigenous technological capability, especially in terms of absorbing external knowledge. For example, there was virtually no mechanism to help diffuse knowledge embodied in patents. The situation has not changed under the stronger protection regime from 1992 onwards. Despite significant investment by transnational corporations (TNCs) since the 1960s, firms have only deepened their technological capabilities in Thailand in the area of production. Most have failed to move to more sophisticated activities such as product design and R&D locally. The spillover impacts of upgrading local capabilities have also been relatively small. In a nutshell, there is no co-evolution of intellectual property rights (IPR) regime and technological capability of firms in Thailand, which is different from the case in NIEs (Intarakumnerd and Charoenporn, 2010).

Interestingly, lately there have been a few incidences of improvement in key sectors like hard disk drive and automotive. The automotive industry in Thailand is quite an exception. It started in the early 1960s when TNCs started their assembly plants there. High demand from assemblers and local component requirements imposed by the Thai government since the late 1960s induced the emergence and growth of local makers of automotive parts and components from the 1970s onwards. After trade liberalization in the 1990s, Thailand has become an important export production base of the automotive industry in the Association of Southeast Asian Nations (ASEAN), with strong automotive part manufacturers. Production is expected to reach two million units a year in 2011, of which more than half of vehicles and parts will be exported. Moreover, Thailand has started to be an attractive location for R&D and product development for emerging markets. Since the 2000s, TNCs' investment strategies have started to change, as they began to invest in more technologically sophisticated activities such as advanced engineering, process and product design, and advanced testing and validation. For all these reasons, the automotive industry is a rather interesting case to study, in order to see how it relates to the non-co-evolution pattern between firms' technological capability and patent regime in Thailand.

This chapter examines the co-evolution of IPR regime and technological capability of automotive firms in Thailand. Specifically we investigate the three following issues. Firstly, is there any atmospheric change in terms of increasing awareness of the importance of patents in the industry after the patent regime became stronger? We observe the rates of patent application and granting. Also, we explore whether or not automotive companies, both assemblers and part suppliers, have *formal* and *systematic* IP strategies and whether these strategies have been integrated with their overall business plans. Secondly, does the stronger patent regime have impacts on the extent and nature of knowledge transfer between transnational corporations and local part suppliers, and, to a lesser extent, between universities and public research institutes and firms? We study the growth rate of licensing between the concerned parties, as well as the frequency and nature of litigation cases. Lastly, does the stronger patent regime have an impact on firms climbing up technological ladders (from production to more sophisticated activities)? Is it easier to obtain licenses for rather simple production technologies than those related to product development and design?

For research methodology, this study collected and analyzed the primary data on Thai IP-related law, regulation and patent registration. We also conducted interviews for case studies of firms in the automotive industry, including both carmakers and part manufacturers. Regulators, policy makers, and university professors specialized in the automotive industry were also interviewed. Furthermore, we analyzed secondary data on Thailand's innovation system, firms' capabilities and learning. This data largely comes from the Thailand R&D/Innovation Survey 2003 done by the National Science and Technology Development Agency (NSTDA), by licensing data from the Bank of Thailand. Our study consists of seven parts including the overall development of technological capability in Thailand, the evolution of the IPR regime in Thailand, the roles of the IPR regime on Thailand's technological catching up, knowledge transfer in the Thai automotive industry and the impacts from changing patent regimes, case studies, discussion and, finally, conclusions.

2. THE OVERALL DEVELOPMENT OF TECHNOLOGICAL AND INNOVATIVE CAPABILITIES OF FIRMS IN THAILAND

Thailand is famous for its agriculture products (such as rice, rubber, tapioca) and service industries, especially tourism. Nonetheless, unlike more successful East Asian NIEs like Korea, Taiwan and Singapore, technological learning of firms in the manufacturing sector has been generally slow and passive, although there were some signs of speedier technological catching up recently. 'Production capacity' in some sectors like automotive, electronics, garment and food processing has improved over time due to passive learning by doing. However, 'technological capability', that is, the ability to create and manage technological changes, which requires more purposeful and active learning, has been rather limited (see Bell and Scott-Kemmis, 1985; Chantramonklasri, 1985; Thailand Development Research Institute, 1989; Dahlman and Brimble, 1990; Tiralap, 1990; Mukdapitak, 1994; Lall, 1998).

The World Bank's study (see Arnold et al., 2000) confirms this long-standing feature of Thai firms. Only a small minority of large subsidiaries of TNCs, large domestic firms and small and medium-size enterprises (SMEs) have capability in R&D, while the majority is still struggling with increasing their design and engineering capability. For a very large number of SMEs, the key issue tends to be building up more basic operational capabilities, together with craft and technician capabilities for efficient acquisition, assimilation and incremental upgrading of fairly standard technology.

The slow technological capability development of Thai firms is quite different from what characterizes Japan, Korea and Taiwan. Firms in these countries have moved rather rapidly from mere imitators to innovators. As early as the 1960s, Japanese firms became more innovative, invested heavily in R&D and relied less on the importation of foreign technologies (Odagiri and Goto, 1993). In general, firms in Korea and Taiwan, where industrialization (beginning with import substitution) started more or less in the same period as in Thailand, were more successful in increasing absorptive capacity (of foreign technology) and deepening indigenous technological capabilities in several industries (see for example, Amsden, 1989; Kim, 1993; Lall, 1996; Hobday, 1995; Kim, 1997). In the electronics industry, for instance, Korean and Taiwanese firms were able to climb technological ladders (from simple assembly to original design and R&D) by exploiting institutional mechanisms such as original equipment manufacturer (OEM) and original design manufacturer (ODM) to help latecomer firms in those countries acquire advanced technology and access demanding foreign markets (see Hobday, 1995).

The low level of technological and innovative capabilities and passive learning of Thai firms can also be illustrated by R&D and Innovation Community Surveys. The surveys have been carried out by the National Science and Technology Development Agency (NSTDA) since the year 1999. R&D surveys were carried out every year but the innovation surveys were conducted three times only, in the years 1999, 2001 and 2003. The numbers of R&D-performing and innovating firms in both manufacturing and service sectors were quite small, at around 6 percent in the year 2006.

Government policies and their implementation towards technological catching up and encouraging the accumulation of indigenous technological and innovative capability of local firms have been largely absent or poorly executed, especially regarding the buildup of enough qualified human capital. There have been virtually no effective government incentives or pressure on TNCs to upgrade their activities technologically and to contribute more to local industrial upgrading. Nevertheless, after the economic crisis in 1997, there has been a positive trend toward the technological development of firms in Thailand. Higher competition in the global market has led to changing behavior of Thai firms focusing on relatively more knowledge-intensive intermediate technologies across all the sectors (Arnold et al., 2000). Several locally owned OEM manufacturers, experiencing external pressure especially from foreign customers that adopted global sourcing strategies, started to develop products under their own designs and brand names (see Intarakumnerd and Virasa, 2004). There has been gradual structural change in R&D investment as well. The government used to play a major role in R&D activities of the country, while the private sector's share in total R&D expenditure was low (around 10 percent in the 1980s). More recently, domestic firms have assumed an increasingly larger role in the country's R&D efforts (reaching almost 40 percent in the 2000s) in response partly to increasing international competition and partly to a supportive policy environment (National Science and Technology Policy Committee, 2006).

The Roles of Transnational Corporations and their Spillover Impacts on Upgrading Technological Capabilities of Local Firms

Thailand is a major recipient of FDI in the region. The total amount of FDI from 1970 to 2006 was US$34,194.23 million. Since 1986 FDI has played important roles in Thailand's industrialization. Before that, compared to investment in neighboring countries like Singapore and Malaysia, private investment in Thailand was based more on domestic resource mobilization and less on FDI. Furthermore, foreign investments in the manufacturing industry during that period mainly took the form of joint ventures with an emphasis on assembly of final goods for the domestic market, while both capital goods industries and parts producing industries remained relatively underdeveloped. From 1986 onwards, FDI became more significant and Thailand has almost doubled its share of net foreign investments in ASEAN. One of the major changes in this period is that a significant amount of FDI went to export industries and to industries that provide intermediate inputs such as electronics parts and components. As a result, Thailand's export performance looked quite impressive during the 1986–96 period, before a major economic crisis in 1997 (Lauridsen, 2004).

Similar to the experience of East Asian NIEs, there was also a significant change in the structure of Thai manufacturing exports. The share of once-dominating resource-based and labor-intensive exports has gone down while that of science-based and differentiated exports has gone up, especially during the 1990s. A range of new 'high-tech' products (especially computers and parts, electrical equipment and integrated products) emerged as key export goods. However, unlike East Asian NIEs, much of Thailand's hi-tech export was in reality manufactured through rather simple, labor-intensive assembly of high-tech components imported from advanced industrialized countries and East Asian NIEs. As a result, in terms of level of technological capability, there was no remarkable movement away from the period of resource-based, labor-intensive light and final-goods-assembly industries before 1986.

A powerful explanation is that while FDI in Thailand has been significant in terms of volume, and although the role of TNCs on technology development of their subsidiaries and of local firms is supposed to be substantial, in fact, the links for technological development between TNCs and their subsidiaries and Thai suppliers were generally rather limited and trivial (Intarakumnerd et al., 2002; Sribunruang, 1986; Kaosa-Ard, 1991). Although foreign investment brings in product management and process technology, transfer of technology has tended to be limited to the operational level. There was no design or product-specific technology transfer. Machinery was imported with minimal instructions on operational procedures given by suppliers, resulting in inefficiently operated and inadequately maintained equipment. TNCs themselves were not active in developing subcontractors or giving technical assistance to local suppliers. The reason behind this was the inefficiency and backwardness of local supporting industries. Equally important, TNCs lacked willingness and effort to devote the resources and time to upgrade local suppliers (see Dahlman et al., 1991). The existence of complaints about these issues is noted in the comprehensive study by Dahlman and Brimble, 1990, and by Kaosa-Ard, 1991.

As a result, there was not sufficient transfer of technology at higher levels such as design and engineering. Little investment from TNCs in Thailand was made in R&D. In 2000, only 39 TNCs, or 1.4 percent of the total number of TNCs operating in Thailand in the manufacturing sector, established R&D centers in Thailand. Most of these TNCs' R&D centers were small and involved largely in adapting their products to local market needs. Nonetheless, the situation has started to change in the past few years. There have been some signs of investment by TNCs in higher technological activities such as R&D, engineering and design in certain sectors such as the automotive and hard disk drive industries (Intarakumnerd et al., 2002).

3. THE EVOLUTION OF THE IPR REGIME IN THAILAND AND THE EFFECT OF TRIPS COMPLIANCE ON ATMOSPHERIC CHANGES

Together with aforementioned development in Thailand's manufacturing sector, Thailand's IPR regime also evolved. Although there are various types of IPR, this study will focus only on patents which are highly related with technology development in developing countries. The purpose of patents is two-fold: to give an incentive to innovators by protecting their inventions for a certain amount of time, and to act as a medium for dissemination of knowledge to the public at large (Foray, 2002). We therefore examine the evolution of the Thai patent regime in this light. This section carefully illustrates the historical development of patent laws and their protection enforcement on one hand, and the availability and effectiveness of mechanisms of diffusion of knowledge embodied in patents on the other.

Prior to the promulgation of the patent law in 1979, there had been no protection for human invention or design in Thailand unless it could fall under other areas of intellectual property. Later on, the Patent Act of 1979 was proposed to promote the research and development of new inventions and designs that are useful to domestic agriculture, industry and commerce, and to offer legal protection to inventors and designers by prohibiting others from copying or imitating their intellectual innovations (DIP, 2006).

In order to protect Thailand's exports, particularly from countries which could pursue trade sanctions on Thailand because of the allegedly inadequate protection of intellectual property (especially the US's Super 301 of the Omnibus Trade and Competitiveness Act 1988), the first amendment to the patent law was completed in 1992. The first amendment signified a change from weak to strong protection. The major changes included expanding the scope of patentable matters to food, beverages, pharmaceutical products or pharmaceutical ingredients, and extending the term of patent rights protection from 15 to 20 years after the filing date (see Kuanpoth, 2006). The amendment has also increased the rights of the holder of a process patent by including a monopoly right to import products produced directly by means of the patented process.

The second amendment was completed in 1999 with an aim to make the law comply with the Trade-Related Aspects of Intellectual Property Rights (TRIPS) agreement and other well accepted international standards. Under this amendment, the group of persons who may obtain patents in Thailand was extended to nationals, residents and those having a legitimate ongoing business address in any country that is a member of the Paris Convention or the WTO. The one-year period from the first application for a patent for the invention anywhere in the world within which patent applications must be filed in Thailand was extended to eighteen months. The number of exceptions to patent rights was reduced. The scope of compulsory licensing was restricted. Finally, a system of petty patents[1] was introduced. For a petty patent, an invention is eligible and accepted for registration if it makes the examiner believes that it is new and industrially applicable. Unlike patents, applicants of petty patents do not have to illustrate distinctive inventive steps. It is noteworthy that petty patents were introduced very late in Thailand in order to encourage local people to invent more and take advantage of this patent protection. This situation is different from that of the NIEs of East Asia, which introduced petty patents much earlier. These countries' first introduction of patent laws was to promote local innovation (UNIDO, 2006).

In comparison with Japanese patent law, especially during the catching-up period of the 1960s–70s, Thai IPR law seems to follow Japan's model by facilitating greater intra-industry technological knowledge flows and spillovers (Intarakumnerd et al., 2001). Firstly, foreign patents are not automatically protected under the current system. Foreigners wishing to protect their assets need to apply for a Thai patent no later than 12 months after filing abroad. Secondly, the system requires that all the patent applications be disclosed 18 months after the applications are filed. Thirdly, applications for patents in Thailand tend to be made earlier in the innovation process because of a first-to-file rule of priority, in contrast to the first-to-invent rule of priority of the US. Lastly, Thai patents have a three-month period of 'pre-grant opposition' when competitors or anybody else can challenge the validity of the prospective patent. In terms of licensing, patent licenses[2] must be in writing and submitted to the patent office, the Department of Intellectual Property (DIP).[3] It is not permissible to restrict the license to Thailand. A licensor may not require a licensee to pay a royalty for use of the patented invention after the patent term has expired.

Thailand has concluded and is currently negotiating a vast number of Free Trade Agreements (FTAs) with a number of countries and trading blocks, including Australia, Japan, Peru, the US, and the European Free Trade Association (EFTA). The FTA with US[4] includes an IP chapter containing TRIPS-plus standards that go beyond what has been already included in TRIPS (see Kuanpoth, 2006). It will include the reduction of the patent registration fee and changes to the registration process to bring it closer to international standards. These measures include using a post-grant opposition system instead of pre-grant opposition, making it more easy for a patent to be granted, and reducing an opponent's chance to make a challenge (Posaganondh and Adsawintarangkun, 2007). As the negotiation with the US is not finished, the TRIP-plus standards have not been implemented yet.

To summarize, Thailand's patent regime has been changed from a weak to a strong regime. Since the late 1990s, the regime moved towards more protection due to the TRIPS agreement, political pressure from advanced countries, and bilateral Free Trade Agreements (FTAs).

As Thai patent laws evolved, so did government bodies implementing them. In 1992, the DIP was established to hold direct authority concerning registration, protection and efforts to increase public understanding of intellectual property rights. In terms of registration, Thailand lacks qualified patent examiners. For instance, only 29 patent examiners took care of 6,261 patent applications in 2006. Consequently, there has been a decline of patents granted in 2005–06 (Posaganondh and Adsawintarangkun, 2007). After Thailand joined the WTO on January 1, 1995, the Intellectual Property and International Trade Court (IP&IT) was established in 1996. This IP&IT Court is equipped with well-trained career judges and associate judges that specialize in the relevant fields such that it can manage the cases which are different from conventional disputes effectively.

In regards to the knowledge diffusion aspect, Thailand lacked purposeful organization, which takes responsibility for encouraging knowledge diffusion, and, hence, the learning of local firms (Intarakumnerd et al., 2002). Previously, the diffusion of IP-embodied information was implemented in a 'passive' manner, as the DIP just sent information (without systematic digestion and classification to match different demands of each industrial sector) to business associations and provincial authorities under the Ministry of Commerce. The Intellectual Property Center (IPC), which later undertook responsibility to diffuse the knowledge embedded in IP, was only just established in 2006. This center is still a part of the bureaucratic DIP, whose main functions are the promotion of IPR registration and protection (not diffusion of knowledge). This is different from the cases in Japan and Korea. In Japan, the National Center for Industrial Property Information and Training (NCIPI) was set up as a part of the Japan Patent Office (JPO) with an aim to provide training services and promote the diffusion of information and knowledge embedded in IPRs. Similarly, the Korea Institute of Patent Information (KIPI), a non-profit organization, was set up in 1995 to support the Korean Intellectual Property Office (KIPO) by providing patent information services for the private sector. KIPI has 350 patent analysts conducting patent research, patent analysis, and patent evaluation (KIPI, 2008). In Thailand, the situation is very different. The Thai IPC has limited resources and capacity in performing the knowledge diffusion tasks. Importantly, it has no capability to analyze Thai and foreign patents, both in effect and outdated, in order to inform local firms of future technological and business opportunities which might arrive from those patents. Another organization of IP-embedded knowledge diffusion is the 'Toryod' website (http:// www.toryod.com) created by the unit for the creation of awareness and exploitation of patent documents for R&D under sponsorship of the Thailand Research Fund Office (RTF) since 1995. The website provides links to searchable patent databases of several countries including patent databases in Thai. However, this project has been operated with limited capacity. The evolution of patent laws and relevant organizations is illustrated in Table 4.1.

Compliance with TRIPS and general public acceptance of the importance of R&D, innovation and intellectual property rights has led to atmospheric changes, especially for government policy initiatives. The Board of Investment (BOI), for instance, has launched a special investment package promoting skill, technology and innovation, or STI. Firms can enjoy one or two years of extra tax incentives if they perform the following activities in the first three years: spending on R&D or design at least 1–2 percent of their sales, employing scientists or engineers with at least bachelor's degree for at least 5 percent of their workforce, spending

Table 4.1   The evolution of Thai patent laws and organizations

	Patent Act 1979	1st Amendment (1992)	2nd Amendment (1999)
Reasons	1. To promote the research and development of new inventions and designs that are useful to domestic agriculture, industry and commerce 2. To offer legal protection to inventors and designers by prohibiting others from copying or imitating their intellectual innovation	To avoid trade sanctions under s.301. In order to meet international standards, the drafters consult a number of relevant sources, e.g. the Paris Convention for the Protection of Industrial Property, the Patent Cooperation Treaty, the WIPO Model Law, the draft Patent Law Harmonization Treaty and the preliminary Draft Agreement on TRIPS	To make Thai patent law officially comply with the TRIPS agreement
Major changes	There was no law in Thailand that protected such creation and, therefore, the rights the plaintiffs raised were not recognized by the Thai legal system	1. The limitation of non-patentable subject matters 2. The longer term of protection, the expanded scope of protection 3. The establishment of a drug price review committee 4. The modification of the process for the grant of compulsory licenses	1. National treatment 2. Priority filings 2. Patent rights (adopted the principle of international exhaustion of patent rights) 3. Petty patents 4. Compulsory licensing 5. The Drug Patents Board
Organization	The Department of Commercial Registration	The Department of Intellectual Property (1992) Intellectual Property and International Trade Court (1996)	Intellectual Property Center (2003)

Source: Adapted from Department of Intellectual Property, 2006.

on training of their employees at least 1 percent of their total payroll, and spending at least 1 percent of total payroll on training personnel of their local suppliers. In addition, the National Science, Technology and Innovation Act, considered as the 'basic law' on science, technology and innovation, was enacted in 2008 to provide a framework for public and private sector institutions to strengthen the nation's STI capabilities. Capabilities to be strengthened include S&T manpower, S&T infrastructure, public awareness of S&T, and S&T management and administration systems. Creating and commercializing intellectual property rights is also emphasized by this new law. Compliance with this law requires management mechanisms for implementation, monitoring and evaluation systems, and flexibility of rolling improvement. According to the law, a new supra-ministerial structure – the National Science, Technology and Innovation Policy Committee – has been founded, to be chaired by the Prime Minister. Members of the Policy Committee include ministers from key ministries relevant to science, technology and innovation, together with respected resource persons. Very recently, after the Abisit Government came to power in 2009, government policies to promote a 'creative economy' based on creativity, talent and the unique culture of Thai people (the so-called 'Thainess') was initiated. Policy makers pay a lot of attention to 'creative industries' like Thai food, Thai craft, Thai massage and spa, Thai films, Thai multimedia software and so on. Again, the issue of intellectual property right creation, protection and utilization is an indispensable part of this new policy.

4. THE ROLES OF IPR REGIME IN THAILAND'S TECHNOLOGICAL CATCHING UP

4.1 Nature of Firms Having Patents

This study uses a firm-level database from the Thailand R&D/Innovation Survey 2003, collected by the National Science and Technology Development Agency (NSTDA). From the 2,582 firms that completed the questionnaire, this study uses the 310 firms that have R&D activities or have been granted patents as our selected sample.

By looking at the characteristics of firms granted patents, we find that the majority of them carried out in-house R&D activities. They were mostly large companies, either subsidiaries of TNCs or their OEM suppliers. They also had more export intensity than firms without granted patents, and had more R&D expenditure. These firms had spent more on 'acquisition of other external knowledge' but less on 'design and other preparation for production/deliveries'. Furthermore, they saw strong IP protection as an important part of the current business environment in Thailand for R&D. Lastly, these firms used university lab facilities more.

Interestingly, the granted patents were not in the main industries (for example, patents were found in the manufacture of musical instruments and weapons). Important information for R&D was from sources within the enterprise and clients but not from patent disclosure, research institutes or universities. Their expenditure for innovation activities was spent largely on acquisition of machinery and equipment, market introduction of innovation, and intramural R&D. The firms rated the following factors as important aspects of a business environment for R&D/innovation: the attitude of people toward innovation, openness of customers, acceptance of failure, and IP protection. Major government programs used for supporting R&D/innovation activities were information services, university laboratory services and testing services.

4.2 Recent Increases in Patent Registration in Thailand

In Thailand, the overall number of patents applied for and granted, either abroad or in Thailand, was very low. In terms of patent registration, it has not been an important issue for local Thai firms since they neither have the capabilities to generate genuine ideas in order to register patents nor incentives to pay attention to patents. Under the weak protection regime, patent registration was not only low but also increased very slowly. In the period 1979–92, there were only 955 granted invention patents. Foreign firms accounted for almost 90 percent of them. Even after the 1992 introduction of a stronger protection regime, which should have provided more incentives for patent registration, the use of patents to protect local invention and design is still low in Thailand. Just more than half of granted patents were for industrial designs, some of which involved rather low technological content. The foreign share of granted patents was still very high, at more than 90 percent (Table 4.2).

It is worth mentioning that under the 2nd Amendment of Thai patent law (1999), the right to apply for patent protection was no longer restricted to Thai nationals and nationals of countries that have reciprocal patent agreements with Thailand. The right to apply for patent protection has been extended to nationals of countries which were parties to international patent treaties or conventions to which Thailand also was a party. Since Thailand is a member of the WTO, and thus TRIPS, nationals of other WTO member countries have received the same protection at the same level as Thai nationals.[5] Consequently, there was a remarkable increase of invention patents after 1999.

Table 4.2 Granted patent by ownership and type of patent (1979–2010) (unit: item)

Year	Granted patents			Design patents			Invention patents		
	Total	Thai	Foreign	Total	Thai	Foreign	Total	Thai	Foreign
1979–92 Weak IPR	3,095 (100%)	742 (24%)	2,353 (76%)	2,140 (100%)	645 (30%)	1,495 (70%)	955 (100%)	97 (10.2%)	858 (89.8%)
1993–99 Stronger IPR	6,204 (100%)	1,081 (17%)	5,123 (83%)	2,296 (100%)	938 (41%)	1,358 (59%)	3,908 (100%)	143 (3.7%)	3,765 (96.3%)
2000–10	19,319 (100%)	6,706 (35%)	12,613 (65%)	10,674 (100%)	6,062 (57%)	4,612 (43%)	8,645 (100%)	644 (7.4%)	8,001 (92.6%)
Total	28,620 (100%)	8,529 (30%)	20,091 (70%)	15,112 (100%)	7,646 (51%)	7,466 (49%)	13,510 (100%)	884 (6.5%)	12,626 (93.5%)

Source: Department of Intellectual Property (DIP).

Although the share of patents issued to Thai residents has increased gradually from 3.7 percent during 1993–99 to around 7 percent during 2000–10, the yearly number of patents issued to local inventors does not demonstrate any sign of significant increase. The high degree of foreign dominance implies that local inventors have low technological capability to develop inventions that meet the basic requirements of novelty, inventive steps, and industrial application.

Apart from private firms, the local science and technology community is a very minor beneficiary of this particular incentive system. There has never been a tradition or practice of using patent information in the basic or advanced education and research arenas such as universities and research institutes, or even in the industry itself. It is only in the past few years that major Thai conglomerates like the CP Group and Siam Cement Group have seriously and actively promoted innovation and the use of the patent system to increase their productivity and competitiveness. Only in the case of Siam Cement Group has the firm paid attention to acquiring its own patents (Intarakumnerd and Charoenporn, 2010).

As mentioned earlier, under the current generally stronger regime, one important mechanism to promote knowledge diffusion and local innovation was introduced, although late. In order to encourage the local people and firms to innovate more and take advantage of the patent protections, the petty patent, a system of utility models, has been incorporated under the second revision of the Patent Act. Petty patents, utility model patents, are granted to inventions that are new and industrially applicable, without the need to publicize inventive steps. The initial term of a petty patent is six years from the date of filing the application with the possibility of two extensions of two years each, as opposed to 20 years for standard patent protection. The introduction of petty patents is an attempt of the DIP to induce local firms to improve their technology capabilities, especially R&D. During 1999–2010, the number of petty patents has grown dramatically (Table 4.3). This supports the idea that at present there are many local people and firms who cannot fulfill the requirements of the standard patent, but can satisfy the requirements of a petty patent.

In addition, the Patent Cooperation Treaty (PCT) came into force in Thailand on December 24, 2009. In the year after the initiation of the PCT, the number of new patent filings in Thailand dropped. This is because Thailand is a receiving country, meaning that most of the patent applications were filed by foreigners that are members of PCT. Therefore, it is expected that the number of new patent filings in Thailand will drop to 60 percent in 2010 and 30 percent in 2011. This is because patent owners can take advantage of the PCT system's 30-month period for the filing of

Table 4.3 *Number of applications and granted petty patents 1999–2010 (unit: item)*

Year	Petty patent applications			Granted petty patents		
	Total	Thai	Foreigner	Total	Thai	Foreigner
1999	114	106	8	6	6	6
2000	335	284	51	125	109	16
2001	464	406	58	381	328	53
2002	565	522	43	386	324	62
2003	511	469	42	300	296	4
2004	635	580	55	407	381	26
2005	752	689	63	618	587	31
2006	973	884	89	791	737	54
2007	582	476	106	915	850	65
2008	396	296	100	725	659	66
2009	217	158	59	498	302	196
2010	10	2	8	397	289	108
Total	5,554	4,872	682	5,549	4,868	687
	(100.0%)			(100.0%)		

Source: Department of Intellectual Property (DIP).

the national phase in Thailand, as compared to the old 12-month priority period.

At the industrial sector level, data from DIP provides a picture of differences across industries in terms of both the process and the importance of the IPR regime. Using the International Patent Classification (IPC)[6] of the WIPO, during 1981–2007, chemistry and metallurgy (25.8 percent), human necessities (22.5 percent), and performing, operations and transporting (20.5 percent) were the leading industries in terms of patents granted (Table 4.4). Considering patents granted for invention to Thai nationals, the most common fields of technology were human necessities (30.9 percent) followed by performing, operations, transporting (18.5 percent), chemistry and metallurgy (16.9 percent), and mechanical engineering (14 percent). Similarly, petty patents, dominated by Thai inventors (85.2 percent), were mostly in the field of human necessities (35 percent) followed by performing, operations and transporting (23.4 percent), and mechanical engineering (12.2 percent). This demonstrates that, unlike in developed countries where most patents are granted in science-based industries such as electronics, more patents in Thailand are granted in supposedly labor-intensive and resource-based industries such as consumer goods and agriculture (in Section A).

Table 4.4   Granted patents and petty patents for invention to Thais by IPC

Section	Granted patents (1981–2010)			Granted petty patents (2000–10)		
	Total	Thai	Ratio	Total	Thai	Ratio
Section A – Human	3,147	312	10%	2,031	1,797	9%
Necessities	13%	19%		23%	23%	
Section B –	5,350	399	7%	2,303	1,995	9%
Performing	22%	24%		26%	26%	
Operations;						
Transporting						
Section C –	4,724	239	5%	924	809	9%
Chemistry;	20%	15%		10%	10%	
Metallurgy						
Section D –Textiles;	3,301	170	5%	990	875	9%
Paper	14%	10%		11%	11%	
Section E – Fixed	498	83	17%	424	383	9%
Constructions	2%	5%		5%	5%	
Section F –	3,205	232	7%	1,104	952	9%
Mechanical	14%	14%		12%	12%	
Engineering;						
Lighting; Heating;						
Weapons; Blasting						
Section G – Physics	1,743	124	7%	720	637	9%
	7%	8%		8%	8%	
Section H –	2,006	79	4%	414	344	8%
Electricity	8%	5%		5%	5%	
Total	23,934	1,638	7%	8,910	7,792	9%
	100.0%	100.0%		100.0%	100.0%	

Source: Department of Intellectual Property (DIP).

Table 4.5 shows the number of granted patents during 1981–90, 1991–2000, and 2001–10. It shows that foreign firms and foreigners have been the driving force behind domestic patent applications in every industrial sector. The share of patents granted to Thai nationals and Thai firms has been small. In fact, the share of patents issued to Thai residents has decreased during 1991–2000 because of an increase in the share of foreign granted patents due to the large inflow of FDI to Thailand, especially from Japanese automobile and electronics TNCs. FDI by TNCs has transferred surprisingly little tacit knowledge and technology through vertical or horizontal spillovers. Only a few companies have set up research

Table 4.5   Granted patents for invention by IPC in 1981–90, 1991–2000 and 2001–10

Section		1981–90	1991–2000	2001–10	Total
Section A – Human	Total	204	1,383	1,538	3,115
Necessities	Thai	13	81	217	311
		6%	6%	14%	10%
Section B – Performing	Total	115	1,073	3,314	4,502
Operations;	Thai	14	30	296	340
Transporting		12%	3%	9%	8%
Section C – Chemistry;	Total	275	1,458	2,622	4,355
Metallurgy	Thai	17	47	144	208
		6%	3%	5%	5%
Section D – Textiles;	Total	17	183	1,840	2,040
Paper	Thai	1	3	124	128
		6%	2%	7%	6%
Section E – Fixed	Total	35	181	282	498
Constructions	Thai	12	18	53	83
		34%	10%	19%	17%
Section F – Mechanical	Total	66	378	2,149	2,593
Engineering; Lighting;	Thai	16	33	154	203
Heating; Weapons;		24%	9%	7%	8%
Blasting					
Section G – Physics	Total	11	357	1,115	1,483
	Thai	3	9	95	107
		27%	3%	9%	7%
Section H – Electricity	Total	11	533	1,289	1,833
	Thai	1	9	63	73
		9%	2%	5%	4%
Total	Total	734	5,546	14,149	20,429
	Thai	77	230	1,146	1,453
		10.5%	4.1%	8%	7%

Source: Department of Intellectual Property (DIP).

establishments in Thailand and the scope of the research being done in Thailand is limited (NESDB and World Bank, 2007). In 2005, technology payment as a percentage of gross domestic expenditure on R&D (GERD) was 767.5 percent. This is relatively high in comparison with other hi-tech products exporting countries and it means that manufacturers in Thailand still depend largely on the purchase of foreign technologies. Thai firms have not developed their own indigenous technological capability development effort.

There is a continually increasing trend in royalty fees, trademarks and

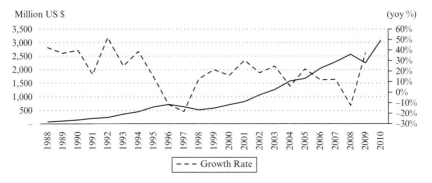

Source: Bank of Thailand.

Figure 4.1   Royalty fees, trademarks and copyrights, 1988–2010

copyright, especially after 1999 (Figure 4.1). This may be due to the fact
that production in Thailand recently has tended towards high-technology
products, particularly in the electronics industries and automobile industries, and this production requires importing foreign technologies.

The increase in patent litigation in Thailand

Thailand recognized the imposition of 'criminal' penalties for violation
of intellectual property rights explicitly even before the TRIPS agreement. Intellectual property law in Thailand, moreover, goes beyond the
minimum standard of TRIPS because it provides criminal sanctions for
infringement or violation of rights at all levels, even levels lower than
a commercial scale. This is quite different from other countries whose
intellectual property right litigations are considered as 'civil' cases. As a
result, the administration of intellectual property rights in Thailand relies
on police authority. The infringement or violation of intellectual property
rights is normally considered a criminal act in accordance with the laws
concerned. However, there is not a great deal of patent infringement litigation in Thailand, presumably because of the lack of a formal discovery
mechanism and the expense necessary to prepare and prove a case against
what has not yet been culturally viewed as a criminal activity. Moreover,
expensive and long-lasting registration processes, as well as delayed court
procedures, are among the many causes that lead to a low capability to
enforce the policy.

During 1998–2010, intellectual property infringement has disposed
4,832 cases, of which 3,755 were criminal cases and 1,077 were civil
cases. Most intellectual property infringement cases related to copyright
infringement. Patent infringement is a small part of intellectual property

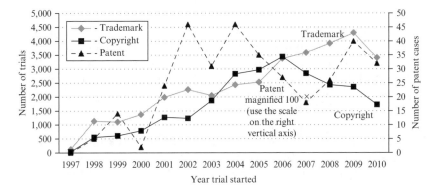

Source: CIPITC case statistics, www.cipitc.or.th.

Figure 4.2   Intellectual property infringement cases disposed

infringement. During 1997–2010, patent infringement cases were more criminal cases[7] (130) than civil cases (59). Nonetheless, the number of cases has increased annually, signifying a stronger IP protection regime (Figure 4.2).

Analyzing patent cases at the Central Intellectual Property and International Trade Court (CIPITC) during 1997–2010, this study found that the overall number of patent cases is still growing at approximately 30 percent per year. When the full-text CIPITC civil decisions were classified according to the IPC technical field, it was found that the most popular technical field is Human Necessity (A) followed by Mechanical Engineering (F). The least popular technical field is Physics (G).

From 1998 to 2010, there were 216 patent law-related civil cases brought to the Supreme Court. These included cases of patent infringement (59), breach of licensing agreement (52), cancellation against patent application decision (24), cancellation against patent registration (25), cancellation against petty-patent registration (22), petty-patent infringement (21), cancellation against the Board of Patent's decision (3), breach of patent contract (2), and breach of technology transfer contract (1).

The patent revoking cases involved the issues of lack of novelty and lack of inventive steps, unfairly widening the scope of patent. Thailand's patent law still allows the practice of pre-grant opposition, which, in theory, should induce competitors to monitor patent filing as early as possible, thereby promoting knowledge diffusion and 'active' learning of firms in Thailand. In practice, there are few cases of pre-grant opposition (less than 5 percent of total patent filing) due to lack of enough competition in the market. Interestingly, oppositions were mostly carried out by Thais for filings made by other Thais (either individuals or firms). There were a few cases of foreign inventors against Thais (8 from 216 cases) and, in most cases, the foreign inventors won. It was rare to see Thais challenge foreigners. Thai firms have limited technological and innovative capabilities to compete and learn from foreign competitors, and they can only compete with each other in a small number of product markets (Intarakumnerd and Charoenporn, 2010).

It is worth mentioning that Thai patent rights must be granted before the right-holder may sue others for infringements. A design patent does not protect an element that cannot be visually perceived by potential consumers. Designs cannot cover functional aspects, which could be protected by a utility patent or a utility model.

It is a normal practice for a plaintiff or a defendant, or both parties, to appeal the CIPITC decision to the Supreme Court. Approximately 10 percent of the cases took advantage of the alternative dispute resolution provided by CIPITC. Patent cases involved almost all technical fields. There were very few patent licensing litigation cases. On average, it took approximately 24 months to complete a trial (the worst case took four years). The average case time has been increasing annually.

The Thai Patent Act empowers the court to order the infringer to pay damages to the patent holder up to the amount the court deems appropriate, relying on the adverse effect of the injury, including the loss of benefits and the expenses necessary to protect the rights of the patent holder. Even so, the burden of proof in a civil infringement case is unfavorable to the patent holders. The patent holders have to convince judges with very solid evidence. Consequently, of the 216 patent infringement (civil) cases, there were only eight cases in which the court ordered the infringer to pay damages to the patent holder. As the court used a 'narrow' definition of loss (actual damage not including opportunity cost), most compensations were less than 100,000 baht (around 3,333 US$).

Regarding criminal cases, there were 31 patent infringement cases that reached the Supreme Court from the years 1998 to 2009. The plaintiffs (patent holders) won only around 25 percent of all cases. Most cases were among Thais. Only five cases involved foreign patent holders suing Thai infringers. Though these are criminal cases, only one case led to a six-month imprisonment (with one year reprieve).

This analysis of litigation cases illustrates that even though Thai patent laws have become stronger and the number of litigation cases has increased, court decisions are still not in favor of the patent holders.

To conclude, the Thai IPR regime, in general, has played little role in the process of technological catching up. This is also true for the country's strategic sectors such as hard disk drive, automotive and pharmaceutical sectors. Our study shows that Thailand's IPR regime, in general, has been changed from a weak to a strong regime due to external factors such as pressure of developed countries, especially the US, rather than co-evolving with the level of local technological capability development. Besides the late introduction of petty patents, Thailand's IPR system has given opportunities for technological diffusion from advanced countries and 'learning by imitating' during the period of 'weak' regime; most firms, however, failed to move from 'duplicative imitation' to 'creative imitation' and innovation.

This is quite different from the experiences of Japanese and East Asian NIEs. At one point, the Thai IPR regime was a 'weak protection' but not a 'pro-diffusion' one. In effect, it was not really a 'catching up mode' of IPR regime. The difference from East Asia NIEs can be explained by the lack of the 'preconditions' of technological catching up. Beyond laws and regulation, these include the accumulated sufficient indigenous absorptive capacity of firms in the country, the mechanisms of knowledge diffusion and utilization, and an innovative enabling environment (Intarakumnerd and Charoenporn, 2010).

5. KNOWLEDGE TRANSFER IN THE THAI AUTOMOTIVE INDUSTRY AND IMPACTS FROM CHANGING PATENT REGIMES

5.1 An Overview of the Automotive Industry in Thailand

The automotive industry in Thailand started in the early 1960s under an import substitution policy and a revision of the investment promotion law to encourage automotive assembly in Thailand. Automotive TNCs tend to prefer FDI to non-FDI channels because it seems to be a more effective means of securing their proprietary assets. During 1961–69, nine assembly plants were set up as joint ventures between Thai and foreign carmakers. To boost investment in the domestic production of automotive parts, in 1969 the Thai government imposed a minimum local content requirement of 25 percent on automotive assembly. Before the local content requirements, some Japanese parts-makers had already entered Thailand to produce spare parts. New vehicles (both passenger cars and commercial vehicles) were purchased through CKD (complete knock down) imports from Japan. After the requirement was enacted, carmakers had to start purchasing locally. However, Japanese carmakers could not rely on Thai locally owned firms, and they requested affiliated Japanese automotive part suppliers to build plants locally and supply to them.

In 1978, with an aim to reduce the trade deficit and boost the industry, a localization policy was formulated. In addition to import bans and raising tariff rates on CKD and CBU (complete built up), the Thai government limited the number of automotive models and increased the local content requirement from 25 percent to 50 percent for passenger cars. Since the Thai automotive industry suffered low demand in cars in the early 1980s, the carmakers preferred in-house production to subcontracting for casting machine activities and produced automobiles themselves to utilize their excess production capacity. To further boost the development of the parts industry, the government raised the local content requirement to 54 percent for passenger cars and 60–72 percent for pick-up trucks. This policy gave rise to new investment in automotive parts. It also facilitated the transfer of technology to the Thai automotive industry.

FDI inflows in the automotive industry were more or less unchanged from 1970–85, with annual inflows amounting to less than $5 million. However, later during the period 1986–95, the annual average value of inflows increased dramatically. In the late 1980s, the appreciation of the Japanese yen pushed up the cost of major automotive parts imported from Japan. The yen appreciation triggered the relocation of Japanese parts producers to Thailand in order to reduce production costs. As indicated by the huge increase in FDI inflows, the increased degree of TNC involvement in the Thai automotive industry took place for both carmakers and part suppliers. Following their customers, Japanese part suppliers established new affiliates for manufacturing new and more sophisticated parts from the late 1980s, when Japan experienced dramatic currency appreciation.

In the 1990s, after more than 30 years of protection, there was a sign of market liberalization. The pressure to liberalize came from the General Agreement on Trade and Tariffs (GATT) which demanded a reduction in tariff rates on both CBU vehicles and CKD kits. The Thai government allowed assembly to expand their capacity and repealed prohibitions on imports of all types of vehicles.

Lower domestic automotive prices, combined with economic expansion, spurred the rise in sales during the period 1991–96. To maintain a rise in sales, the carmakers expanded their capacity. The carmakers increased procurement of subcontracted parts due to an increase in domestic vehicle demand and to satisfy local content requirement. Carmakers in Thailand expanded business transactions with joint venture suppliers and indigenous Thai suppliers. This period is also the first in which cars produced in Thailand were exported to the world market, especially one-ton pick-up trucks. Thailand has become the second largest production base of pick-up trucks after the US.

Recognizing the potential of Thailand as an export hub in the Southeast Asian region, Ford Motor, under the name of Auto Alliance Thailand (AAT), established their operation base assembly plant in 1997. General Motors Thailand, which waited for local content abolition in January 2000, began their operation in June 2000. Accordingly, the more assembly plants that were set up, the more foreign automotive part suppliers established their production bases in Thailand.

Since the mid 1990s, several world-class non-Japanese multiple-parts manufacturers such as Dana (1994), TRW Steering & Suspension (1998), Visteon Thailand (1998), Johnson Controls (1999), Delphi Automotive Systems (2000) and Tenneco Automotive (2002) have established their factories in Thailand (Figure 4.3). From 1994–97, the value of Board of Investment promoted projects was four times higher than the recorded value in the period 1990–93. The increased foreign investment in the automotive industry brought in new lines of automotive parts not previously produced in Thailand (such as transmission systems).

Thailand faced economic crisis in 1997. The automotive sales in 1998 dropped 76 percent from 1996 sales. The automotive parts industry was also affected by a contraction in sales. The Thai government announced a new excise tax rate and import tariff. Moreover, the Thai government abolished the local content requirement in 2000. Carmakers tried to export both finished cars and automotive parts. Part suppliers had to improve themselves to reduce production cost. Procuring more parts and raw material locally is one way of cutting costs.

Importantly, to help affected companies improve their liquidity positions, the Board of Investment removed the restrictions on foreign shareholding in November 1997. Prior to this, the policy required the majority ownership to be held by a Thai national. Many investors, mostly Japanese, took advantage of this new policy. From November 1997 to September 2000, foreign partners in 164 automotive firms have changed their shareholding structure from minority share to majority share (Charoenporn, 2001). FDI inflows in the Thai automotive industry further increased after the 1997 financial crisis and reached a record high by 2007. Since the 2000s, TNCs' investment strategies in the automotive industry have started to change. Since 2003, large TNCs have begun to invest in R&D in Thailand (for example Toyota Motor Asia Pacific Engineering and Manufacturing Co., Ltd; Nissan Technical Center Southeast Asia Co., Ltd; ISUZU Technical Center Asia Co., Ltd; and Honda R&D Asia Pacific Co., Ltd). Nonetheless, the R&D activities of these companies focus on modification of their already designed products to fit local demands and to exploit local advantages, such as analysis of appropriate local natural raw materials and parts to meet international standards or the standards of importing countries such as the European Union.

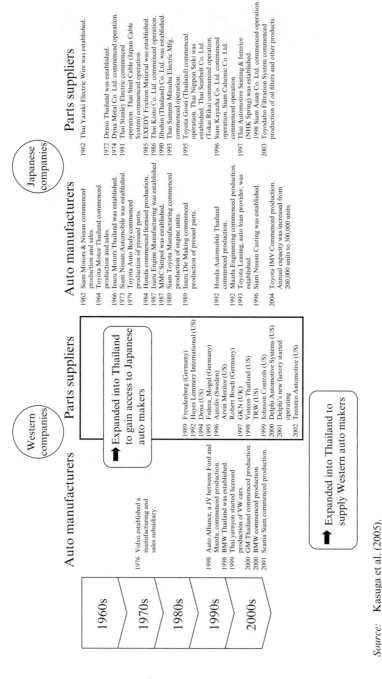

Source: Kasuga et al. (2005).

Figure 4.3   History of Thai expansion by Western and Japanese auto-related companies

As described above, the automotive industry in Thailand has developed under the Thai government's policy changes from protectionist import substitution policy (during 1960–85), to liberalization and export promotion (late 1980s–90s) and then to the stage of globalization and technological upgrading from 2000s to the present (Figure 4.4). From 1987–2005, almost 300 additional foreign part suppliers entered into Thai auto parts manufacturing. Thailand has already become one of the key production bases of most global players from Japan, the US and Europe.

Currently firms in the industry can be classified into three groups: 12 car assemblers; approximately 635 first-tier suppliers; and around 1,700 second- and third-tiers suppliers which include the supporting companies. Most of them are SMEs (Figure 4.5). Most assemblers are subsidiaries of TNCs. They are dominated by Japanese TNCs and the big three US car companies, namely Daimler Chrysler, General Motors (GM) and Ford, whose prime objective is to produce and export one-ton pickups from Thailand.

The Thai automotive industry has become more export oriented since 1996. Units of vehicle export increased from 14,000 units in 1996 to 152,800 in 2000. An increase in vehicle exports continued. In 2010, Thailand produced 1,645,304 cars of which 896,065 were exported, at a value of US$13,500 million (Figure 4.6). Due to a sufficient pool of qualified engineers and technicians, and an extensive supplier network enabling integrated production, Thailand is clearly the strongest automotive production base in Southeast Asia. Thailand has become the third largest auto-manufacturing base in Asia. Thailand specializes in manufacturing and exporting one-ton diesel pickup trucks, a type of vehicle with scale economies and somewhat slower model changes, thus providing a potential basis for domestic parts production. The pickups alone accounted for more than 50 percent of total vehicle exports throughout the period 1999–2004. More recently, passenger cars have accounted for an increasing share of exports.

For automotive parts, nowadays, a comprehensive range of parts is locally manufactured.[8] However, there are some components that are still not produced in Thailand, including passenger car engines, fuel injection pumps, transmissions, differential gears, injection nozzles, electronic systems, and electronic control units. Indigenous Thai suppliers are mainly in 'non-functional' parts such as body parts, accessories and others, while foreign suppliers are concentrated in the group of 'functional' parts, requiring higher manufacturing and design capabilities to produce, such as engine, electrical transmission, and suspension parts (Table 4.6).

Indigenous Thai part suppliers have low technological capabilities and are largely dependent on technology provided by joint venture (JV) partners or licensers, but they cannot absorb the transferred technology

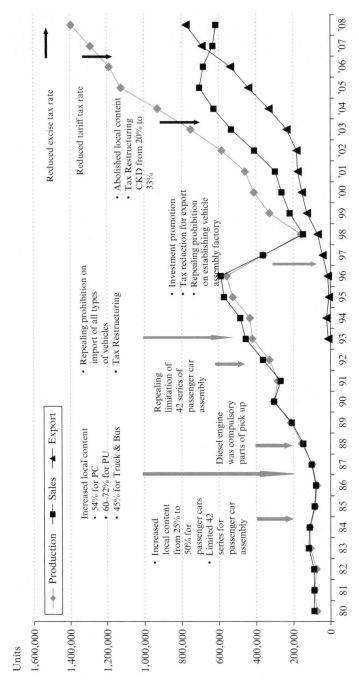

Source: Thai Automotive Institute.

Figure 4.4   Thai automotive development and government policies

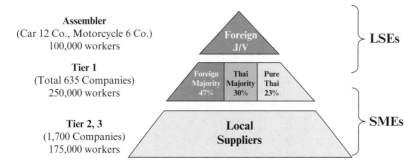

Source: Thai Automotive Institute (TAI), updated July 2010.

Figure 4.5 *Structure of manufacturers in the automotive industry in Thailand*

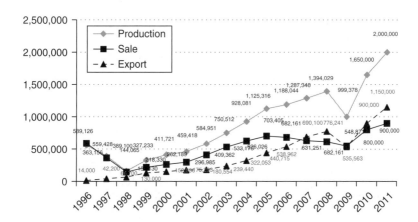

Source: Thai Automotive Institute (2011).

Figure 4.6 *Production, domestic sales and exports of automobiles in Thailand, 1993–2010*

due to a lack of skilled labor (Brooker Group, 2002, pp. 2–14). In addition, the College of Management, Mahidol University (2006) has examined the technological capabilities of six groups of automotive component suppliers, namely, suspension and brake, interior, exterior, engine, electronic, and drive transmission. Their results show that, in general, component suppliers in Thailand could be classified into two categories based on level of technological capabilities. Those in suspension and brake, interior

Table 4.6   Number of automotive OEM part suppliers classified by part

Part group	Thai	Thai majority	Foreign majority	Total
Engine	20	8	35	63
Electrical	15	10	27	52
Drive/ Transmission	17	6	29	52
Suspension/ Brake	13	1	21	35
Body	57	17	47	119
Accessories	18	2	19	39
Others	214	24	111	349
Total	354	68	287	709

Source: Thai Automotive Institute (2011).

and exterior had relatively higher capabilities. They have the potential to compete regionally and internationally. The other three, in engine, electronics and drive transmission components, have lower capabilities, since their underlying technologies are more sophisticated and require proprietary knowledge belonging to TNCs.

5.2   Knowledge Transfer in the Automotive Industry in Thailand

Foreign carmakers have played an important role in disseminating important technology that has enhanced the technological capability formation and growth of Thailand's supporting industries (Techakanont and Terdudomtham, 2004). TNCs are actively transferring technology through information sharing and advising local suppliers. Many TNC part suppliers, especially Japanese ones, are involved with local part suppliers through a technology-licensing contract or as minor shareholders. However, they have expressed their intention to be co-owners and/or majority shareholders. Their prime objective is to take full control of the parts manufacturing operation. This tendency of strengthening their involvement with local parts suppliers has been observed since the late 1980s.

As the Thai automotive industry has become more export-oriented, local content of locally assembled vehicles has increased naturally. To a certain extent the increased importance of vehicle exports can be regarded as a structural change. Especially when the foreign ownership restriction was abolished during the beginning of the crisis in 1997, these foreign major shareholder TNCs started bringing updated and more cutting-edge technology together with close supervision by foreign technicians. This did not occur when the TNCs were involved through technology licensing channels or were minor and less active shareholders (Kohpaiboon, 2006).

Moreover, considering the new national specialization strategy of TNCs, car assemblers did not have full information on producing a vehicle because it had not already been produced somewhere else. This is sharply different from in the past when vehicle models already launched somewhere else were replicated in developing countries. Assembling activities are not involved in product development and engineering. However, under the new strategy, car assemblers and parts suppliers have to jointly work out all necessary information for the manufacturing process based on input prices available at selected production sites to minimize total costs of a vehicle. Hence, higher technological capability from their part suppliers is required, as they are expected to participate in the product development and product engineering (Kohpaiboon and Poapongsakon, 2010).

The content of the inter-firm technology transfer has gradually enhanced from simple 'operational technology' to a higher level of 'process engineering technology'. According to Techakanont's research, there has been another shift towards 'product engineering capabilities' since the year 2000 (Techakanont, 2002). Nonetheless, few local suppliers with long-term relationships to assemblers, with willingness to participate in product developments in Japan and who own efforts in human resource development, are given the opportunity for higher-level technology transfers. It can be argued that OEM suppliers that survive in the new environment are likely to be large firms that are able to access longer-term financial support in order to comply with the new requirements.

To survive, indigenous Thai part suppliers, as the technology transferees, need to increase their own technological capabilities, especially absorptive capacities. It has been reported that most local suppliers have not been able to deal well with these changes and have stepped down to a lower tier; some may lose orders in the future if they remain at the same technological level they currently maintain.

Indigenous Thai parts suppliers recognize the need for their own product development, due to either an eroding comparative advantage or the loss of important customers, which have in many cases moved to China. They are forced to upgrade their skills and to enter the original brand manufacture (OBM) market with their own product developments. They used various means to achieve this goal including the recruitment of retired foreign R&D engineers, licensing, joint ventures with European firms and intensified cooperation with customers.[9] Moreover, information from international exhibitions is also considered important. Some firms utilize external knowledge, e.g. from designers or universities, in order to develop technologically simple OBM products (Berger, 2005, p. 192).

There has been intense competition among TNC carmakers which has considerably affected the pattern of TNC involvement in the automotive industry worldwide since the late 1980s. Global auto assemblers have responded by developing global networks of production sites, each of which specializes in the manufacture or assembly of a small number of components and/or vehicles. Today's operations are devoted to regional or global export markets. This strategy demands lower prices, better quality, rapid delivery, and much greater responsibility on the part of components producers. Assemblers have therefore shifted to greater reliance on a smaller number of increasingly large parts producers (Doner et al., 2004).

These changes make it much more difficult for small indigenous parts producers to produce OEM parts, much less develop their own designs or brands. The global industry thus offers the potential for an expansion in local automotive production. But the industry's globalized nature and rising production standards also pose real challenges to indigenous participation in this production.

The playing field for indigenous suppliers in the TNCs' production networks is becoming very limited, especially for OEM suppliers. Where OEM is concerned, bulky auto-body-related stamping parts would be the available playing field for indigenous suppliers. With long experience in assembly, Thailand would have strengths in press parts and related die, molds and jigs which require relatively less technological capability, especially in regards to product design (Kohpaiboon, 2006). To maintain their position as OEM suppliers, indigenous suppliers must acquire a certain level of product design knowledge in understanding two-dimensional drawing and manufacture parts at internationally competitive prices. In this regard, the issue of IPR may be important to indigenous Thai parts suppliers in the future.

5.3 Impacts from Changing Patent Regimes in Automotive Industries

5.3.1 Patent registration in the automotive industry

The analysis of granted patents in the automotive industry (represented by IPC classification B60: Vehicles in general) indicates that during 1981–2011 there were 333 granted patents out of 1,583 patent applications. The number increased from four patents during 1981–91 to 46 during 1992–99, and to 283 during 2000–11. However, there were no patents in IPC B60 belonging to a Thai inventor before 1991, only one patent during 1992–99, and nineteen during 2000–11. Most patents are in vehicle parts (IPC B60R). This evidence shows that a strong patent regime does not encourage indigenous invention.

Most of the granted patents belonged to Japanese carmakers and their subsidiaries. These companies applied for patent registration, which had

Table 4.7   Grant patents and petty patents of IPC B60 (1980–2010)

IPC Code	Items	Grant patents		Petty patents
		Total	Thai	Thai
B 60 B	Vehicle wheels	7	0	15
B 60 C	Vehicle tires	74	0	11
B 60 D	Vehicle connections	3	1	13
B 60 F	Convertible vehicles	0	0	0
B 60 G	Vehicle suspension arrangements	7	0	3
B 60 H	Air-treating devices of vehicles	17	1	2
B 60 J	Windows, windscreens and doors; protective covering	0	0	26
B 60 K	Propulsion units or transmissions in vehicles	37	1	13
B 60 L	Electric equipment for vehicle	10	1	1
B 60 M	Power supply lines	0	0	0
B 60 N	Vehicles passenger accommodation	23	3	2
B 60 P	Vehicles adapted for load transportation	6	1	40
B 60 Q	Signaling or lighting devices	22	3	6
B 60 R	Vehicle parts	85	10	124
B 60 S	Servicing of vehicles	10	1	16
B 60 T	Vehicle brake control systems	24	0	3
B 60 V	Air-cushion vehicles	1	0	0
B 60	Vehicles in general	326	22	275

Source: DIP.

already been registered in Japan, to DIP under their corporate headquarter names. This is coincident with the WTO-induced change in Thai patent law in 1999 (especially the 'national treatment'), allowing parent firms registered in WTO member countries to apply for patents in Thailand (before, only subsidiaries registered in Thailand were allowed to do so).

On the other hand, regarding petty patents, there are 275 petty patents granted to Thai inventors. Of these, 26 are for protective covering (B60J); 40 are for modification of vehicle (B60P); and 124 were granted for vehicle parts (mostly simple accessories parts) (Table 4.7). Thai inventors are composed of individuals, companies, and public organizations (such as the Office of Vocational Education Commission).

It is worth mentioning that TNC carmakers and suppliers have patented various kinds of invention beside IPC B60. Patents have also been registered in IPC B62 – land vehicles for travelling (14 items); IPC F02 – combustion engine (14 items) and IPC F16 – engineering elements or unit (for example gears, 19 items). They also have patents related to basic

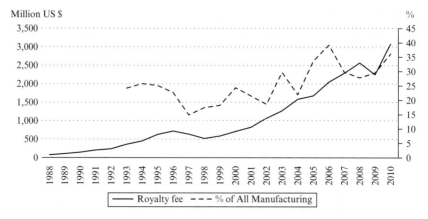

Source: Bank of Thailand.

Figure 4.7   Royalty fees from manufacture of vehicles and transportation equipment, and ratio to all manufacturing sectors

technology such as patents on the process of the substance, and physics, etc. Similar to the study of Miyazaki and Kijima (2000), an analysis of patents in Thailand has confirmed that the Japanese carmakers (Toyota, Nissan, Honda, Mitsubishi Motors, and Mazda), in order to meet changing social expectations and environmental pressures, have been building competencies in key areas related to safety, environment, and driving comfort, which are necessary to maintaining their leadership in the industry.

5.3.2   Royalty fees and licensing in the automotive industry

Data from the Bank of Thailand shows that the value of royalty fees, trademarks, and copyright of the manufacture of vehicle and transportation equipment has increased continuously and rapidly since 1999 (Figure 4.7). These royalties constitute approximately one-third of total royalty fees, trademarks and copyright of all industrial sectors. Half of the value of royalty fees, trademarks and copyright for total transportation equipment belongs to the manufacture of parts and accessories for motor vehicles and their engines.

The study of Pitkethly (2001) finds that Japanese companies have a positive attitude toward taking active steps towards licensing out technology. Japanese companies actively use IP in both licensing and continuous learning, whether through licensing or patent information management. Also, they will license out technology not only to Western countries but also to a significant number of Asian countries.

Regarding the situation of the automotive industry in Thailand, most of the automotive-related patents in Thailand belong to Japanese companies. In general, the licensing fees are paid differently between subsidiaries of Japanese TNCs and independent local suppliers. Local suppliers must pay the licensing fee at around 2–5 percent of revenue, while TNCs' subsidiaries need not pay the loyalty fee. This licensing practice can be seen as a technology transfer mechanism, but the differential treatment may be an obstacle for independent local firms to compete with TNCs' subsidiaries on an equal footing. They need to make an extra effort to technologically catch up with subsidiaries producing the same or similar types of automotive parts. Nonetheless, this practice is similar to what happens in other countries such as Taiwan. Carmakers, especially Japanese, generally do not want to see local suppliers compete with their long-term suppliers.

5.3.3   Patent infringement and litigation in the automotive industry

Thailand presents a major challenge to IPR owners because of its role as a manufacturing and export hub for fakes. Major problems of intellectual property violations are trademark and copyright infringement and design patent infringement. Thai law enforcement and the Customs Departments have responded to the calls for more effective action against the trade in fake goods, particularly in the automotive sector[10] (Kelly and Taweepon, 2006). In 2004, the Thai Department of Special Investigation (DSI), the so-called Thailand FBI, established a specialized Bureau of IP Crime. For IP enforcement matters, the DSI is in charge of investigating criminal IP offences provided that the injured person is capable of demonstrating a prima facie case of infringement valued at a threshold of more than 500,000 baht (approximately US$12,500) calculated based on the value of genuine original goods. There was a series of raids by DSI, for example in the case of copying and infringement of the DaimlerChrysler and Yamaha (Japanese motorcycle)[11] brands.

Counterfeit or imitation products, which are generally sold in the market, are becoming widely accepted by users because they are cheaper than genuine products. Some counterfeit products have been sold even at the automotive service centers. They were priced close to the genuine products and created profit for the vendors while consumers could not differentiate the products. These fake products cause damage to the performance of motor vehicles. In the case of fake oil filters and fuel filters, not only are they not durable, but also they are inefficient. They cause wear of the piston and cylinder, lower the rate of acceleration, and increase fuel consumption. Counterfeit brakes can cause longer breaking distance and loss of control, or generate high heat and even flames. These things affect the safety of the life and property of drivers and pedestrians.

The Thailand Automotive Institute (TAI) found that the value of motor vehicles damaged by counterfeit and pirated products around the world is up to US$350 billion, or about 7 percent of world trade. This is especially the case in the industrial machinery division, which includes the automotive industry. In Asia alone, the loss is approximately US$7.5 billion. There is a drive by the vehicle manufacturers and governments of various countries to ensure the protection of innovation.[12]

The analysis of the CIPITC database showed that there were only 67 litigation cases related to the automotive industry during the years 1998–2010. Most litigation related to trademark violation, international trademark infringement and breach of contract by Thais. The top ten major counterfeited parts were filter, brake pad, frame, clutch, radiator, lamps, fuel pump, shock absorber, ignition coil, and water pump. Damage value was higher than 1,000 million baht. The use of counterfeit auto parts was argued as an obstacle to the development of the country's automotive industry. However, the problem of intellectual property infringement was evaluated as a minor one for both domestic and foreign automotive parts companies (Bongsebandhu-phubhakdi et al., 2009).

Out of 67 cases, there were 20 of patent litigations. Most were cases of reversing administrative decisions on patents/design patents (or their applications), and revoking patents by foreign patent holders. There were also cases between foreign patent holders and Thai inventors as well as between Thai inventors. There were six cases of petty patents, and again most were cases of petty patent revocation by foreign patent holders because of low quality and lack of novelty. Not surprisingly, petty patent infringements are frequent between Thais, as it is much more popular and within reach for Thais to apply for a petty patent.

Out of these 67 cases, 31 reached the Supreme Court. Like the overall picture, most cases involved Thais suing Thais. Only a small number of cases ended with a court decision forcing the defendants to pay the plaintiffs for their losses. There was only one case of patent infringement (for motorcycle products design) in which the court ordered a Thai infringer to pay damages to a foreign patent holder, and the compensation was rather small (50,000 baht or US$1,600). Many cases were settled by compromise between the two sides. In terms of duration, the cases won by defendants (infringers) took much longer than the cases won by plaintiffs (patent holders). As for criminal cases, only six reached the Supreme Court. Four of them involved transnational corporations suing local firms for infringement on motorcycle products. One case was won by a transnational corporation. However, only a very small fine was charged to the Thai infringer. The other three cases have not yet been decided.

The number of litigation cases has increased recently. Most cases were settled before verdicts with dispute resolution. Looking at the case details, even when Thai suppliers were sued for infringement, they were rarely banned from using the technologies. In other words, infringement suits were more commonly used to get the alleged offenders to pay royalties than to put them out of business.

6. THE CASE STUDIES

To elaborate on the above general findings on knowledge transfer in the Thai automotive industry and the impacts from changing patent regimes, our case studies include four carmakers, three foreign suppliers, and four indigenous Thai suppliers (see details in Appendix Table 4A.1).

6.1 Carmakers

Recently carmakers' investment strategies in the automotive industry have started to change. Since 2003, large Japanese carmakers began to invest in R&D in Thailand. Incidentally, there has been an emergence of awareness of the importance of IP management of Japanese carmakers in Thailand, especially after the economic crisis in 1997 when Thailand was viewed as a significant global exporting hub of these companies. This is evident in an increasing patent application trend of Japanese carmakers since 2000. Under the 2nd Amendment in 1999, the right to apply for patent protection was no longer restricted to Thai nationals and nationals of countries that had reciprocal patent agreements with Thailand. The right to apply for patent protection was also extended to nationals of countries which are parties to international patent treaties or conventions to which Thailand is also a party. Since Thailand is a member of the WTO and thus TRIPS, nationals of other WTO member countries receive the same protection accorded to Thai nationals.

Regarding litigation, carmakers and leading global suppliers may try to defend their position, not by threatening suit on grounds of patent product infringement, but by protecting their process technology. Sometimes, they choose not to apply for patents in order to keep the process technology secret, in which case trade secrets matter more than patents. The global carmakers have been outsourcing R&D activities for non-core components such as electronics and communication control systems, but have retained R&D initiatives for core components such as engine and chassis control systems, because the latter are core components of automobiles. Some carmakers have even attempted to control the excessive outsourcing that has been found to occur in engine control systems (Genba et al., 2005). Therefore, carmakers mainly file patents for a group of engine parts, chassis and transmission parts, safety parts (such as airbags) and exhaust systems.

Toyota

Toyota Motor (Thailand) (TMT), a subsidiary of the Japanese multinational Toyota Motor Corporation (TMC), established Toyota Technical Center – Asia-Pacific (TTCAP), which later became Toyota Motor Asia Pacific Engineering & Manufacturing (TMAP-EM) – to operate as an R&D base for Toyota's global operations, by offering product design and modification for regional conditions and providing testing and validation services. The real emphasis of the center in Thailand is on material development, design and engineering to fit local needs, and parts (e.g. strength and durability) and vehicle testing. Since they focus mainly on technical support for the production line and all engineering improvement has to be approved by TMC, TMAP-EM does not have its own patents. Patenting is not a main focus of TMT.

On the other hand, TMC has had 87 patent applications and has been granted 19 patents in Thailand. These patents consist of method of production, details of material, and product designs and inventions. Interestingly, TMT was granted only one petty patent, on 'assembly jigs', in 2007. In 2009, TMT and TMAP-EM were granted another petty patent, on a kit for punching residual liquid plastic out of the mold and a process for draining the mold. This confirms that TMT began to be interested in using IP management, beginning with the petty patent which may be appropriate to the capabilities of a production base in Thailand.

Nissan

Nissan Technical Center South-East Asia, a subsidiary of the Japanese multinational Nissan Motor Company ('Nissan'), is responsible for development activities of Nissan in the ASEAN-4 market (Thailand, Malaysia, Indonesia, and the Philippines) to ensure that all specifications meet local market requirements of each country and the standard of Nissan, to promote parts localization in the ASEAN region, and to promote ASEAN production units and parts overseas. However, these activities are still limited to the 'testing' of certain 'non-functional' components. Unlike Toyota, investment in this technical center is much lower and it has no expensive equipment. There are no patents generated from activities in Thailand, as most activities are limited to testing. There are, nonetheless, co-development works with suppliers, mostly Japanese, in Thailand. This might lead to patenting. However, suppliers will be the ones who file and own these patents. During 1996–98, the Thai subsidiaries Nissan Motor Co. Ltd and Nissan Diesel Co. Ltd had 18 and 13 applications respectively. Nonetheless, since 2003, the parent company Nissan has had 20 applications for design patents.

As regards licensing, before 2003, when its majority shares were owned by the Pornprapha family, Nissan (Thailand) had to pay royalty fees of 5 percent of sales of key components to Nissan. After 2003 (the liberalization phase), Nissan (Thailand) has been 100 percent owned by Nissan. No more royalty fees have been paid. Technical assistance from Japan became natural, since they were considered as the same company. For example, engineers from both sides worked together in developing kits for testing activities in Thailand.

Honda

The Japanese multinational Honda Motor Co., Ltd ('Honda') set up distributors in Thailand under the name Honda Cars (Thailand) Co., Ltd (HCT) in 1983. Recently, Honda established two R&D centers in Thailand: Honda R&D Southeast Asia Co., Ltd (2004) – a research and development center for motorcycles and related products in the ASEAN – and Honda R&D Asia Pacific Co., Ltd – a four-wheel vehicle research and development center for the Asia and Oceania region. These two centers aim to develop autoparts, and conduct style research and prototype testing for CBU units. Since Honda's four-wheel development center has just started its activities in Thailand, it is quite different from TMAP-EM of Toyota. It has no systematic training courses. Employees are allowed to initiate things by themselves on a trial and error basis. No big decisions have been made in Thailand on the main functions of cars. These big decisions need technical approval from Honda in Japan. The motorcycle R&D center, on the other hand, is doing more advanced development activities including designing a new model for the whole of south-east Asia. Regarding patents, during 1981–2000, the parent company Honda applied for 104 patents for motorcycles and automobiles in Thailand. Out of these applications, Honda has been granted 61 invention patents and 12 design patents (which are mostly motorcycle design). Interestingly, there is no patent or petty patent under the name of the two Honda R&D centers in Thailand.

Isuzu

Isuzu Motor (Thailand) set up Isuzu Technical Center of Asia Co., Ltd, claimed as the first automotive R&D company in Thailand, in 1991 with the policy to train Thai engineers in automotive design. The center started by designing local parts and was appointed by Isuzu's head office in Japan to be a research center of Asia. It also has a plan to expand to Europe and America in the future. The center is now working closely with a design center in Japan. The center trained its Thai engineers by sending them to Japan for on-the-job training for two to three years. Since 2000, Isuzu Motor (Thailand) has been granted 5 automobile design patents (pick-up truck; bus; bumper; radiator grill; lamp) from 23 design patent applications.

From the case studies of carmakers, we find that carmakers in Thailand received knowledge from their parent companies in Japan. Factory visits and on-the-job training are major modes of technology transfer. Explicit knowledge transfer through patent disclosure is seldom found in Thailand. Automobiles are complex systems, and their product quality depends largely on engineering which is based considerably on tacit knowledge. In the automobile industry, the profit from innovation mainly comes from the lead-time of innovators, combined with their ability to continually improve the products ahead of later adopters, and their marketing advantages. Effective imitation is costly and time-consuming even if no patents are being enforced.

Interestingly, American carmakers (GM and Ford) and their major suppliers (Delphi, Visteon, TRW etc.) have no patents under their names in Thailand.

6.2   Foreign Parts Suppliers

Not only foreign carmakers but also foreign parts suppliers are involved in patenting. However, technological development and patenting-related activities are different between large and smaller foreign suppliers.

DENSO Corporation

DENSO Corporation is a leading and large global supplier of advanced automotive technology, systems and components, headquartered in Japan. It set up a technical center in Thailand which is a part of a new company, DENSO International Asia Co., Ltd (DIAT), in 2007. The DIAT technical center has 40 persons (including supporting staff). However, the real activity is not yet R&D. Rather, it is the testing of new products and drawing the blueprints under specifications given from Japan. A testing center is a very important component of R&D. These activities will continue for at least five years before real R&D work can start. This is a learning period. After ten years, it will be ready to have full function R&D. During 1985–96, Nippondenso, registered in Japan, was granted 19 invention patents (both products and process inventions). After 1997, the group used DENSO Corporation, the global name, instead of Nippondenso, to file patents in Thailand. DENSO

Corporation applied for 149 inventions and has been granted 30 invention patents.

Kasai Kogyo

For small foreign part suppliers, the case of Kasai Kogyo, a first-tier supplier of interior parts to Nissan, shows that transfer of technology, mostly production-related, from the Japanese HQ to the subsidiary in Thailand (Kasai Teck See Co., Ltd) was carried out through licensing. There are license agreements between the two parties, but no upfront payment. Only a running royalty of 2.5–3 percent per year is applied to the subsidiary's products sold under the licenses from the mother company. At the other end, the relationship between Kasai Kogyo (Thailand) and Thai-owned second-tier suppliers is focused on trading of qualified parts. In the process of assigning local companies to produce parts for Kasai Kogyo, there are meetings to discuss specifications and how to make the parts. In this process, the Thai second-tier suppliers learn from the company. Engineers from Kasai Kogyo have been sent to these Thai suppliers when the latter faced problems they could not solve by themselves. These are channels of technology transfer between Japanese first-tier suppliers and Thai second-tier suppliers through on-the-job training and problem solving.

Patents have no role in this kind of technology transfer process, as most technologies are in the tacit form which requires close interaction between engineers of both sides. Therefore, there is no dispute or litigation on patent cases. Patent disputes are between Kasai and its competitors (especially those selling products in replacement markets), not between the company and its suppliers. Interestingly, Kasai Kogyo applied for invention patents for a 'vehicle cover sheet' in 2009.

From the case studies of foreign suppliers described above, it is clear that the carmakers design and develop car models, and produce them by assembling parts procured from specialized first-tier suppliers and using the equipment supplied by specialist machine-makers. These specialist first-tier suppliers (most foreign companies or joint ventures) are happy to supply to new carmakers as long as these carmakers are willing to pay prices that cover production and R&D costs. It is mostly these specialist suppliers that own patents for parts and machines and hence, by buying from them, newcomers can circumvent patent-related constraints. Nowadays, suppliers need to have the capabilities to participate in new car model development processes which are mostly done in Japan. This makes it hard for most Thai suppliers to climb up the technological ladders from second-tier to first-tier suppliers.

Therefore, in Thailand the majority of patents in IPC B60R (Vehicle parts) belong to global suppliers and originated from home countries (especially Japan). Under the modularization system, first-tier suppliers need capabilities over a range of technological fields that are wider than the range of activities that might be actually covered in-house. Unlike large foreign first-tier suppliers like DENSO, the small foreign suppliers in Thailand like Kasai Kogyo still need support from their parent companies. Innovative activities of these smaller foreign companies in Thailand are, therefore, contained at the level of technical problem solving.

6.3   Indigenous Thai Suppliers

Most TNCs and foreign joint ventures are linked to a certain degree into the vertical supply chain and share related information with regard to *specific* product-related issues, especially for new products. However, only a few of them co-operated closely with Thai suppliers in *broader* product, process, or human resource development activities.

Thai Summit Group
Summit Auto Seat Industry Co., Ltd (SAS) is a 100 percent Thai-owned company established in 1972. SAS is under the umbrella of Thai Summit Group, a major Thai supplier of auto parts. SAS is one of the most competitive local first-tier suppliers and is able to compete against multinational competitors. To catch up with the technological changes at the global level, the company continues to invest in new technologies. Most investment decisions are made internally by the management team following the two-step process. The first step is to study new technologies. After understanding them, the company confers with the customers and, if possible, the company will propose the use of a specific technology. Once customers have agreed, the company will then decide to invest. For example, the company recently made an investment in a new hydro-forming system after conferring with customers and visiting some of the leading factories abroad.

At the other end, SAS works with lower-tier suppliers to improve the quality of their products and parts. SAS also has developed linkages with a local university, King Mongkut's University of Technology North Bangkok, to organize training courses for the company's staff. In some cases, the linkage expanded to the level that the company and the university worked together to develop new products. This university and industry linkage is quite uncommon in Thailand. As a result, SAS has developed design capability, rapid prototyping, and simulation analysis. It has upgraded itself from an ordinary part producer to a sub-system integrator, that is, designing and integrating parts and components into a sub-system to sell to carmakers. In regard to patents, there were only a few invention patents applied for under SAS, including a device for pickup car floor holding (in 2009) and equipment for increasing carrying area for motor vehicles (in 2010). In addition, another firm in Thai Summit Group, Thai Summit Harness, which defines itself as a replacement equipment manufacturer (REM) automotive-part supplier, had one invention patent on 'electrical harness for automobile' in 2005.

Thai Summit R&D Next Technology Co., Ltd (TSRD) is a manufacturer of tooling (die and jig) established in 1995. TSRD experienced strong price competition from producers from China and India. As a result, TSRD needed to invest more in building up its technological capabilities to upgrade its parts. To survive in the competitive mold production and tooling business, the company had to reduce the costs of engineering, manufacturing, and improving activities. TSRD then focused on the development of simulation test engineering to design a product by using computer simulation instead of the actual prototype production. This computer simulation reduced several steps of the testing process.

At present, TSRD employs about 430 people, many being engineers. Besides the indigenous effort, the company took over a Japanese tooling company in Japan and employed many foreign experts to work for the company. TSRD also has a joint R&D with customers. Nonetheless, products and technology developed from this partnership cannot be patented. They are results of co-development, and one party cannot own a patent. However, TSRD could secure an order from this customer, which is the most important issue. TSRD is continuing its own R&D effort and is still trying to buy other foreign companies to access new technologies.

The Somboon Group
The Somboon Group (SG) is one of the biggest first- and second-tier automotive part suppliers in Thailand. It was established in 1975 and aims to be a leader in automotive parts manufacturing in the ASEAN region, providing end-to-end services, and growing alongside its customers. SG consists of four companies: Somboon Advance Technology Plc (SAT), Bangkok Spring Industrial Co., Ltd (BSK), Somboon Malleable Iron Industrial Co., Ltd (SBM) and International Casting Products Co., Ltd (ICP). Examples of major customers are Auto Alliance, Dana, GM, Hino, Honda, Isuzu, Kubota, Mitsubishi Motors, Nissan, Toyota and Yongkee.

SG is active in leveraging external sources of knowledge. It has various kinds of technical relationships with international organizations. In 2009 SG conducted training using a professor from Osaka University whom a Japanese partner recommended. The firm also used a consulting service from an international organization. The consulting service was mainly in the form of email communication and sending products for testing. In addition, under recommendation of its Japanese customer, SG paid Japanese first-tier suppliers in Japan for their technical advice (TA), such as asking for help when SG was developing a new process. However, the knowledge transferred by this method is mainly tacit knowledge through on-the-job training and getting advice. The TA relationship is a long-term one. SG set up a team just to work with this TA project in order to maximize knowledge transfer.

In 2009, SG decided to stop using TA and invested in spring design and production by itself because the TA service was not satisfactory when it concerned new product development (not only process improvement). This can be seen as a limitation of using TA. Once a company wants to develop a new product, it cannot rely only on seeking others' advice. It needs to build up its own capabilities, especially in design. Initially, customers were worried whether SG could succeed or not. In the end, SG succeeded, and planned to provide TA to other firms in other countries, which had also used the TA services from the same Japanese firm as SG. However, since SG stopped using the TA service from the first-tier Japanese suppliers, the linkage that SG had had with its Japanese customers has also gone. This illustrates that the Japanese automotive network is rather closed and based on trust. If a local company wants to continue selling parts to Japanese carmakers, the company needs to keep its TA relationship with first-tier Japanese suppliers of those carmakers. To circumvent this problem, SG is planning to set up an office in Japan to develop closer relationships with its customers. Regarding patents, although the Somboon Group has long experience of technological development, until now there are no patents or petty patents belonging to the group. This illustrates that patents are not as important as other means of technology transfer, especially seeking TA, employing foreign engineers and acquiring foreign firms.

Daisin
The company was established in 1979 to manufacture aluminum-casting parts for the automotive industry as a foreign joint venture with Nissin Kogyo Co., Ltd (the Thai partner being a major shareholder with 67 percent ownership). The case of Daisin demonstrates the necessity of 'active' investment for indigenous technology capability development (not passively relying on assistance from foreign partners like other Thai firms) and the significance of working closely with suppliers and carmakers (Honda Motor Thailand) in order to gain their support for capability development.

The story begins with the company hiring a retired Japanese engineer. This engineer helped the company to improve its production capability and to negotiate with Nissin to significantly lower its royalty fees. Later, the company also acquired external knowledge besides partnership with Nissin by hiring other Japanese technical consultants to help in developing its own design capability. (In fact, Nissin was quite reluctant to help.) Eventually, the company could work closely with customers (carmakers) to suggest the new design for a hand brake and a new lighting system. Honda and Toyota invited Daisin's engineers to Japan as their guest engineers to jointly develop a new brake. Daisin now has become an ODM for several carmakers. This is quite exceptional for Thai suppliers. Moreover, the company used its design capability from being an ODM in the automotive industry in order to diversify its products into other markets such as long-tail boats, a small rice miller, and a wood-cutting machine. These businesses provide much higher profit margins to the company, as it does not have to be constrained by the global production network of Japanese carmakers. As in other cases, until now, Daisin has not applied for any patents in Thailand.

Sammitr Motor Manufacturing (SMM)

SMM began as a limited company in 1967 to produce car and truck body parts, molds and fixtures for auto-makers. The production line was later extended to accommodate other related industries like agriculture machines.

To maintain leadership and a competitive edge, the company has assigned an R&D unit to develop, upgrade and present new products which can better meet and exceed customer needs since 1997. Not only does the company strive to develop in-house personnel with knowledge and expertise in automobile engineering and alternative energy, but also the company has joined hands with local and foreign leading research institutes like China Chong Qing Automobile Research Institute (CCARI) and Thailand's National Metal and Materials Technology Center (METEC).

Results from R&D output are mostly tacit knowledge embedded in the ability to improve production processes and develop new products. The company also has joint R&D projects with carmakers to develop new parts. These joint activities also help in securing purchasing orders from carmakers. Successful projects are, for example, the production of light-weight trailers, special-purpose trucks, natural gas vehicle (NGV) trucks, NGV conversion kits and a multipurpose truck with 100 percent biodiesel engine (B100).

SMM patents only inventions that can sell, because patenting has costs. The company perceives that patent registration in the past was time consuming, but that it has become faster now. To speed up the R&D and patenting processes, the company also worked with academic and research institutes, which could guide them with research methodologies to ensure better results. Since 2000, SMM has applied for 28 design patents and was granted five, including a roof joint lock device for pickup truck roof, a cylinder hydraulic for pickup truck, rice harvesting machines and equipment, and a set of support rolled steel. Recently, SMM also focused on applying for petty patents because their approval process was much shorter. Since 2002, SMM was granted four petty patents covering an automatic door lock device, a two-point fixed jig, a leaf spring to reduce hardness and noise, and vehicle lock devices.

Regarding litigation, SMM has sued some Thai firms, especially those selling products in replacement markets, for IP infringement. SMM received some compensation from negotiations with these companies. On the other hand, SMM has never been sued for IP infringement. SMM's motivations in patenting are to protect knowledge and technology and use it as a weapon to negotiate with local firms in the case of infringement. In particular, SMM acquired design patents for the protection of its product designs which can be easily imitated, especially in replacement markets. SMM does not aim to sell the patent or licensing. Having patents indicates its technological capability to be a supplier of carmakers.

Patent information disclosure is also viewed as an important source of knowledge. For example, it used information from an expired foreign patent to develop a process for a durability test of hydraulic systems in 2010.

The case studies of indigenous suppliers elucidate the following observations.

First, OEM arrangements help local firms, like other latecomer firms, to acquire basic production knowledge and access to the competitive global automotive market. In this beginning stage, the most important knowledge transfer channel is in the form of technical assistance from either carmakers or foreign higher-tier suppliers. Patents are not an issue at this stage. Learning from patent information disclosure, even on production processes, is also difficult, since it requires absorptive capacity to understand and assimilate knowledge embodied in patents.

Second, because of stronger competition and global sourcing strategies of global carmakers, suppliers have been forced to take on the role of sub-system integrator. This is quite a tall order for many local suppliers. Summit and Somboon groups have been partially successful in this regard, but most local suppliers have failed. Therefore, these companies have to supply their parts to these sub-system integrators, many of them being global players like Denso.

Third, since the profit margin of local OEM suppliers is so small, several of them have used experiences and knowledge gained as OEMs to diversify either to other sectors like Daisin and Sammitr or to the local REM market, which offers higher profit margins. Nonetheless, exporting these REM parts is not easy due to licensing conditions set by foreign technology owners on price, quantity, territory, duration, and field of use.

Fourth, at a later stage those local suppliers that had developed a certain level of capability (for example, Thai Summit Group, Summit Auto Body, Somboon Group, Sammitr Motor) started filing design patents and petty patents, but mainly in non-functional parts, usually not even OEM parts contracted by their customers (global carmakers). These critical parts are proprietary knowledge and have been patented by global suppliers/ sub-system integrators.

Lastly, these design and petty patents (which are granted more easily) are intended to (a) discourage other local part makers from entering their markets, especially REM, and (b) enhance their prestige as capable part suppliers, thereby inducing more orders from carmakers or higher-tier suppliers (global sub-system integrators). The findings from the case studies are summarized in Table 4.8.

7. DISCUSSION

To answer whether there is co-evolution of the IPR regime and technological capability of automotive firms in Thailand, we review what we have discussed in previous sections in terms of changes in IPR regime, government policies to promote the automotive industry, and the building up of technological capabilities of firms in the industry (summarized in Table 4.9).

From Table 4.9, one can see the evolutions of the IPR regime, automotive sector promotion policies, and technological capability development of automotive firms. Nonetheless, the co-evolution of IPR regimes and technological capabilities of firms is rather small. Other policies such as local content requirement and liberalization had more impact. The main reasons for TNCs' investment in the automotive sector in Thailand from the 1960s and 1970s were market driven and the availability of cheap skilled human resources. At the time, Thailand had no patent law to protect their intellectual property rights following their investment. Similarly, TNCs' investment in technical centers after 2000 has little to do with the second amendment of patent law, a result of TRIPS. They

Table 4.8 Summarized findings from the case studies

Case	Knowledge transfer	Patenting	Licensing/litigation
MNC carmakers	Receiving technical support from parent company Sending engineer teams to help suppliers (foreign and indigenous) without charge but expecting cost reduction and quality improvement in return In late 1990s, started using modularization and global sourcing concept, together with encouraging suppliers to develop their own capabilities as sub-system integrators.	An increasing patent application trend by Japanese carmakers since 2000. Besides design patents, they filed patents for their core technologies e.g. engine, transmission, suspension, and production processes. No patents from their Thai-based R&D/technical centers (only TMAP-EP has a petty patent) Recently started being interested in using IP management.	Not trying to sue on the grounds of infringement of product patent, but by protecting their process technologies. Claims against unscrupulous local and Chinese competitors for alleged violations of IPR (faked spare parts). Forced Thai government to enforce IPR protection, especially on trademarks.
Foreign part suppliers	In the past, they relied on blueprints from carmakers (customers) and parent companies Sent engineer teams to help lower-tier suppliers After 1997, leading ones started to bring in updated/cutting edge technologies together with close supervision by foreign technicians Recently, large ones became system integrators	Large ones are active in patenting to protect their products in the Thai market, but this is not the case for small ones. Those patented inventions and designs were originated in home countries. Minor improvement might be done locally. There is a correlation between rates of patent application and amount of FDI and rates of car model changes	No need to pay license fees if they are subsidiaries or majority owned by foreign shareholders. They preferred to have licensing agreements with local firms rather than totally shutting down their activities

| Indigenous (Thai) part suppliers | OEMs get technical support from carmakers and Japanese global suppliers through technical agreement in return for fees. Transferred knowledge is mostly about production process technology through on the job training and advice (IPR is not an issue). Recently, some started investment in technology capability development, hired retired foreign engineers and took over foreign firms. Diversification to other REM and other sectors Without technological capability some have been downgraded to 2nd or 3rd tier suppliers | Have a few patents (mostly design but rather active in petty patents since 1999) Only patent 'nonfunctional' parts Parts co-developed with carmakers cannot be patented Most outputs from R&D and technological improvement cannot be patented | Pay royalty fees to their foreign customers/partners Those having higher technological capability and other sources of knowledge can negotiate to reduce licensing fees Petty and design patents are used to discourage other local firms from entering the market and attract more orders |

Table 4.9 The evolutions of the IPR regime, automotive-related policies, and technological capability of automotive firms

IPR regime	Automotive industry-related policies	Technological capability of automotive firms
Before 1979 No Patent Law	1960s Thai automotive industry was born from import substitution policy 1970s Promoting Thailand as an automobile assembling base of TNCs 1969s Increased local content requirement from 25% to 50% for passenger cars & limited to 42 series for passenger car assemblies	• Before regulation on local content 1969, production was almost exclusively CKD (completely knock down) and semi-knocked down (SKD) • Local content rates: bare chassis with engine (15%); windshield chassis (20%)
Patent Act of 1979	1980s Region's best automobile assembler • 1984 Increased local content requirement to 54% and 70% • Diesel engine became compulsory parts	1980s • 1981–1990: only 4 patents (IPC-B60) and none owned by Thais • Passenger car must use 54% local content; pick-up truck use 72% local content and must use locally produced engine (cylinder blocks; cylinder head; crankshaft; camshaft; connecting rod) • Suppliers received technological support and blueprints from carmakers

The 1st amendment Patent Act (1992)	1990s Region's most liberalized automotive industry with the strongest part manufacturers	1990s
• An extension of the term of patent rights protection	• Repealed limitation of 42 series of car assembly (1991)	• Western part suppliers expanded into Thailand to gain access to Japanese carmakers
• The right to apply for patent protection was restricted to Thai nationals	• Repealed prohibition on import of vehicles (1993)	• After 1996, Thailand exports cars and parts to the world market
• Pre-grant opposition	• Tax restructuring (1993)	• After 1997, TNCs started bringing updated and more cutting-edge technology together with close supervision by foreign technicians
• National treatment	• Investment promotion & tax reduction for export	• 1992–1999: only 46 patents (IPC-B60) and just 4 for Thais
• Establishment of the Department of Intellectual Property (1992)	• Repealed prohibition on establishing vehicle assembly factory	
• Establishment of the Intellectual Property and International Trade Court (1996)	• Removed the restrictions on foreign shareholding in November 1997	
	• Establishment of Thai Automotive Institute (1998)	
The 2nd amendment Patent Act (1999)	2000 to present Liberalization and strong production base of Asia	2000 to present
• National treatment: the right to apply for patent protection will no longer be restricted to Thai nationals	• Abolished local content in 2000	• Increase in patent litigation
• Priority filings	• Tax restructuring CKD from 20% to 33%	• Carmakers actively applied for patents (design and invention)
• Introduction of petty patents	• Reduced tariff tax rate	• Carmakers and some 1st tier suppliers set up R&D and technical centers in Thailand
• Establishment of Intellectual Property Center (2003)	• Reduced excise tax rate	• Indigenous Thai firms started to build up technological capabilities beyond production
	• AHRDP (major sector-level training schemes in collaboration with TNCs) during 2001–02	• Thais applied for 275 petty patents
		• 2000–11: only 283 patents (IPC-B60) and 19 for Thais

wanted their development activities to be closer to their main production bases according to their globalization strategies. The national treatment clause might encourage them to file invention and design patents in Thailand. However, these patents would be products of their development activities in home countries, not from their technical centers in Thailand. Knowledge transfer between headquarters and subsidiaries in Thailand has increased, while royalty payment has decreased or has completely gone. Nonetheless, this is not a result of a changing patent regime but rather an increase in the ownership of parent companies after liberalization policies in the late 1990s. However, one component of the changing patent regime might have had some impacts. Introduction of the petty patent in 1999 encouraged indigenous firms (and TNCs) to start filing this type of patent catering for incremental innovations, though most patents were in non-functional parts and for the purposes of attracting more orders from TNCs and fending off local competitors, especially in replacement markets.

Furthermore, the three following key findings answer the questions set in the introduction to this chapter.

Firstly, there are 'some' atmospheric changes in terms of an increasing awareness of the importance of patents in the industry after the patent regime became stronger. The rates of patent application and granting have increased gradually, especially after 2000. This is coincident with the WTO-induced change (TRIPS) in Thai patent law in 1999, allowing parent firms registered in WTO member countries to apply for patents in Thailand. However, for the past few years, the rate of patent granting has increased slowly due to the lack of patent-examining capacity of DIP.

There is not a great deal of patent infringement litigation in Thailand, presumably because of the lack of a formal discovery mechanism and the expense necessary to prepare and prove a case against what has not been culturally viewed as a criminal activity. However, the overall number of patent cases is still growing at approximately 30 percent per year.

This study finds that automotive companies, both carmakers and part suppliers, recently have started formal and systematic IP strategies. Many Japanese carmakers and leading part suppliers have established their R&D and technical centers in Thailand. They have also registered invention and design patents in Thailand, although under the name of parent companies in Japan. Technological activities taking place in R&D centers of the Japanese carmakers and suppliers in Thailand are mainly for testing and validating products to make them suitable for local needs, and improving production processes. Moreover, the results of these development activities must be approved by the engineering teams of carmakers and suppliers in Japan (and patenting in Japan).

However, several TNCs' affiliates are becoming active in terms of R&D and innovation. Considering the time lag between R&D/innovation activities and the filing of a patent, the data suggests that TNCs in Thailand may increase their patent activity in the near future. For instance, in the last few years, Toyota Motor Thailand has started filing petty patents for inventions by Thai engineers.

In addition, leading indigenous part suppliers recently recognized the importance of IP strategies and have integrated them into their overall business plans. However, the majority of inventions by indigenous Thai suppliers tend to be minor improvements. Therefore, petty patent (utility models) have been more popular among Thai supplier inventors. It is unclear how much protection these utility models actually provide. Only a few foreign inventors applied for utility models, suggesting that they regard utility model protection to be insufficient for their exported products. However, petty patents may have had announcement effects, advertising to the customers the genuineness of the products, convincing banks and other financial institutions, and appealing to government agencies. They may have been valuable for small indigenous part suppliers that lack credibility. Moreover, there are cases where (design) patent protection or petty patent protection encouraged R&D investment even if the purpose of R&D was improvement rather than new invention.

Secondly, the stronger patent regime has had 'small' impacts on the extent and nature of knowledge transfer between TNCs and local part suppliers. Thai indigenous suppliers, as licensees, had to pay the licensing fee at the same rate before the Patent Act amendment according to TRIPS in 1999. Thai suppliers agreed to or were forced to pay high royalties to patent-holders based in developed countries (such as Japan). The growth rate of royalty fees shows the technology dependency of Thai suppliers. Licensing necessarily implied the payment of royalty, which weakened the competitive position of the indigenous firms trying to catch up with foreign firms. As OEM suppliers, indigenous suppliers still had to pay royalty fees although patents had already expired. This money should have been used for supporting their technological development activities. Therefore, what is more important than patents here is the OEM arrangement between suppliers and customers. It helps latecomer firms to access global and competitive production networks, but it can be an obstacle if these firms are not active in developing indigenous capabilities and leveraging other sources of knowledge.

The stronger patent regime does not have obvious impacts on the extent and nature of knowledge transfer between universities and public research institutes and firms. Thai suppliers will patent only commercial products, but patenting has its cost. University professors (or researchers of public research institutes) are quite interested in basic science and academic journal publication. Indeed, a general lack of focus on developing indigenous capabilities either in-house or with universities does not encourage university–industry links (UILs). However, there have been some exceptional efforts to establish such links recently such as in the cases of Sammitr and Summit groups. In these cases, IPR is not seen as an obstacle blocking linkages.

Lastly, the stronger patent regime has impacts on firms climbing up technological ladders from production to more sophisticated activities. As earlier mentioned, production technologies and skills are mainly tacit in nature. Transfer at this level is by means of technology assistance in the forms of training (mostly on the job) and giving advice. IPR is not an issue. Nonetheless, higher level technologies such as design and development are proprietary knowledge of carmakers and global suppliers (sub-system integrators) who own patents in their home countries, and, increasingly, in Thailand. Case studies of indigenous firms illustrate that 'automatic' or 'passive' transfer of knowledge is almost impossible. Successful firms like Daisin gained this capability neither from their joint venture partners, nor their customers (carmakers). It had to follow an 'independent' learning route by building up its own capabilities as well as leveraging external knowledge from other sources outside its existing production networks. Similarly, in order to build such capabilities, Summit Group had to collaborate with a local university, take over a Japanese firm, and recruit foreign engineers together with setting up its own R&D center. Stronger patent regimes can be an obstacle and indigenous firms have to be 'active' learners in order to climb up technological ladders.

8.   CONCLUSIONS

This study has explored the co-evolution of the IPR regime and technological capability of automotive firms in Thailand. We find that there is only a *small extent* of co-evolution. Other government policies and changes in TNCs' strategies and the market in general are much more important factors shaping technological capability development of firms in the sector. Specifically, we discover the following. Firstly, there have been some atmospheric changes in terms of an increasing awareness of the importance of patents in the industry after the patent regime became stronger. Secondly, the stronger patent regime has slight impacts on the extent and nature of knowledge transfer between TNCs and local part suppliers. It has no obvious impacts on the extent and nature of knowledge transfer between universities and public research institutes on one hand and firms on the other. Last but not least, the stronger patent regime *has impacts* on firms climbing up technological ladders from production to more sophisticated activities. To be able to climb up the technological ladders, local latecomer firms need to develop their own independent effort based on active learning in the building up of indigenous technological capabilities and leveraging external sources of knowledge besides their existing production networks, in order to circumvent difficulties partly generated by the stronger patent regime.

NOTES

1. The term of a petty patent will be six years from the date that the application is filed in Thailand. The term may be extended twice, for a period of two years each. The term of protection for petty patents will be shorter than those for ordinary invention patents, however, it is equivalent to that for design patents.
2. Patent license agreements are governed by the provisions of the Patent Act B.E. 2522 (A.D. 1979), as amended in 1992 and again in 1999, and Ministerial Regulation No. 25 B.E. 2542 (A.D. 1999) issued under the Patent Act, the Ministerial Regulations, and the general laws of contract under the Civil and Commercial Code.
3. Under Section 41 of the patent Act (No. 3) B.E. 2542 (A.D. 1999), a license agreement of a patent must be in writing in compliance with the requirements, procedures, and conditions prescribed by the Ministerial Regulations, and it must be registered with the Patent Office.
4. The negotiation process has been suspended after the military coup in September 2006.
5. Parties who do not meet any of the above criteria may, under the Amendment, still apply for patent protection in Thailand if they are foreign applicants who are domiciled or have an ongoing, functioning industrial or commercial enterprise in either Thailand or a country which is a member of an international patent convention or treaty to which Thailand is a party.
6. The IPC provides for a hierarchical system of language independent symbols for the classification of patents and utility models according to the different areas of technology to which they pertain. At the top of the hierarchy are the following eight sections: (A) Human Necessities: includes agriculture, foodstuffs and tobacco, personal or domestic articles, health and amusement; (B) Performing Operations; Transporting: includes separating and mixing, shaping, printing, transporting; (C) Chemistry; Metallurgy; (D) Textiles; Paper; (E) Fixed Constructions: includes building and earth or rock drilling, mining; (F) Mechanical Engineering; Lighting; Heating; Weapons and blasting: includes engines or pumps, engineering in general; (G) Physics: includes instruments and nucleonics; (H) Electricity: includes basic electric elements, generation, conversion or distribution of electric power, basic electronic circuitry, electric communication technique, electric technique.
7. During 1997–2010, most intellectual property criminal cases were trademark infringement (57.2 percent or 33,201 cases) followed by copyright infringement (43.5 percent or 24,675 cases) and patent infringement (0.2 percent or 130 cases). Similarly, most civil cases were trademark infringement (53.2 percent or 354 cases) followed by copyright infringement (38 percent or 253 cases) and patent infringement (8.9 percent or 59 cases).
8. Parts manufactured in Thailand include engines (diesels, motorcycles); engine components (starters, alternators, pumps, filters, hoses, gears, flywheels); body parts (chassis, bumpers, fenders, hoods, door panels); brake systems (master cylinders, drums, discs, pads, linings); steering systems (steering wheels, gears, columns, pumps, linkages);

suspensions (shocks, coils, ball joints); transmissions (gears, casings, rear axles, drive shafts, propeller shafts); electrical/electronics (alternators, starters, speedometers, lamps, motors, flasher relays); interiors/exteriors (seats, mats, weather strips, console boxes); and others (windshields, seat belts, radiators, wheels, compressors).

9. Whereas foreign-owned firms had higher capabilities in project management, quality control, and linkages with materials and technology suppliers, Thai-owned firms had higher capabilities than foreign-owned firms or joint ventures in terms of making investment decisions, product development, linkages with customers and markets, and linkages with supporting institutes (College of Management, Mahidol University, 2006).

10. The issue of copying in the automotive sector has attracted attention in the media and WTO and other international business groups. Several TNC automotive manufacturers including GM, Toyota and Honda filed well-publicized claims against unscrupulous Chinese competitors for alleged violations of IPR, for example, the case of *GM Spark* vs *Chery QQ*. Honda faced a similar problem with the CRV and the Shuanhuan Laibao SRV as many parts including the doors and hood were interchangeable between the models.

11. A Malaysian-owned motorcycles assembler was seized under the authority of the Thai Patent Act because the bikes were slavish copies of patented Yamaha designs and inventions with a value of more than 45 million baht (Kelly and Taweepon, 2006).

12. The Office of Industrial Economics, Ministry of Industry in collaboration with the Department of Intellectual Property, Ministry of Commerce, Thai Automotive Industry, and the Working Group on IPR under the APEC Automotive Dialogue held seminars 'The 1st APEC Automotive Dialogue IPR Seminar' and 'Best Practices of Intellectual Property Rights Protection in the Automotive Sector' on November 13, 2007. The conference aimed to raise awareness about the importance of intellectual property in relation to the automotive industry and automotive parts and to coordinate information to solve the problem of infringement of intellectual property between the private and public sector agencies involved.

BIBLIOGRAPHY

Amsden, A. (1989), *Asia's Next Giant: South Korea and Late Industrialisation*, New York: Oxford University Press.

Arnold E. et al. (2000), *Enhancing Policy and Institutional Support for Industrial Technology Development in Thailand, Volume 1: The Overall Policy Framework and the Development of the Industrial Innovation System*, December, World Bank.

Bell, M. and D. Scott-Kemmis (1985), 'Technological capacity and technical change. Report on technology transfer in manufacturing industry in Thailand', draft working paper nos 1, 2, 4 and 6, Science Policy Research Unit, University of Sussex, Sussex.

Berger, M. (2005), 'Upgrading the system of innovation in late-industrialising countries – the role of transnational corporations in Thailand's manufacturing sector', Dissertation, Kiel University, Germany, March.

Bongsebandhu-phubhakdi, C., T. Saiki H. and Osada (2009), 'Management of technology in Thai automotive parts companies', *Journal of Advances in Management Research*, 6 (2), 128–43.

Brimble, P. and R.F. Doner, (2007), 'University–industry linkages and economic development: the case of Thailand', *World Development*, 35 (6), 1021–36.

Brooker Group (2002), 'International competitiveness of Asian economies: a cross-country study – Thailand paper', report for Asian Development Bank.

Chantramonklasri, N. (1985), 'Technological responses to rising energy prices: a study of technological capability and technological change efforts in energy-intensive manufacturing industries in Thailand', unpublished D.Phil. thesis, Science Policy Research Unit, University of Sussex, Brighton.

Chantramonklasri, N. (1994), 'Science and technology development for industrial competitiveness in Thailand: problems and lessons', *TDRI Quarterly Review*, **9** (2), June, 24–30.

Charoenporn, P. (2001), 'Automotive part procurement system in Thailand: a comparison of American and Japanese companies', unpublished Master's thesis, Faculty of Economics, Thammasat University, Bangkok, Thailand.

College of Management, Mahidol University (2006), 'Assessment of technological and innovative capability of strategic cluster (automotive), a Final Report submitted to National Science and Technology Development Agency', July (in Thai).

Dahlman, C.J. and P. Brimble (1990), 'Technology strategy and policy for industrial competitiveness: a case study of Thailand', Industrial Series Paper No. 24, April, The World Bank.

Dahlman, C. et al. (1991), *Technology Strategy and Policy for Industrial Competitiveness: A Case Study of Thailand*, Decision and Change in Thailand: Three Studies in Support of the Seventh Plan, Washington, DC: World Bank.

Department of Intellectual Property (DIP) (2006), *Information for Thailand's Intellectual Property Right*, written by Administrator from Thailand IPR Service Centre, downloaded from http://www.ipthailand.org/en/index.php?option=com_content&task=category&sectionid=6&id=57&Itemid=52.

Doner, R.F., G.W. Noble and J. Ravenhill (2004), 'Production networks in East Asia's auto parts industry', in S. Yusuf, M.A. Altak and K. Nabeshima (eds), *Global Production Networking and Technological Change in East Asia*, Washington, DC: Oxford University Press.

Foray, D. (2002), 'Intellectual property and innovation in the knowledge-based economy', *Isuma: Canadian Journal of Policy Research*, **3** (1), 71–8.

Genba, K., H. Ogawa and F. Kodama, (2005), 'Quantitative analysis of modularization in the automobile and PC industries', *Technology Analysis & Strategic Management*, **17** (2), 231–45.

Hobday, M. (1995), *Innovation in East Asia: The Challenge to Japan*, Aldershot, UK and Brookfield, VT, USA: Edward Elgar.

Intarakumnerd, P. (2004), 'Thailand's National Innovation System in transition', paper presented at the First Asialics International Conference on Innovation Systems and Clusters in Asia: Challenges and Regional Integration, 1–2 April, Bangkok, Thailand.

Intarakumnerd, P. et al. (2002), 'National Innovation System in less successful developing countries: the case of Thailand', *Research Policy*, **31**, 1445–57.

Intarakamnerd, P. and P. Charoenporn (2010), 'The roles of IPR regime on Thailand's Technological Catching-up', in Hiroyuki Odagiri, Akira Goto, Atsushi Sunami and Richard R. Nelson (eds), *Intellectual Property Rights, Development and Catch-Up: An International Comparative Study*, New York: Oxford University Press, pp. 378–411.

Intarakumnerd, P., and Virasa, T. (2001), 'Broader roles of RTOs in developing countries: from knowledge-creators to strengtheners of National Innovation

System', Science, Technology and Innovation Policy Research Department, National Science and Technology Development Agency (NSTDA), Thailand and College of Management, Mahidol University, Thailand, NSTDA Working Paper.

Intarakumnerd, P. and T. Virasa (2004), 'Government policies and measures in supporting technological capability development of latecomer firms: a tentative taxonomy', *Journal of Technology Innovation*, **12** (2), 1–19.

Intarakumnerd, P. et al. (2003), 'Thailand's National Innovation System (NIS) in the context of East Asian economies: initial findings', paper presented at the seminar on Innovation Systems in Asian Economics, 4–5 September.

Kaosa-Ard, M. (1991), 'A preliminary study of TNCs' hiring and localization policies in Thailand', *TDRI Quarterly Review*, **6** (4), December.

Kasuga, T., T. Oka, Y. Higa and K. Hoshino (2005), 'The expansion of western auto parts manufacturers into Thailand, and responses by Japanese auto parts manufacturers', *JBICI Review*, **11**, 1–35.

Kelly, E. and S. Taweepon (2006), 'IP issues for Thailand's automotive industry', *Asia Law IP Review*, October, 33–6.

Kim, L. (1993), 'National system of industrial innovation: dynamics of capability building in Korea', in R. Nelson (ed.), *National Innovation System: A Comparative Analysis*, Oxford, UK: Oxford University Press.

Kim, L. (1997), *Imitation to Innovation: The Dynamics of Korea's Technological Learning*, Cambridge, MA: Harvard Business School Press.

Kohpaiboon, A. (2006), 'Global integration and Thai automotive industry', Discussion Paper No. 16, Faculty of Economics, Thammasat University, Bangkok (available for downloading at http://www.econ.tu.ac.th/Research/Discussionpaper).

Kohpaiboon, A. and P. Nipon (2010), 'Industrial upgrading and global recession: evidence of hard disk drive and automotive industries in Thailand', Discussion Paper No. 22, Faculty of Economics, Thammasat University, Bangkok (available for downloading at ww.econ.tu.ac.th/Research/Discussionpaper).

Korea Institute of Patent Information (KIPI) (2008), http://eng.kipi.or.kr/en_kipi/index.jsp, downloaded August 4, 2008.

Kuanpoth, J. (2002), 'Technology transfer in Thailand', in Christopher Heath (ed.), *Legal Rules of Technology Transfer in Asia*, London: Kluwer International.

Kuanpoth, J. (2006), 'TRIPS-Plus intellectual property rules: impact on Thailand's public health', *Journal of World Intellectual Property*, **9** (5), 573–91.

Lall, S. (1996), *Learning from the Asian Tigers: Studies in Technology and Industrial Policy*, London: Macmillan.

Lall, S. (1998), 'Thailand's manufacturing competitiveness: a preliminary overview', in proceedings of the Conference on Thailand's Dynamic Economic Recovery and Competitiveness, Papers for Session 4, Bangkok, 20–21 May.

Lauridsen, L. (2004), 'Foreign direct investment, linkage formation and supplier development in Thailand during 1990s: the role of state governance', *European Journal of Development Research*, **16** (3), 561–86.

Miyazaki, K. and K. Kijima, (2000), 'Complexity in technology management: theoretical analysis and case study of automobile sector in Japan', *Technological Forecasting and Social Change*, **64**, 39–54.

Mukdapitak, Y. (1994), 'The technology strategies of Thai firm', unpublished D.Phil. thesis, Science Policy Research Unit, University of Sussex, Brighton.

National Economic and Social Development Board (NESDB) (2004), 'A study for determining the direction for writing the operation plan for human resources development for key industrial and service sectors (demand side)', unpublished Final Report, Bangkok, Thailand.

National Economic and Social Development Board (NESDB) (2007), 'National productivity enhancement plan', PowerPoint presentation, January 26.

Odagiri, H. and A. Goto (1993), 'The Japanese system of innovation: past, present and future', in R. Nelson (ed.), *National Innovation System: A Comparative Analysis*, Oxford: Oxford University Press.

Pitkethly, R.H. (2001), 'Intellectual property strategy in Japanese and UK companies: patent licensing decisions and learning opportunities', *Research Policy*, **30**, 425–42.

Posaganondh, V. and S. Adsawintarangkun (2007), personal communication, The Department of Intellectual Property, 7 July.

Sribunruang, A. (1986), *Foreign Investment and Manufactured Exports from Thailand*, Bangkok: Chulalongkorn University Social Research Institute.

Tanasugarn, L. (2007), 'The first 10 years of patent cases in CIPITC: results of preliminary analyses', *IP&IT Journal*, Special Issue: 10th Anniversary, 19–37.

Techakanont, K. (2002), 'A study on inter-firm technology transfer in the Thai automotive industry', unpublished PhD dissertation, Hiroshima University.

Techakanont, K. and T. Terdudomtham (2004), 'Evolution of inter-firm technology transfer and technological capability formation of local parts firms in the Thai automobile industry', *Journal of Technology and Innovation*, **12** (2), 151–83.

Thailand Automotive Instiute (TAI) (2011), http://www.thaiauto.or.th/statistic/vehicle_production.asp, downloaded May 1, 2011.

Thailand Development Research Institute (TDRI) (1989), *The Development of Thailand's Technology Capability in Industry*, Vols 2–5, Bangkok: TDRI.

Tiralap, A. (1990), 'The economics of the process of technological change of the firm: the case of the electronics industry in Thailand,' unpublished D.Phil. thesis, Science Policy Research Unit, University of Sussex, Brighton.

United Nations Industrial Development Organization (UNIDO) (2006), 'The role of intellectual property rights in technology transfer and economic growth: theory and evidence', working paper for Strategic Research and Economics Branch, UNIDO, Vienna.

APPENDIX

Table 4A.1   List of interviews

Company	Establishment (ownership)	Products and activities
Carmakers		
Isuzu Technical Center of ASIA (ITA)	1991 (100% Japanese)	The 1st R&D center in Thailand aiming to develop Thai engineers in automotive design
Toyota Motor Asia Pacific Engineering and Manufacturing (TMAP-EM)	2003 (100% Japanese)	R&D base offering product designs and modifications for regional conditions and to provide testing and evaluation services
Honda R&D Southeast Asia	1997 (100% Japanese)	R&D on motorcycle and multi-purpose engine (e.g. agricultural machinery)
Honda R&D Asia Pacific	2005 (100% Japanese)	R&D for the Asia and Oceania region; developing automotive parts; style research; CBU prototype testing
Nissan Technical Center South East Asia (NTCSEA)	2008 (100% Japanese)	Technical center fulfills requirements of each ASEAN country and of Nissan, and to promote parts localization
Foreign part suppliers		
DENSO International Asia Co., Ltd (DIAT)	2007 (100% Japanese)	The technical center based in Thailand of DENSO Corporation (the world leading supplier producing air conditioning systems, power-train control systems, engine-related components)
Kasai Teck See Co., Ltd (consolidated subsidiary of Kasai Kogyo)	2007 (100% Japanese)	The global first-tier supplier of door trim, console box head lining, and noise insulation

Indigenous part suppliers

Summit Auto Seat Industry Co., Ltd (SAS)	1972 (100% Thai)	The supplier of seat, interior trimming parts of automobile and motorcycle; exhaust system, body parts, roll formed parts, mechanism parts
Thai Summit R&D Next Technology Co., Ltd (TSRD)	1995 (100% Thai)	The supplier of tooling (die and jig) and R&D for automotive, motorcycle, and electronic parts; agricultural products tool
Somboon Group	1975 (100% Thai)	The supplier of iron casting parts, spring
Daisin Co., Ltd	1979 JV with Nissin Koygo Co., Ltd (67% Thai shareholder)	The supplier of aluminum casting parts for automotive industry such as bracket sub assembly, cover clutch, outer tube
Sammitr Motor Manufacturing (SMM)	1967 (100% Thai)	The supplier of car and truck body parts as OEM; producing molds and fixtures for auto makers and other related industries like agriculture machinery

5. The national patent regime and indigenous innovations in compliance with TRIPS: a case study of China[1]

Song Hong

1. INTRODUCTION

China is a transition economy moving from a planned economy to a market one. Under the planned economic system, with the concepts of public ownership and public property right dominant, awareness of protecting intellectual property used to be very weak, and as a result legislation in the field fell far behind. As a backward country, during the era of the planned economy, China made breakthroughs in certain fields such as nuclear weapons, hydrogen weapons, man-made satellites, and the aerospace industries as well. In the meanwhile, China achieved a very high level of education for its citizens, and set up a relatively complete and sound innovation system which kept science research separate from production. During this period, China made a great number of break-throughs and developments in the high-tech core fields as well as the key segments. By making full use of the existing technologies and equipment and by improving and updating imported equipment and machines, China gradually mastered the designing and functioning of this equip-ment, improving its imitating and learning capability greatly. In this way, China established a relatively sound national economic system in the whole country.

Since its economic reform and opening to the outside world, with private enterprises developing and state-owned enterprises reforming, development of the market economy encouraged more and more indi-viduals, enterprises and research units to make innovations for the sake of economic interests. The patent protection laws also provide legal and institutional supports to such activities. China not only protected intel-lectual property by the Patent Law, but also gradually adapted the law to the international code. Since 2006, when China enacted the 'Intellectual Property Protection Strategy', it has entered a new stage in which it began to actively and voluntarily protect intellectual property. After more than 30 years of economic reform and opening, China has emerged as a worldwide innovative power in many fields.

The research question of this chapter explores the relationship between protection of intellectual property rights (IPR) and domestic innovation activities in China. For the innovation activities, we use patents as the main index, even though it is not a perfect one. Sometimes, the increase of patents is related to innovation, sometimes it is not. Sometimes people invent something or make an innovation without applying for patents, sometimes the reverse is true. However, we choose patents, firstly, because this is a comparative study, using the same index; secondly, because there just is no better alternative.[2] Linda Yueh (2009) tried to find if patent protection and the IPR regime have promoted China's innovation. Her conclusion was that factors such as economic development level (GDP per capita) and national innovation system (institutions and scientific talent) played key roles in fostering China's innovation activities, to which patent protection and the IPR regime also contributed a lot. According to Xibao Li (2012), the number of China's patent applications increased dramatically in the past decade. One of the reasons behind this lies in the government's encouraging and supportive policies toward patent application. Lan Xue and Zheng Liang (2010), using the patent database, give a detailed account of changes in China's patent applications, and also some explanation about the relationship between TRIPS and patent applications. In addition to looking at the relationship of patent protection, development of IPR regime and China's domestic innovation from a macro perspective, we also conducted case studies in China's auto industry, in order to give a more detailed observation at industrial as well as enterprise level of China's patent protection in compliance with TRIPS and the innovation activities by local auto enterprises. The chapter is divided into six sections following this introduction: Section 2 gives a brief introduction to China's economic development, technological innovation activities, evolution of China's intellectual property protection system; Section 3 is about formation of China's patent protection regime in compliance with TRIPS; Section 4 presents case studies of China's auto industry, which will give an introduction to China's intellectual property protection and innovation activities at the industrial level; Section 5 is about China's patent protection in line with TRIPS and its impacts on the innovations of China's auto enterprises; Section 6 concludes.

2. ECONOMIC DEVELOPMENT, TECHNOLOGICAL INNOVATION ACTIVITIES, AND CHANGE OF CHINA'S PATENT PROTECTION REGIME

2.1 Economic Development and Technological Innovation Activities

2.1.1 Technology importation on a large scale: 1949–57

Soon after socialist China came into being, China set up its science and technology research system based on the Chinese Academy of Sciences, with integration of three additional parts: tertiary education institutions, industrial sectors and local science and research institutions. Aided by the Soviet Union, in 1953 China began its First Five Year Plan, including 156 pivotal construction projects, most of which were imported in a package from the Soviet Union. Confronted with the pressures of national survival and a hostile international environment, China had to concentrate all its available resources to developing the defense industry as well as the core defense technologies, which were a highlighted characteristic of China's scientific, defense and economic development at that time.

2.1.2 Technology imitation, learning and innovation in the period of a closed economy: 1958–76

After the fulfillment of the First Five Year Pan in 1957, with Sino–Soviet relations strained and eventually breaking, China had to rely on itself. China began to formally adopt the development principle of independence and self-reliance in 1963. For fifteen years after that, China underwent an embargo imposed by both the Western countries and the socialist group led by the Soviet Union, with its whole economy trapped into a closed-up stage. Even worse, during the period of the Cultural Revolution (1966–76), the State Scientific and Technological Commission was dissolved, regular science and research activities broke down, and as a result, development of China's science and technology was interrupted. Nevertheless, in the period from 1956 to 1976, China had many remarkable achievements, such as explosion of the atom bomb in October 1964, explosion of the hydrogen bomb in June 1967, and the successful launch of satellite Dong Fang Hong No. 1 in April 1970.

2.1.3 Economic development: 1977–95

In September 1977, the State Commission of Science and Technology was formally restored. The national innovation system gradually departed from the traditional model (state dominant with the military coming first), and seemed on a track of combining science, technology and economic development together.

With the reform of the science and technology regime, China implemented a series of mandatory plans in order to push science and economic development together. Science and technology were deployed at three levels: technologies best serving economic development; newly emerged high technologies and high-tech industries; and basic science research. These levels formed a framework for China's new era science and technology development strategy (Ministry of Science and Technology, 2009, 2010).

2.1.4 Market reform and a new type of national innovation system (Strategy of revitalizing China through Science and Education): 1996–2005

In the 1990s China's economic reform entered a new stage. China clearly set the goal of building up a socialist market economy in 1992, and developed and implemented the Strategy of Revitalizing China through Science and Education in 1995. Thus, under the conditions of a market economy, construction of a new type of national innovation system was carried out.

Firstly, China step by step put the legal system of protecting IPR in place, which included protection of patents, trademarks, copyrights, computer software, integrated circuits, new species of plants, and prevention of unfair competition, so as to seek a fair and reasonable solution to disputes over the ownership of research achievements and IPR, and resolve the problems of how to transfer, utilize and distribute profits earned from IPR. Secondly, China sought to reform the science and technology (S&T) regime, with a policy of maintaining stability at one end while letting go at the other. Maintaining stability meant providing constant support to basic research, high-tech research and major strategic research. Letting go meant releasing control of various development oriented science research institutions, allowing them to be directed by market needs, encouraging them in commercialization and industrialization of S&T achievements, and helping them best serve economic development needs. This could be seen as an intensive adjustment and revolution occurring in China's science and research institutes. Thirdly, China strengthened human resources training and expanded dramatically the enrollment of undergraduate and graduate students. Lastly, China also made efforts to improve its evaluation and incentive system of scientific research, export inspection system of secret technology, and so on.

Guided by the new type of national innovation system, China carried out some innovation programs and plans.

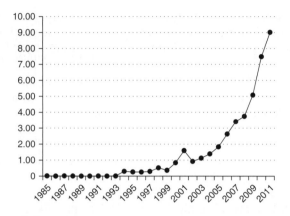

Source: WIPO Statistics Database.

Figure 5.1   China's share of PCT applications (%)

2.1.5   Moving towards an innovative nation: since 2006

In 2006 China proposed a strategy for enhancing indigenous innovation capacity and making a new-type innovative nation. An overall plan on China's S&T reform and development in the next fifteen years, based on the guideline of indigenous innovation, targeted leapfrogging, supporting economic development, and looking to the future. At the same time, the country as a whole also entered a new development stage.

After more than 30 years of reforming and opening, especially efforts in the last 20 years or so, a new market-oriented national innovation system was set up in China. In 2011, China became an important source of innovation second only to the US, Japan and Germany in terms of share of Patent Cooperation Treaty (PCT) patent applications (Figure 5.1). Moreover, in the PCT applications ranking list for enterprises, ZTE and Huawei, two enterprises from China, won the first and third places respectively in 2011.

2.2   Economic Development and IPR Protection

Along with economic development, especially development after the opening-up and reform era, Chinese government and indigenous enterprises continually deepened their understanding of IPR. First, China had to introduce patent protection. In a traditional socialist country, due to dominance of public ownership, people have little knowledge of IPR, nor of property rights over intangible assets. In the early stage of China's opening-up reform, when it imported foreign technologies, many of its foreign counterparts would take advantage. Even worse, some foreign enterprises cajoled China into buying invalid patent technologies at the price of protected ones. Once China had patent law, it could legally set limits on multinationals' pricing power over technology transfer to protect the interests of domestic enterprises. Second, China had to protect domestic enterprises through protection of indigenous IPR and intangible assets. At the initial phase of opening to the outside, lots of Chinese state and collective enterprises lost their indigenous brands and products, so losing control of their accumulated specific technologies and intangible assets in their efforts in technology importation. The reason was that Chinese people, equipped with limited knowledge of brands, technologies, and other intangible assets under the planned economy, did not yet recognize their commercial value, let alone protect them. Because of this, with joint enterprises increasing, well-known domestic brands vanished from sight, and people had to get used to international brands which sounded not only unfamiliar to them, but also weird and awkward. This is especially true in the commodity products such as beverages, washing powder, toothpaste and so on. Third, there was a rising demand for indigenous patents and inventions. With opening-up to the outside and reform policy developing further, China's traditional state and township enterprises made one transformation after another, growing into new-type private enterprises, whose awareness of brand and know-how was strengthened. Innovation capability also improved (Table 5.1).

At the same time, thanks to foreign direct investment (FDI), especially labor-intensive FDI from neighboring areas such as the Four Asian Dragons (Hong Kong, Singapore, South Korea and Taiwan) and Japan, China rose to be the processing and manufacturing center of East Asia, even of the whole world. Accumulation of know-how, brands and patents has been accelerated dramatically. Now it is clear that a strong awareness of protecting indigenous IPR has become an internal driving force for pushing China's IPR protection.

Generally speaking, China's patent protection system, developing from nothing, has undergone the following five phases:

1. Planned economy: public ownership was dominant and no laws or regulations on IPR protection existed;
2. 1978–84: opening-up to the outside world and economic reform were just at the initial stage and the first Patent Law was published;
3. 1984–92: first revision of the Patent Law;
4. 1992–00: second revision of the Patent Law;
5. 2000–05: third revision of the Patent Law (OECD, 2005, 2008; Liu et al., 2011).

Table 5.1 Issuance and revision of China's Patent Law

Phases of patent law issuance and revision	Scope of patent protection	Term of patent protection (years)	Phases of patent dispute implementation	China's economic development stages	Negotiations on IPRs between China and the US
1949–77	No	No	No	Development of a Planned Economy	Suffered in a long-term embargo of Western countries; relations with the Soviet Union getting worse; in a closed state
1978–84, Patent Law was delivered	Invention; utility model; design	15; 5–5 plus 3; 5–5 plus 3	Litigation period was 2 years	Technology importation and innovation: (a) importation; (b) commercialization; (c) attend WTO and TRIPS	During Den Xiaoping's visit to the US in 1979, both countries signed Sino–US S&T Cooperation Agreement, Sino–US Cooperation Agreement on High Energy Physics, which touched upon IPR protection Soon after, both countries signed Sino–US Trade Arrangement, which also contained IPR protection. China heard this concept for the first time and began to accelerate IPR legislation

				Innovation
1985–92, first revision of Patent Law	Invention; utility model; design	20; 10; 10	Litigation period was 2 years. Scope of compulsory license: taking public welfare into consideration	1991–92, China and US started negotiations on IPR. China amended No. 24 article, extending protection to food, beverages, spice, medicine and other material manufactured through chemical methods. 1992 edition of Patent Law was issued
1993–2000, the second revision of Patent Law	Invention; utility model; design	20; 10; 10	Litigation period was 2 years. Enactment of compulsory license became more restrictive	1993–94, both countries continued their negotiations on IPR; negotiation extended to 1996
Since 2001, the third revision of Patent Law	Invention; utility model; design	20; 10; 10	Litigation period was 2years. More rigid provisions on compulsory license	In 2005, China and the US opened a new run of negotiation on IPR, their third round table discussion on IPR.

Source: Information collected by the author.

2.3   Links between Pressure Inflicted by the Developed Countries and China's Development of IPR Protection

Due to its level and experience of economic development, China had to put up with huge pressure from the Western countries, mainly the US, in its efforts to constitute a patent law. To some extent, we could say that China's issuance and revision of the law were actually pushed by the Americans (Yang Guohua, 1998). The influence of the US is evident in the following aspects.

2.3.1   Development of Sino–US economic trade relations pushes China to improve IPR protection legislation

Initial stage of bilateral economic trade relations: patent law taking shape   The opening-up to the outside world and reform that started in 1978 mainly meant opening to the Western countries, among which the US was the most important for China. In 1979, during Deng Xiaoping's visit to the US, the leaders of the two countries laid down a sound foundation for future Sino–US economic trade development. In 1980, the Sino–US Trade Agreement was signed, which contained some content on IPR. For example, the sixth article in the Agreement specifies that both countries will afford each other equal national treatment in the protection of patents, copyrights and trademarks. Soon after that, China launched legislation for protection of IPR: it joined the World Intellectual Property Organization (WIPO) in 1980; published the Trademark Law in 1982; and promulgated the Patent Law in 1984 (enforced on April 1, 1985).

Pressures exerted by Section 301 after 1988   In the 1980s, the US made great efforts to promote IPR protection on the world scale. Besides actively promoting TRIPS worldwide during the Uruguay Round in GATT (General Agreement on Tariffs and Trade), the US constituted new laws leading to stronger protection of IPR, and also carried out trade retaliation against international IPR violators. In April 1988, the US Congress passed a new revision of the Omnibus Trade and Competitiveness Act, bringing in an additional retaliatory article, namely Special 301 provisions, which allow the US to impose trade sanctions against those countries whose protection of US IPR is considered neither adequate nor effective. The US government made China a target of Special 301 as soon as it was decreed.

The US Trade Representative (USTR) placed China on its Special 301 priority watch list in 1989. From April to May, representatives from both countries held talks on how to protect US IPR, and reached a memorandum of understanding (MoU) in Washington DC on May 19, 1989. In this MoU, China made commitments that it would: formulate a Copyright Law consistent with international code, in which computer programs as a special type of work would be protected; amend Patent Law so as to extend patent duration and scope; and join international conventions on IPR protection.

After signing the MoU, China made significant progress in its IPR protection legislation. In July 1989, China accessed the Madrid Agreement Concerning the International Registration of Trademarks; in September 1990, China promulgated Copyright Law; on June 4, 1991, China decreed Regulations on the Protection of Computer Software.

1991–94: Negotiations and disputes, bringing patent law closer to TRIPS   On May 26, 1991, USTR designated China a Special 301 priority foreign country, whose IPR practices were considered to be the most serious or harmful to the US. According to Special 301, the US would initiate a six-month investigation of China, and if both sides could not reach an agreement by November 26, 1991, the US would adopt unilateral trade sanctions against China. China responded vigorously, saying that it was unfair for Americans to put China under the pressure arising from Special 301, while ignoring Chinese people's constant efforts to protect IPR and the many consultations attended by both sides on IPR protection. What the US had done to China was totally unacceptable, for which China had to express its regret. The Chinese government said that all trade disputes including disputes over IPR should be resolved through consultation.

By the end of November 1991, the two governments held four rounds of consultations, but to no avail. A trade war loomed on the horizon. Just then, the Uruguay Round reached an agreement on IPR, which provided a reference standard for Sino–US negotiations. After another two rounds of tense negotiations, they eventually signed the Sino–US Memorandum of Understanding (MoU) on IPR on January 16, 1992, which temporarily brought an end to Sino–US friction over IPR.

To honor its commitment made in the MoU:

1. China accessed certain international conventions, such as the Berne Convention for the Protection of Literary and Artistic Works (Berne Convention) in October 1992, and the Convention for the Protection of Producers of Phonograms Against Unauthorized Duplication of Their Phonograms (Geneva Convention) in April 1993. According to China's legal principle, these international treaties have binding force in China's domestic law, specifying that if there is a difference between the relevant domestic law and the two treaties, provision of the treaties

shall prevail, except for those on which China has made a reservation; it also made corresponding revisions to the domestic laws, in which it enlarged the scope of patents to all chemical inventions, including pharmaceuticals, chemicals, products and methods, stipulating that without licensing of the patent owner, no one could manufacture, utilize or sell patent products; it also extended duration of a patent to 20 years, and added a provision whereby if any entity which is qualified to exploit the invention or utility model has made requests for authorization from the patentee of an invention or utility model to exploit its or his patent on reasonable terms and such efforts have not been successful within a reasonable period of time, the Patent Office may grant a compulsory license to exploit the patent for invention or utility model;

2. China amended its Copyright Law in September 1992. In light of the Berne Convention and Geneva Convention, China made relevant revisions to its Copyright Law as well as Regulations for Implementation of Copyright Law, and also promulgated a number of regulations with legal effect. China strengthened protection of computer software, and, to conform to the conventions, it maintained protection of computer software without formalities, and extended duration of protection to 50 years;

3. In February 1993, China made revisions to Trademark Law;

4. China decreed the Anti Unfair Competition Law in Sepetember 1993. To ensure enforcement of the Paris Convention, emphasizing protection of industrial property, and to effectively prevent illicit competition, China pledged to prohibit use of any unfair method to disclose, obtain and use another's business secrets without getting consent from the legal owner of the secrecy.

The commitment made by the US in the MoU was to end the investigation initiated against China under Special 301, and to take China off the Special 301 list. As we have seen, in this MoU, China made very concrete commitments, and completely enforced them.

2.3.2   Enforcement of laws

The US and Special 301   Having seen China's improvement in forming the domestic IPR regime, the US began to shift its attention to legal enforcement in China. The primary policy tool was still Special 301. According to the provisions of Special 301, a country not implementing the agreement is deemed to be an anti-trade-agreement country, and incurs another Special 301 investigation. On June 30, 1994, the USTR once more designated China a priority foreign country, and wasted no time declaring an investigation. The USTR claimed that, although China had made significant progress by enacting new IPR laws, enforcement of its laws and regulations was sporadic at best, and virtually non-existent for copyrighted works, resulting in a high rate of piracy. It seemed that China was not sincere in curbing piracy. In addition, there were still some hidden trade quotas and a lack of transparency in regulations that denied market access for the US IPR products to China. Hence, this time the investigation was focused on China's enforcement of IPR laws and regulations, which marked a shift signifying that the Americans would pay more attention to the effectiveness and adequacy of China's enforcement of IPR laws than before. According to Special 301, the investigation would last six months. During the period, both countries held a few rounds of talks. China took some effective measures, including closing down pirating factories and checking through the retail stores to confiscate and dispose of counterfeit goods, giving a heavy blow to piracy of computer software etc. However, there was still big gap between the two sides. On December 3, 1994, the USTR stated at the conclusion of the investigation that China's enforcement of IPR laws and regulations was unreasonable, not only causing a huge burden, but setting limits on US business. The USTR issued a draft list of products including garments, sneakers, toys, and electronic products imported from China, valued at $2.8 billion, which would be subject to the punitive duty of 100 percent, the highest retaliatory value throughout its history (Table 5.2).

China expressed its great regret and strong dissatisfaction at the US unilateral declaration of retaliation against China, demanding that the US give up its wrong position on IPR issues, and work with China in a more active and constructive way, through conscientious consultations, to seek a decent settlement for both sides. Simultaneously, in line with its Foreign Trade Law, China in turn threw back an anti-sanction list of US products. It was the first time they had made legal battle over the trade dispute.

Meantime, the threatened trade war between the two powers raised concern in the entire industrial business circle on both sides, as well as the world as a whole. The USTR delayed the investigation to February 4, 1995, so that representatives from both sides had enough time to reach an agreement, which was eventually concluded on February 26, 1995. In this agreement, China made commitments in three aspects: to take intermediate measures to curb piracy all over the country; to adopt long-term measures to ensure effective enforcement of IPR protection; and to provide greater market access of IPR holders to China. The US promised to stop its Special 301 action, with no more trade sanctions against China.

Table 5.2   IPR protection and US Special 301: China's position,
          1989–2011

	Watch list	Priority watch list	Priority foreign country
1989		1	
1990		1	
1991			1
1992	1		
1993			
1994			1
1995	1		
1996			1
1997			Section 306 monitoring
1998			Section 306 monitoring
1999			Section 306 monitoring
2000			Section 306 monitoring
2001			Section 306 monitoring
2002			Section 306 monitoring
2003			Section 306 monitoring
2004			Section 306 monitoring
2005		1	
2006		1	
2007		1	
2008		1	Section 306 monitoring
2009		1	
2010		1	Section 306 monitoring
2011		1	Section 306 monitoring

Source: USTR, special 301 reports, various issues.

According to the provisions of Special 301, if the US signed a binding treaty with a foreign country, where the country agreed to remove or step by step remove the concerned laws, policies or practices, the USTR would put an end to the Special 301 investigation. The US committed to provide technological assistance in IPR protection; to work with China, through continuous consultations, to tackle their disputes over market access of other goods, foreign competitive products and agricultural products etc.; and provide relevant assistance.

The agreement concluded in the last negotiation was still on the way to implementation, when new pressure emerged. On April 30, 1996, the USTR stated that China's enforcement of the agreement was insufficient, especially in the shutting down of pirate factories and giving market access to American audio-visual producers. As a result, China was once again placed on the Special 301 priority watch list. On May 15, the USTR announced a list of Chinese products, valued at $3 billion, which would be subject to a punitive import tariff. At the same time, China in turn declared its own retaliatory list of American products. Both sides began to hold talks which attracted worldwide attention.

After bitter negotiation, the two sides reached agreement on June 17, 1996. China took action to curb piracy of either authorized or underground CD factories, targeting products such as CDs, CD-ROMs, LDs and VCDs. In a special enforcement period, China launched effective investigations against the pirate producers, shutting down factories and confiscating pirated products. China strictly prohibited the export and import of pirated product such as CDs, CD-ROMs, LDs and VCDs, and made efforts to put CD factories under more effective supervision, including suspending permission for construction of new CD factories, strengthening authorization of copyright, introducing SID code, and checking licenses of CD producers, so as to put the market in order. As for market access, China made commitments in phonograms, movies and software. In turn, the US agreed to remove China from the priority watch list, with no sanction against it.

In the ensuing eight years, the US kept China under Section 306 monitoring, according to which, once China is deemed to be not implementing the Sino–US agreements, it will suffer US trade retaliation.

WTO   After being admitted to the WTO in 2001, China had to improve its enforcement of laws by WTO mechanisms. After 2005, in addition to the bilateral channels, the US began to push forward China's enforcement of IPR protection under the multilateral framework. In that year, the USTR once again placed China on the priority watch list, and started new rounds of talks involving IPR issues.

In the ensuing seven years (to 2011), China has been one of the countries on Special 301, the priority watch list, subject to supervision of Section 306.

It should be noted that most of the negotiations, disputes, even threats of trade retaliation between China and the US were focused on copyright, especially audio visual works, for example DVDs, VCDs and computer software, with little on patent products.

In brief, improvement of China's patent legislation accompanied the process of its opening-up. Development of Sino–US economic trade relations, especially their disputes over IPR issues, played as one of the most important external driving forces. At the same time, China's economic development also highlights the importance of IPR protection. The domestic enterprises began to ask for such protection. Since the 1990s, with China's opening up and reform developing further, and the multinationals' impacts increasing, more and more domestic brands were merged and vanished. This was often the case with beverages and everyday items (washing powder, toothpaste, shoeshine etc.), which led to a rising demand from China's indigenous firms for protection of independent brands and patents. On the other hand, the multinationals also pressed the Chinese government hard to protect their copyrights, patent products and trademarks as well. With economic development and economic restructuring in particular at a turning point, China's patent regime moved to an independent development stage, which could be seen very clearly in the third amendment of Patent Law.

3. BUILDING A PATENT REGIME COMPLYING WITH TRIPS

In 2001, China became a member of the WTO and signed the TRIPS agreement. In order to join the WTO, China made a widespread adjustment in laws, regulations and policies. After twice revising the Patent Law, China made great efforts to improve patent protection. Thus, it did not have to do much to adjust the Patent Law to the TRIPS agreement (Li Shunde, 2000).

3.1   China's Patent Law and TRIPS: Necessary Adjustments

3.1.1   Opportunity for review

Most of the countries practice a registration or formal examination system for utility model and design. This is almost the same as in China, except that the final declaratory judgments for annulment suit and infringement action must be made by the court in the form of judiciary verdict. According to China's Patent Law, the decision of the Patent Reexamination Board in respect of any request, made by the applicant, the patentee or the person who made the request for revocation of the patent right, for reexamination concerning a utility model or design is final (article 43 of the Patent Law), and not allowed to be brought up before a court. This content is different from international common codes, and does not conform to the relevant provisions of TRIPS. According to Section 4 of Article 41,

> parties to a proceeding shall have an opportunity for review by a judicial authority of final administrative decisions and, subject to jurisdictional provisions in a Member's law concerning the importance of a case, of at least the legal aspects of initial judicial decisions on the merits of a case. However, there shall be no obligation to provide an opportunity for review of acquittals in criminal cases.

In Section 5 of Article 62,

> final administrative decisions in any of the procedures referred to under paragraph 4 shall be subject to review by a judicial or quasi-judicial authority. However, there shall be no obligation to provide an opportunity for such review of decisions in cases of unsuccessful opposition or administrative revocation, provided that the grounds for such procedures can be the subject of invalidation procedures.

Chinese Patent Law made corresponding adjustments in light of provisions of TRIPS.

3.1.2   More restrictions on compulsory license

In TRIPS, there are many restrictions on compulsory license. For example, in Section (a) of Article 31, 'authorization of such use shall be considered on its individual merits'; according to Section (b), use of the subject matter of a patent without authorization by government or third parties authorized by the government may only be permitted in situations of national emergency or other circumstances of extreme urgency, or in the case of public non-commercial use. China's Patent Law has similar contents. Article 14 in China's Patent Law is about 'planning license', which is a product of the planned economy. Both GATT and WTO are based on the market economy principle, and only if a planned-economy country makes a successful transition to a market economy one can it function well under the world trade framework built on GATT and WTO. Therefore, China's Patent Law should be taken as a very unique compulsory license, which is not only in contrast with but also conflicts with compulsory licenses under TRIPS, and needs to be removed completely.

3.1.3   More action to reduce imminent infringement

So-called imminent infringement refers to infringement which has not happened yet, but seems imminent. To hold back imminent infringement is good practice. Section 3 of Article 50 in TRIPS has clearly defined and set limits on using it. China lags behind in this field, and should catch up.

3.1.4   Ignorance can be forgiven principle

According to Section 2 of Article 62 in China's Patent Law, where any person uses or sells a patented product not knowing that it was made and sold without the authorization of the patentee, it shall not be deemed an infringement of the patent right. Such an 'ignorance can be forgiven' principle is very rare in foreign patent laws, trademark laws, and copyright laws. In regard to TRIPS, this is just a unique situation which can only occur to layout design of IC and business secrecy, as the former is extremely complex, minute and indiscernible, while for the latter secrecy makes it hardly knowable. Patent infringement committed by people who know nothing about it should be considered as a benign infringement, but one whose primary feature is still illegal, just exempt or partly exempt from legal responsibility for compensation resulting from infringements. China lacks such a rule, and should add it into its existing laws.

3.1.5   Compensation for loss principle

According to Article 45 of TRIPS, the judicial authorities shall have the authority to order the infringer to pay the right holder damages adequate to compensate for the injury the right holder has suffered because of an infringement of that person's IPR by an infringer who knowingly, or with reasonable grounds to know, engaged in infringing activity. The judicial authorities shall also have the authority to order the infringer to pay the right holder expenses, which may include appropriate attorney's fees. In appropriate cases, Members may authorize the judicial authorities to order recovery of profits and/or payment of pre-established damages even where the infringer did not knowingly, or with reasonable grounds to know, engage in infringing activity. In contrast, Article 60 of China's Patent Law is very simple, with only an outlined principle of compensation for loss, and no detailed content.

3.1.6   Abuse of patent ownership

According to Section 1 of Article 48 in TRIPS, the judicial authorities shall have the authority to order a party at whose request measures were taken and who has abused enforcement procedures to provide to a party wrongfully enjoined or restrained adequate compensation for the injury suffered because of such abuse. The judicial authorities shall also have the authority to order the applicant to pay the defendant expenses, which may include appropriate attorney's fees. According to Section 2, in respect of the administration of any law pertaining to the protection or enforcement of IPR, Members shall only exempt both public authorities and officials from liability to appropriate remedial measures where actions are taken or intended in good faith in the course of the administration of that law. In contrast, China's Patent Law has no such restriction targeting patent abuse by patentee, which China is supposed to make up soon.

3.1.7   Patent rights should include offering for sale

'Offering for sale' sometimes refers to sales promotion and marketing, and sometimes refers to supply for sale, which includes a wide range of acts related to selling a kind of product with strong willingness displayed through various channels and in various ways, such as product exhibitions, product demonstrations, free trial etc. It is clearly stated in Section 1 of Article 28 in TRIPS that a patent shall confer on its owner exclusive rights which include offering for sale. However, China's Patent Law has no such content, which is expected to be integrated into the law.

Generally speaking, after China joined TRIPS the amendment of the Patent Law had two adjustments of importance. Firstly, that part of content involving three kinds of patentee with Chinese characteristic was removed (Article 6 of 1992 Patent Law), with no more emphasis on the difference between owner and holder arising from various ownership of their working units. Such an adjustment resulted from the principle of IPR as private property right embodied in TRIPS, based on the overall situation where China is admitted into WTO, and its state enterprises' reform is further deepened. Secondly, in terms of decision of reexamination, the past law treated invention in a different way from utility model and design (if not satisfied with the decision of reexamination, an applicant of a patent for invention can bring it to the court, while for a patent for utility model or design, the decision is final: the applicant cannot bring a lawsuit to the court) (Article 43 of 1992 Patent Law). The law was changed, with equal treatment to the three: any applicant of a patent can institute legal proceedings in the people's court within three months from the date of receipt of the notification only if he or she is not content with the decision of reexamination. The amendment fully followed the primary legal principle of judicial final settlement, resolving almost all the difference between China's Patent Law and TRIPS.

The People's Republic of China conducted an intensive work programme to examine and revise the IPR laws, administrative regulations and department rules relating to the implementation of the WTO Agreement and China's accession commitments. A list of China's IPR laws, administrative regulations and department rules to be revised and abolished was notified to the Working Party. Part I of the list contained eight laws and regulations. Part II of the list contained four department rules to be revised or abolished for the same reason. This list included the names of laws, regulations and department rules, reasons for revision or abolishment, and dates of implementation (Table 5.3).

To sum up, the formulation and revisions of China's patent regime underwent several dramatic changes when it was first constituted in 1985 and China made efforts to join WTO. After going through these two periods, China's patent protection regime and policy framework were almost in place. Thus, in 2001 when China became a member of WTO and TRIPS, its legal system and institutions did not have to change too much.

Table 5.3   Revision of China's IPR laws in conformity with the TRIPS Agreement

Laws, Regulations and Rules	Date of implementation
Part I Laws and Administrative Regulations	
1. Copyright Law of the People's Republic of China	Upon accession
2. Regulations for the Implementation of the Copyright Law of the People's Republic of China	Upon accession
3. Regulations for the Protection of Computer Software	Upon accession
4. Trademark Law of the People's Republic of China	Upon accession
5. Detailed Rules for the Implementation of the Trademark Law of the People's Republic of China	Upon accession
6. Regulations of the People's Republic of China on the Protection of New Varieties of Plants	Effective as of October 1, 1997
7. Law of the People's Republic of China Against Unfair Competition	Effective as of December 1, 1993
8. Regulations on the Implementation of the Integrated Circuit Layout Design	To be effective as of October 10, 2001
Part II Department Rules	
1. Interim Rules on the Administration of Patents in Agriculture, Animal Husbandry and Fisheries	To be abolished upon accession
2. Notice on the Interim Regulation on the Protection of Copyright of Books and Magazines	To be abolished upon accession
3. Notice on the Issuance of the 'Detailed Rules of Interim Regulations on the Protection of Copyright of Books and Magazines', 'Publication Intention Contracts' and 'Publication Contracts'	To be abolished upon accession
4. Interpretation of Article 15(4) of the 'Interim Regulation on the Protection Copyright of Books and Magazines'	To be abolished upon accession

Source: WTO, WT/ACC/CHN/49, 1 October 2001 (01–4679), Report of the Working Party on the Accession of China.

Since 2005, with China moving towards an innovative nation, in its newly amended Patent Law in 2009, the patent protection level has been raised even higher than TRIPS, which not only reflects China's progress in legal system and institutions, but also reflects the requests for China to be an innovative nation.

4. PATENT PROTECTION AND TECHNOLOGICAL INNOVATIVE ACTIVITIES OF CHINA'S AUTOMOTIVE INDUSTRY

With China's per capita yearly income surpassing $3,000, cars have begun entering its ordinary households' consumption package starting from 2003 and 2004. In 2009, China's volumes of both car production and sales exceeded those of the United States and ranked the first in the context of the global financial crisis. Its car sales volume reached 10.12 million units in 2011, of which 2.95 million (29.1 percent) were home brands, and the remaining 70.9 percent were transnational brands. From a historical perspective, it is a marvelous achievement for both China's car industry and its home brands.

4.1 Early Period – Reverse Engineering (RE) and Imitation (1949–77)

During this period, China produced two local brands of car, the Hongqi and Shanghai.

4.1.1 Hongqi brand
The Hongqi brand is the earliest and senior official car model in China, and once enjoyed a high reputation. A 1955-version Chrysler sedan, borrowed from the Jilin University, was the model. China's First Automobile Works (FAW) completely dismantled it and conducted a manual survey and drawing of every one of its components. On the basis of this work, together with a series of improvements with Chinese characteristics, a high-grade limousine model was produced. Its power system and equipment were almost the same as the Chrysler limousine. Afterwards, FAW's designers carried out five systematic revisions and tests and finally confirmed the Hongqi-branded car as CA72. It was the first formal Hongqi-branded high-grade limousine with China's serial number. On October 1, 1959, the Hongqi-branded car formally made its debut appearance at the country's military parade to celebrate the tenth anniversary of the establishment of the new China.

4.1.2 Shanghai brand
If Hongqi-brand limousines served as special vehicles for senior leaders, then Shanghai-brand cars are mostly for China's junior officials. Under the stimulation of successful car production by the FAW in 1958, the Shanghai Municipal government organized several relevant factories to make larger efforts for car manufacturing. In that year, a Benz 220S car was transported to the Shanghai Automotive Manufacturing Factory for

a 'live dissection' in an extremely delicate and complicated process. Tens of the most powerful Shanghai-based industrial enterprises participated in the dismantling of the Benz limousine. In such a 'great cooperation', every participating enterprise was assigned the research and manufacturing of a specific component. After several years' delay, in 1963 the first Shanghai-brand car was born. During its lifetime up to 1991, a total of 77,054 cars were manufactured. Despite an imitated outside shape design, the cars established a brand of China's own. For a long period, Shanghai-brand sedans bolstered domestic car demand.

The entire environment facing China's economic development before the reform and opening-up seriously restricted the development of its automotive industry. The country's economic environment at that time mainly displayed the following characteristics: (1) the planned economy; (2) suffering strict and long-term economic sanctions and blockades from Western countries; (3) serious setbacks in China–Soviet relations in the 1960s. Such adverse economic circumstances prompted China to promote the development of its independent automotive industry.

From a domestic perspective, the development of China's auto sector also faced numerous unique conditions during this period:

1. At that time, official consumption dominated the country's auto demand, while private demand did not exist. Under these circumstances, car demand in China was very limited. Oversupply would result in waste, and under-supply would fail to spur the development of the auto industry. Such unique demand conditions also meant that consumers usually did not find fault with the form of cars, and instead, focused more on their quality.
2. On the one hand, such an imitation-based manufacturing model restricted supply, given the limited imitation capability. On the other hand, the country's auxiliary capabilities and its whole industrial foundation were still at a comparatively weak level, negatively restricting its supply capability. A backward supply industry caused some car components, such as quality iron and steel, to be in short supply.
3. The whole manufacturing process was still a handcraft workshop-based production model. For those components that should have been produced in a streamlined, large-scale and standardized system, the manual operations resulted in certain discrepancies in quality and similarity.

While Hongqi-brand cars were basically manually made because of the very limited number of targeted senior officials, Shanghai-brand vehicles, which were largely targeted at middle and low-level officials and thus had a larger demand, were made on a semi-manual basis. Generally, under the demand of government-dominated consumption, China's automotive industry gained initial development during that period of time. But compared with developed countries that enjoyed full-fledged market economic situations, China's development lagged far behind.

4.2   Technological Introduction and Joint Ventures (1978–2000)

At the end of the 1970s, China's economy embarked on market-based reforms, and domestic demand for automobiles proceeded to rise dramatically. The country's limited foreign exchange was spent on the import of vehicles, which deeply distressed decision-makers. With the aim of import substitution or even the export of local cars for earning foreign exchange, the Chinese government began considering the development of the country's automotive industry, especially car manufacturing, through technological cooperation or in the form of the establishment of joint ventures. In the 1980s, the technological development of China's car industry pressed ahead mainly through two forms. The first was the introduction of car models and production equipment to build domestic car production capabilities. The second was the establishment of joint ventures in the form of joint funding to manufacture introduced car models.

4.2.1   Self-production through the introduction of car models and technologies

Daihatsu technologies and the 'Xiali Model'   In 1984, Tianjin Automobile Industry Company signed an agreement with Japan's Daihatsu on the introduction of a set of complete technologies for manufacturing the Hijet 850, a kind of minibus, and Charade 1.0, a mini two-box car. The Chinese name, *pinyin* 'Xiali', is used to name the car model.[3]

Xiali-brand cars were one of the most sold vehicle brands in China in the late 1990s, ranking second only to Santana. The annual sale volumes of Xiali-brand cars reached 100,000 in 1998 and 1999, and production capacity reached 150,0000 cars and 200,000 engines. This had become a modern car manufacturing plant with a certain scale.

Audi 100 technologies and the 'Hongqi Model'   FAW signed an agreement with Volkswagen on May 17, 1988, on the transfer of Audi products and technologies to update its Hongqi-brand car. It stipulated that FAW would introduce third-generation Audi 100 cars from Volkswagen, and start from SKD (semi-knocked down) and CKD (completely knocked down) car assembly, before gradually raising the local content level. After reaching certain standards, these introduced products will be allowed to use their own Hongqi brand.

4.2.2 FDI for joint ventures

In the 1980s, the development of China's automobile industry was dominated by the model of 'introducing foreign direct investment to set up joint ventures'. During this period, the Chinese government approved the establishment of joint ventures by FAW, the Second Automobile Works Co. (SAW) and Shanghai Automobile Industry, the country's most important auto bases. These joint ventures have since become the main force of China's car sector to date.

Shanghai–Volkswagen: Santana   In October 1984, Shanghai Automotive Industry Corporation (SAIC) set up a joint venture with Germany's Volkswagen for the manufacturing of the Santana, with both holding 50 percent of shares.

After its establishment, the Shanghai-Volkswagen had its first Santana assembled in 1985, and achieved an output of 1,733 units the same year. The output of Santana kept growing in the following years. However, this kind of production put huge pressures on China's balance of payments. In 1989, a special office aimed at promoting the localization of Santana was set up. With efforts from various parties, Santana's local content ratio had been raised to over 90 percent by 1996. Correspondingly, the Santana components manufacturing system was gradually built up, which laid a solid foundation for the introduction of new car models and their development.

FAW–Volkswagen: Jetta   In 1991, the FAW signed an agreement with Volkswagen for the production of Jetta vehicles, with FAW holding 60 percent of shares and Volkswagen 40 percent. Later, the proportions were adjusted to 50 percent each.

Shenlong Fukang: Fukang vehicles   On May 18, 1992, the Dongfeng Automobile Company and the French Citroen Automobile Company set up the joint Dongfeng Peugeot Citroen Automobile Company Ltd in Wuhan, Hubei province, with a 70 percent to 30 percent share-holding proportion between the Chinese and French sides. It was planned to be a modern auto manufacturer with a capacity of 300,000 cars and 400,000 engines. The project was divided into two stages, with the establishment of a manufacturing base of 150,000 cars and 200,000 engines as its first stage.

With such kinds of joint-venture projects, China's car industry has realized a mass and modernized production. The three car models later basically realized an annual output of more than 100,000 units. It is huge progress in both manufacturing technologies and assembly lines. At the same time, the three car models have also basically realized localized production and correspondingly set up an auxiliary components manufacturing network.

4.3 Post Entry into the WTO – Competition between Joint Venture and Home Brands (2001–)

Under the protection of tariffs and non-tariff measures, investments made by transnational companies in China were typical of market-sourcing before China's WTO entry. In China they produced mainly car models that were outdated and eliminated by the car markets in developed countries, and their manufacturing equipment was also far behind the world advanced level. Car models remained almost unchanged for decades. However, due to a policy of protection and the lack of competition, these enterprises enjoyed a monopoly over China's car market at that time. Despite achieving mass production scale, their prices still remained far higher than international levels. Take the year 2000 as an example. That year, China exported 523 cars, while importing 21,620, compared with the 605,000 units manufactured and 617,000 units sold in the country. It means that China's car exports only accounted for 0.086 percent of its output in 2000. As far as the production scale of individual car models is concerned, Santana and Jetta later basically reached an annual output of 100,000 units.[4] However, their prices were three to four times those of the international market. For example, the international price of Jetta was $5,000 at that time,[5] but the domestic price was as high as 160,000 yuan, almost $20,000. In 2000, the mainstream car models on China's auto market were all ones that were popular on the international market two or three decades earlier. For example, Santana, produced by Shanghai-Volkswagen, was launched on the domestic market in 1985, but it was the 1981 version on the international market. Jetta made its debut in China in 1992, but it was a 1985 version on the international market. Similarly, the Fukang, Alto and Xiali, which were respectively launched on the domestic market in 1996, 1991 and 1986, enjoyed popularity on the international market in 1991, 1984, and 1980. A typical case is Santana, a car model that prevailed on the international market in the 1980s, which took 30.88 percent of China's market share in 2000.

After China's WTO entry, changes in supply–demand relations in China's vehicle market as well as China's reduced limitations on foreign direct investment have caused transnational companies to make some adjustments to their China-bound investment strategies.

First, transnational companies that established a market-sourcing investment base in China needed to make big adjustments, either phasing out their investment and increasing vehicle exports to China's market, or improving their current investment facilities through investment expansion, technological upgrading or introducing new models. The latter of the two options became the preferred choice for many transnational companies. There are several reasons underlying such a choice. First, product exports to China are not a particularly feasible option. Although China made its commitments for tariff and non-tariff reductions, a transition period of five to six years was given for their final implementation. Furthermore, import barriers at the domestic car market still remained relatively high, making it very difficult for transnational companies to pursue their export strategies. Second, current China-bound transnational investments mainly stem from the US and European transnational companies, whose manufacturing bases are mainly distributed across the US and European nations. For them to export vehicles to China from a remote homeland or overseas manufacturing base is by no means a wise option. Third, the scale of China's car market and its strategic significance also prompted transnational companies in their choice. There was another kind of transnational company, represented by the US-based General Motors (GM) and Japan's Honda, which had arranged for their China-bound investment strategies much earlier, in line with the new landscape following China's WTO entry. In its pursuit of joint ventures with Shanghai Automobile Company in 1998, GM offered to Chinese partners some conditions that other transnational corporations did not agree on and thus gained a 50 percent share in the joint venture. These conditions included an all-round transfer of its component technologies to the newly-built joint venture, an investment of $40 million to set up five technological training agencies, and placing a large portion of Buick design work in China. Conditions accepted by GM were unacceptable to Volkswagen in its negotiations with the Chinese side about Santana's production. Because of its unwillingness to transfer more of its international components manufacturing capacity to China, Volkswagen once had strained relations with SAIC. Also, due to its unwillingness to pay a higher price, Chrysler lost to Mercedes-Benz in their competition for a multi-purpose vehicle project in Zhanjiang, Guangdong province. For the same reason, more cautious Toyota also let slip an earlier chance to set up a joint venture with SAIC.

Due to their long attempt to meet China's car market through exports to the country, Japanese and South Korean car corporations have always remained inactive in China-bound direct investment.[6] Such a choice is reasonable, considering the two countries are adjacent to China and their exports to it do not have high transport and logistical costs. The reduction in China's tariffs and non-tariff barriers following its WTO membership also lowered the cost of exports to China. However, the US and European transnational companies have held a more favorable position than Japanese and South Korean counterparts through direct investment, and thus have gained huge market shares in China. Such practices have posed a severe challenge to the established strategies adopted by Japanese and South Korean enterprises. After years of 'wait and watch', Japanese and South Korean enterprises finally woke up and began large-scale investment in China, represented by Toyota, Renault-Nissan and Hyundai. All these newcomers have begun to set up joint ventures in China for the manufacturing of whole car series and car models, with a projected annual output of 300,000 to 500,000 units within five years.

There are also differences between these new and old transnational car companies in terms of their China investment strategies. In a fast-growing market, incoming transnational companies usually want to introduce some new products and lower their prices in a bid to increase their market shares and gradually weaken the dominant market position held by earlier comers. This is exactly the case with China's automobile market. In 2000, Volkswagen held a 53.57 percent share of China's auto market and the proportion declined to 35.20 percent in 2003.[7] In 2002, there were more than 40 brands and 200 car models in China, 60 percent of which were introduced car models.[8] Quite a number of new vehicle models have completely adopted the CKD or SKD manufacturing forms.

After China's WTO entry, the basic auto development strategy adopted by transnational companies has basically been as follows: investment in China; expanding investment; the launch of new products; a full-series product investment; lowering prices.

Under such a strategy, however, transnational companies, as one party of China-based joint ventures, have conducted few innovative activities locally. Instead, what they have tended to do is to introduce new car models and at most make some adapting adjustments. The Chinese manufacturers, as the other party of joint ventures, have been in a more passive position, trying to subsist on preferential government policies.[9] What they have mainly done is to pursue as much cooperation as possible with transnational companies to set up joint ventures. As a result, it is very common that a specific local automobile group sets up multiple joint ventures with several transnational car companies.

Why did China's local large-size automobile groups fail to conduct their independent investment in the context of changed market conditions? The CEO of FAW, China's largest vehicle manufacturer and second largest car manufacturer, gave his representative viewpoint on this question.[10] First, the strategy of adoption of joint ventures is mainly based on the insufficiency of funds and technological backwardness on the Chinese side, and the lack of ability for independent expansion. A second reason for the failure to pursue joint technological development lies in the small scale of Chinese vehicle manufacturing. At that time (2000), FAW had an annual output of only 120,000 units. The capital accumulation produced by such a small output volume would make it difficult to maintain a large amount of fiscal input for the research and development of next-generation products. It is also difficult to compete with the new-generation product R&D injected by some transnational corporations, which have a huge capital accumulation as the result of their millions of vehicle production and sales. In the context of economic globalization, only with a production capacity of millions of vehicles can Chinese auto firms be qualified to say 'we can go along with our development road and engage in our self-designed things'. Even with such a capacity, they would still need to hold an open approach and participate in international labor division and cooperation. Otherwise, they would go backwards. In terms of its truck manufacturing volume, FAW already ranked the world's third or fourth, but it still failed to set up independent product development and technological innovations. The reason is attributed to both systematic and technological problems.[11] This is also proved by the merger and expansion crusade made by FAW and SAIC in recent years. Despite its mergers and newly-established enterprises, what have been produced by FAW are basically foreign brands, such as Mazda. The only self-developed brand is Hongqi, but with a common sales performance, while enterprises merged by SAIC, such as SGMW and SGM Huayue, all produce transnational brands.

From the perspective of the role played by the Chinese partner, what contributions have they made, if any? Carlos Ghosn, Chairman and CEO of the Renault-Nissan Alliance, said in 2003 of the role of Chinese partners:

> Chinese partners usually hold 50 percent shares in joint ventures they set up with foreign automobile manufacturers. This is the price Nissan-alike foreign companies must pay in their effort to enter a booming Chinese car market. The reason why foreign car manufacturers provide Chinese partners with products and special technologies is to add value to the established joint ventures. By contrast, their Chinese partners have contributed almost zero to the actual operation and management of joint ventures except for offering some low-cost labor and sales channels.

Such a structure and status quo will not change in a short period, but also are not expected to last long.[12]

From the point of view of those small and medium-sized indigenous carmakers that have established independent product development capabilities, the failure of joint ventures, especially for the Chinese partners, to conduct technological development efforts should be attributed to the form of joint ventures itself. It is their belief that such joint venture arrangements make it impossible for the Chinese side to learn new product exploration or technologies, a result that is decided by the rights distribution pattern between Chinese and foreign partners in joint ventures. First, in typical joint venture arrangements, foreign transnational companies keep a firm control over applied technologies and usually charge technological concession fees, or the Chinese side must pay again for the use of introduced technologies. Second, foreign transnational companies keep control of brands, and joint ventures have to pay for their purchase or privileged utilization. Even if the vehicle model is not designed especially for China's market, joint ventures also have to hand in enough money for their development. Third, foreign transnational companies enjoy pricing power. Foreign partners in joint ventures have a dominant say on the prices of products. Fourth, transnational companies also control the components purchasing network and confirm the qualification of goods suppliers, a power that joint ventures cannot enjoy. In their interviews, Chinese staff of joint ventures usually label the highest-level Chinese management personnel as 'yes-men', which means they enjoy no other rights but expressing their endorsement of the proposals raised by their foreign partners. Also, joint ventures are only a product-manufacturing process, not involving research and development. Take the braking system for example. From the perspective of designing, numerous data and experiments are surely needed to design an ideal braking system. But in joint ventures, transnational companies only offer the finished braking system and try to resolve problems that occur, but decline to disclose how these problems are resolved. This is also the case with the introduction of vehicle models. For example, Volkswagen introduced to China the Polo and Santana, but tries to keep their design a secret. In their joint ventures, Chinese partners usually have no chances for in-depth participation in the development of products, and certainly no chance for study.[13] In short, under the joint-venture arrangement, China-based joint ventures have in most cases become an assembly room of transnational companies or their factory and workshop, and there have been no chances for the Chinese side to engage in innovative activities.

There was no IPR protection in the imitations and innovations by China's car industry from 1949 to 1977. Given that all these activities were conducted in a closed situation, no IPR lawsuits were filed against the country. From 1978 to 2000, China's car industry made its headway through setting up joint ventures with foreign vehicle giants. During this period, China's IPR system gradually came into being, but domestic enterprises were still in a subordinate position under such joint-venture arrangements, given that all technologies and patents were under the strict control of foreign cooperative partners. Thus no IPR protection and rights violation cases have emerged. Since China's entry to the WTO and TRIPS, however, things have changed.

5. PATENT PROTECTION REGIME: TRIPS AND INNOVATION BY CHINESE CAR MANUFACTURERS

The Chinese government has long failed to allow more domestic enterprises to enter the car-making industry or establish joint-venture enterprises in order to ensure scale of economy and avoid repetitive competition. After it joined the WTO and opened its market wider, some domestic enterprises have made their way into the sector by various means. Due to policy restrictions and competition pressure, those enterprises must conduct indigenous innovation and develop their own products.[14] In this section, we introduce in detail the indigenous innovation activities of those domestic enterprises.

The TRIPS that this chapter focuses on and the indigenous innovation activities of Chinese car manufacturers are concentrated in this type of enterprise. Reasons behind this focus include: (1) they are enterprises that are conducting serious indigenous innovation among Chinese car manufacturers; (2) the environment in which they developed and grew rapidly in the more than 10 years after China joined the WTO and TRIPS favors IPR protection, which complies with TRIPS; and (3) those enterprises have experienced fast growth and transition and remain at a crucial stage of growth. Their cases are very typical and are worth studying. We elaborate using examples of four enterprises.

5.1   Chery Automobile Co.

5.1.1   Corporate development
Chery is a local enterprise based in Anhui province in central China. The company entered the car-making sector accidentally. In 1995, the local government officials of Wuhu city, Anhui province, traveled overseas on a tour to draw on the development experiences of European countries. They knew that Ford in the UK was looking for a buyer of its car engine production line. Thanks to its confidence in the domestic automobile market,[15] the local government secretly bought the production line in the

name of importing car components, although it was yet to get approval for its entry into the sector (car manufacturing is not allowed without approval of national authorities). In 1997, the local government set up the Chery company. Construction of Chery factories started on March 18, 1997 and in May 1999, the first engine, CAC480, successfully rolled off the production line. The first Chery car made its debut on December 18 of the same year.

As the domestic sedan market grows rapidly, by March 26, 2010, more than ten years after Chery started its car manufacturing, the company has produced 2 million cars. In 2011, Chery sold 643,000 cars, with 160,200 cars exported to other countries. It was ranked the first among domestic companies with self-owned brands in terms of sales for 11 consecutive years and ranked the first in terms of exports for nine consecutive years.

Currently, Chery has had the capacity to produce 900,000 vehicles and engines, 400,000 sets of manual transmission and 50,000 sets of automatic transmission.

5.1.2 Patent lawsuits

Fulwin was Chery's first product and its engine was a Ford product. It entrusted the design of its shell to a Taiwan company. At the end of 1999, Fulwin debuted on the domestic market and became a great success. In 2003, Chery launched three new models, namely, QQ, Cowin, and Eastar. The three models were very popular on the market and sales were impressive. For example, in 2003, 28,585 QQ, 7,534 Cowin, and 7,581 Eastar were sold.[16] However, the success of the three models also incurred patent lawsuits.

In April 2003, the US-based GM accused Chery of copying its Matiz Spark for its QQ model. GM held that the QQ model, which was made by Chery and was going to be launched at that time, is very similar to the Matiz of GM in terms of design, inside decoration, style and size, and most of their components are even interchangeable. GM asked the court to rule that Chery should make public apology and compensate GM 75 million yuan; Chery should also shoulder the lawyers' fees and investigation costs of 5 million yuan and all its illegal sales of QQ should be confiscated. Meanwhile, GM also applied to the patent re-examination committee of the State Intellectual Property Office to demand that the design patent of Chery QQ should be ruled invalid.

In December 2004, GM filed a lawsuit to the Shanghai No. 2 Intermediate People's Court to accuse Chery of illicit competition, because, as GM said, a photo Chery provided to be published in some websites (such as pcauto. com.cn), to prove to consumers that QQ was a safe model, was actually one of a Matiz.

Moreover, GM held that the brand of the company, Chery, was very similar to Chevy, the nickname of the GE Chevrolet, which it was suspected of copying.[17] GM also filed lawsuits against Chery in Malaysia and Lebanon.

The Chinese court conducted investigations and ruled that regarding GM's accusation that the design of Chery's QQ was copying that of GM's Spark, according to the Chinese laws and proof provided by GM, it could not be concluded that Chery had committed infringement or illicit competition. The court suggested that the two sides solve their dispute by judicial means and through the mediation mechanism.

5.1.3   Technological innovation

Technological development for survival   Chery's entry into the car manufacturing industry did not get the approval of the central government, and so Chery could not pin its hopes on any help from the center. Therefore, the company had to rely on itself to conduct indigenous technological innovation in its car production. As a new company that was just established, how did it launch three independently developed models within just three years? Those new models were developed with the help of its team that originally served the Dongfeng Automobile Co. Ltd, formerly called China Second Auto Works.

At the end of 2000, the Dongfeng Automobile Co. Ltd decided to embark on the road of joint venture and canceled its own technological center. There were more than ten engineers in that center at the time and they had to find new jobs. The new car manufacturer Chery invited them to work for it, and, in July 2001, Chery established a development team composed of more than 20 engineers formerly working for Dongfeng. They had cooperated for a long time and together developed various products. They were all capable and had teamwork spirit, and some of them had training in France. They were the backbone of Dongfeng in car development. Soon after its establishment, the team started to design new models for Chery. They worked painstakingly for more than eight months and worked out the Eastar and QQ. The fast pace of development was a result of the team's determination to prove their capability. They worked overtime and one of them even worked for 48 consecutive hours without sleeping, which was a record for the company. After completing work on the Eastar and QQ, they improved the design of the Fulwin and finished the design of the Cowin. Chery launched its first SUV T-11 in 2004 and also upgraded the design of another A-series car.

It should be noted that the team does not wholly belong to Chery. They cooperated with Chery to form the Jiajing Auto Design Co. Ltd. Two thirds of the company's stake was owned by Chery while the remaining stake was held by the development team. The arrangement was because those engineers from China Second Auto Works were worried that Chery might, like their former employer, abandon its design and development arm, and therefore they wanted to maintain independence. By the end of 2003, there were 60 technical staff in Jiajing and the newcomers were mainly college graduates. Although the company's main task now is to design and develop products for Chery, in theory, it could become a specialized design company.

Pressure of patent lawsuits   After it had developed its first car through purchasing an engine production line and entrusting development, and then launched three new car models through hiring the research and development team from the China Second Auto Works, Chery set up its auto engineering research institute, which covers 70,000 square meters, in 2003 to cater to its demand for new product development. It invested 250 million yuan for the first-phase construction of the institute, which had separate R&D centers for engines, passenger cars, and commercial vehicles, and an automobile experiment center. The engine R&D center was composed of the transmission department and engine department. The passenger car R&D center had separate departments for CAE, car model, chassis, car body, and information. The automobile experiment center had a testing department and metering station, and focused on car body, chassis, engine, transmission, electric and electrical appliance and process material research.

Currently, Chery has established an R&D system that combines the strength of industry players, universities and research institutes; it is centered on its automobile engineering research institute, central research institute, planning and design institute and auto testing and experiment center; and it is also based on the coordinative cooperation between Chery and its key component manufacturers and suppliers, and the alliance it has formed with domestic colleges, universities and research institutes. Chery has more than 6,000 R&D staff in the system and has grasped a series of core vehicle assembly development and key component technologies. The company has made several technological breakthroughs by indigenous innovation, including TGDI (turbo gasoline direct injection), DVVT (dual variable valve timing), CVT (continuously variable transmission) and new energy technologies, all of which are leading technologies on the domestic market and have led to the overall technological upgrading of Chery products. The company also attaches great importance to mentality and managerial innovation to continually improve the corporate governance regime and boost corporate innovation, and hires and trains a large number of technical and managerial professionals.

'Indigenous innovation' is the core of Chery's development strategy and also the source of the driving force for its exceptional high-quality development. It has made significant inputs and efforts to improve R&D because, on the one hand, it is a requirement of survival and on the other hand, it is a lesson from the patent lawsuits. In the patent lawsuit with GM, one of the important reasons for Chery to win the case was that the company had applied for 24 patents – GM held that Chery only applied for 12 patents – to protect the IPR of the QQ model even before it was formally launched. After the lawsuit, Chery accelerated its application for patents and has become the No. 1 in terms of the number of patents on the domestic market. By January 20, 2012, it had applied for 5,811 patents – the most among domestic automakers – among which 1,952 were invention patents, 1,898 utility model patents and 1,961 design patents.

Direct impact of TRIPS   From the perspective of Chery, the TRIPS clauses have had a limited impact on the company's innovation activities and many people do not even know the clauses and the changes brought by China's accession into the WTO. However, seen from the perspective of GM, the impact is obvious. If not for the WTO membership or the signing of TRIPS, the possibility that GM could initiate such patent lawsuits is slim.

5.1.4   Challenges ahead

Chery's development used to be based on the following strategies. First, it develops and launches as many products as possible; second, it makes utmost efforts to increase sales – it attaches importance to channel expansion instead of brand building.

The strategy has, on the one hand, led to the rapid expansion of corporate scale, and, on the other hand, also brought various problems and challenges. For example, its internal product development has been fettered by too many product models and there has been repetitive competition among different model development teams; they lack effective integration; and the company has not paid enough attention to details. Its development procedures are not sound and standardized enough and as a result of inadequate system integration, Chery has failed to bring out the advantage of its strength as a whole. Although it attaches importance to the launch of more car models, Chery has yet to establish a module-based product development and manufacturer structure, and it also needs to set up a supplier regime, especially a hierarchical supplier regime. Moreover, Chery's efforts to expand scale and market share have resulted in inadequate internal corporate management and it is yet to reach the level of an internationally advanced enterprise. Meanwhile, its profit margin has been low.

In 2011, as domestic macroeconomic regulation strengthened and the domestic market changed (with consumers tending to purchase high-end products and the impact of branding becoming more significant), Chery's development reached the key stage of transformation and upgrading. Chery's transformation has the following characteristics. First, regarding technological development, it has moved from reverse development to forward development. Second, its production system and management have become more normalized and standardized. Third, the whole company has evolved from a player trying to catch up with its competitors to a mature and stable industry player or even a leader.

Obviously, Chery is facing many difficulties in such a transition. Take Chery's R&D system that has moved from reverse engineering to 'forward development'.[18] When it conducted reverse development, it needed to churn out targeted products and components through imitation and did not need to know why. However, in the forward development, it needs to know all the technical qualifications and conduct testing and experiments. Meanwhile, the procedures of forward development are very strict, which is very different from those of reverse development. Xie Baoxin, vice-president of Chery's automotive engineering institute, was well aware of such difference. He explained it using the example of an English-language automobile R&D procedure document. He said that some years ago, few of the heads of Chery's R&D department could understand the document; later, after some years of study, many people have grasped the whole automobile development procedure. In the new development phase, Chen Anning, new head of Chery's R&D department, hoped to change some traditional ways of conducting R&D and establish a more standardized R&D regime so that Chery can depend on the strength of the whole system to produce high-quality cars. He found that Chery has done a good job in making single auto parts, such as engines, transmissions and chassis. His task is to find a way to foster the overall and in-depth system integration capabilities of Chery, so that the R&D decision of every car model can be more rational, thus bringing the company more returns: in his words, '(We have) many gold grains, and how can we melt them into a gold bar?'

To sum up, in the past more than ten years, Chery has made a successful transition from imitation-based expansion to innovation-supported growth. The process of such a transformation can be divided into the following steps.

1. Entrusted development – entrusting the development of its own models to foreign professional R&D companies and allowing a small number of its own engineers to participate in the development to

foster its own R&D team. Its car model development capabilities thus were gradually established after entrusted development of two or three models.

2. Breakthrough in making of core components, such as those in the design and development of engines, transmissions and chassis.
3. System integration. Car manufacturing is a system integration process and needs the coordination and integration of all sub-systems. 'Now Chery has realized an overall product development mode from core technological innovation breakthrough to system integration-based innovation,' said Chen Anning, deputy general manager of Chery. He said Chery has attached greater importance to details in product design and strengthened its capabilities of making various product assemblies match each other so as to achieve 'seamless interface' and balanced development of products.
4. Brand and sales network construction. Chery is advancing in that direction in its new strategic transition.

As its corporate scale expands and innovation capabilities grow, Chery has had increased demand for IPR protection. For example, when it needs to rely on brand influence for further development, it certainly needs to protect its brand; similarly, when it needs to rely on high-quality products for its development, then its demand for IPR protection also rises accordingly. Therefore, after achieving such a transition, Chery, like other multinational carmakers, will become a company that sincerely supports and demands IPR protection and supports TRIPS.

5.2   Zhejiang Geely Holding Group Co.

A car is but a sofa with four wheels and an iron shell on it. (Li Shufu, chairman of Geely)

5.2.1   Corporate development

Geely is a legendary company and a Chinese private car manufacturer in the real sense. It was launched in 1986 and started with production of refrigerator components. In 1994, it entered the motorcycle manufacturing industry and went on to enter the passenger car industry in 1997. However, due to government regulation, it was not until 2001 that the company was granted the license for car manufacturing. In the short period of just more than ten years after it entered the sector, Geely has expanded rapidly to grow into one of China's largest passenger car manufacturers. In 2009, it successfully purchased Volvo, a world-renowned automobile company. In 2011, Geely sold 421,385 cars.

5.2.2 Patent-related lawsuits

In August 2003, Japan's Toyota held that the Merrie brand of Geely was similar to the Toyota brand and that it had used the word 'Toyota' in its marketing activities, which should be seen as illicit competition. Therefore, it formally sued Geely and demanded compensation worth 14.07 million yuan. This was called 'China's No. 1 Case' regarding IPR in the car industry. In November 2003, the Beijing No. 2 Intermediate People's Court ruled against Toyota and overruled all Toyota's demands. Geely won the case.

After the ruling, commentators held that although it did not win the case, Toyota had gained its ends, because it had made it clear to the public through the case, which was widely reported by various media outlets, that Geely has nothing to do with Toyota. In this way, it thwarted the attempt of Geely to rely on its links with Toyota to market and improve its own brand. Meanwhile, it was also a warning to Geely that patent and design infringement was not allowable and that Geely could pay a price for that.

5.2.3 Technological innovation

In 2001, when Geely first entered the passenger car industry, China was poised to join the WTO. Therefore, Geely grew in a patent system that is largely in line with TRIP.[19] Moreover, among the Chinese carmakers that conduct indigenous innovation, Geely has faced the most severe and challenging environment. First, Geely is supported mainly by the single business of passenger car manufacturing and receives little support from other businesses. Second, it is not a central government-supervised or local government-supervised State enterprise, and therefore it cannot get support from the government; it even has to face various government restrictions. Third, private enterprises cannot have any access to preferential policies that are devised for joint ventures.[20] How has such an enterprise risen within a short period of time?

First, such an unfavorable environment has pushed Geely to the wall and it would not survive and expand without innovation. It is such an environment that has forced Geely to figure out various methods to conduct innovation from its beginning. Such efforts helped Geely to dispel the myths around joint ventures and multinationals conducting innovation. For example, it used to be believed that domestic enterprises could not conduct innovation and were incapable of carrying out such innovation activities. Another myth that has been disproved is that only after a car manufacturer has made 3–5 million cars can it be qualified and able to conduct innovation. The story of Geely and other private enterprises proves that miracles can happen so long as one dares to break the ice.

Second, how has Geely conducted innovation? Li Shufu, chairman of Geely, summed up the company's development strategy as follows:

> [Geely] has started with the simplest technology, the training of qualified professionals, and the making of components, with R&D and sales as the pillars spearheading corporate development; and it has made efforts to gain advantage in making economical cars and occupying the low-end market before entering the mid-end market; and after succeeding in the domestic market, it has entered the international market to rapidly accumulate its R&D capabilities and inputs to form core competitiveness continually and export two thirds of its production to make Geely a world-known brand.[21]

Three main points stand out:

1. Self-design of earliest car models. Geely entered the passenger car industry through acquiring a Sichuan firm producing mini-cars. The acquisition brought the earliest car manufacturing resources and personnel source for Geely. Through imitating the Xiali model of China First Auto Works, Geely designed its own car model, which was inexpensive and close to the general level of carmaking at that time in terms of design and technology. Many links of the production were even semi-mechanized.
2. Encouraging participation of more personnel to form its own component supply system. When he entered the car-making industry, Li Shufu had little more than 100 million yuan as the initial funding. He altogether invested 400 or 500 million yuan at most after he financed from his brothers. He adopted the method of de facto private financing to engage more investors to realize his 'car-making dream'. He persuaded some business owners and friends to invest together and form an alliance, in which he focused on car manufacturing while others invested in workshops to make components for Geely.
3. Core component R&D and breakthroughs. The lawsuit initiated by Toyota against Geely affected the supply of engines for Geely, making the company more aware of the impact of having to rely on external sources of engine supply. Moreover, since the core components had to come from external sources, especially from multinationals like Toyota, prices were very high, generally two or three times the cost of self-production and supply. Therefore, Geely was determined to conduct indigenous development of core components to break through the bottleneck of core technologies. By 2006, the huge investment in the R&D of core components had helped Geely successfully grasp the technology of making CCVT engines and the blow-out

monitoring and brake system, and gradually establish its own core component system. In March 2009, Geely successfully purchased Australia's DSI, the world's second largest transmission manufacturer, which strengthened Geely's capabilities in R&D and production of transmissions. Meanwhile, Geely has managed to improve its R&D capabilities through attracting high-calibre professionals from both domestic and overseas firms. In 2004, it invited Shim Bong Sup, then vice-president of Korean carmaker Daewoo in charge of R&D, to join Geely and appointed him as Geely's vice-president to take charge of corporate R&D and its research institute. After more than ten years of efforts, Geely has essentially broken through all technological bottlenecks and gradually entered the phase of indigenous development. The car models produced by Geely have received 4-star and 5-star Euro NCAP ratings and rank among the best cars in terms of safety.

By the end of 2011, Geely owned 3,837 patents, among which 387 were invention patents, 2,927 utility model patents and 523 design patents. In terms of the number of invention patents held, it is ranked No. 2 among domestic carmakers after Chery.

5.2.4 Challenges ahead

Like other domestic carmakers, Geely is gradually stepping toward a standardized modern enterprise. In such transition, the fierce direct competition with multinationals in the domestic middle- to high-end market will become a challenge for Geely. There are many uncertainties and it is unknown whether Geely will succeed.

However, Geely has shown some positive signs in that respect. First, Geely has developed popular mid- and high-end car models, such as Emgrand EC7 and EC8. Second, the acquisition of Volvo could improve its brand image and add to its technological capabilities and production experiences in the manufacturing of high-end car models. It is justifiable to believe that Geely can revitalize itself through renewed efforts.

5.3 Great Wall Motor Company Limited

5.3.1 Corporate development

The Great Wall Motor Company Limited is a private enterprise from Baoding city, Hebei province. It has grown out of a township enterprise and first produced coaches and trucks before concentrating on SUV and pickup production. Since 2006, it has started to produce passenger cars. It was listed on the Hong Kong Stock Exchange in 2003.

By 2011, Great Wall Motor had 30 holding subsidiaries with more than 42,000 employees. Its product line includes the Haval SUV, Voleex sedan and Wingle pickup series and it is capable of satisfying its own demand for core components, such as engines and transmissions.

In 2011, Great Wall Motor sold a total of 486,811 vehicles, up 22.5 percent year-on-year. Among the vehicles sold, 164,379 were Haval SUVs, 200,696 were Voleex sedans and 121,176 were Wingle pickups. The three types of exports all increased to a varied degree. It exported 83,117 vehicles in the same year, up by 50 percent year-on-year.

5.3.2   Patent lawsuits

The development of Great Wall Motor has been greatly influenced by State-owned ZX Auto, which is in the same city and is one of the Chinese forerunners in making SUVs and pickups. In 1996, ZX Auto led its domestic counterparts to realize large-scale exports. In a sense, Great Wall Motor was copying the development model of ZX Auto. Without the development and corporate accumulation of ZX Auto, Great Wall Motor might have not been in existence, since initially its technical, R&D and sales staff all came from ZX Auto. After they came to Great Wall Motor, they simply copied the practice of ZX Auto. At that time, the protection of patents and IPR was very weak and the Great Wall Motor has thus gradually grown up.

However, in the sedan manufacturing sector, Great Wall Motor has been hit by patent lawsuits filed by multinationals against its alleged copying of other companies' models. On November 28, 2003, when Great Wall Motor was listed in Hong Kong, the *Financial Times* reported that Nissan was poised to sue the company, alleging that the front face of Great Wall Motor's Sing SUV was 'exactly the same'[22] as Nissan's Paladin model. Great Wall Motor lost the case.

In April and July 2007, Italy's Fiat sued Great Wall Motor in Torino, Italy and China's Shijiazhuang city, Hebei province, accusing it of copying Fiat's Panda in making its Peri model, Great Wall Motor's first sedan model. In April of the same year, Toyota also sued Great Wall Motor, alleging that the latter's Florid model was similar to the design of Toyota's Yaris. Great Wall Motor won those patent lawsuits.

However, after going through the patent lawsuits with multinationals, Great Wall Motor has realized the importance of IPR and become serious in its model design. Just as Mr Li Shuli, Great Wall Motor's patent affairs chief, said: 'Those companies that have paid a real price in intellectual property right lawsuits and have been involved in related affairs with multinationals would all realize the importance of intellectual property right.'

5.3.3   Innovation

Great Wall Motor has a 5,000-member R&D team and has hired more than 500 experts and managerial professionals across all related fields in China and abroad. Meanwhile, it has cooperated extensively and closely with universities, famous design companies and engineering companies in China and abroad. However, in reality, the majority of its backbone R&D staff is self-trained R&D professionals. Many of them do not have a high educational level but have rich experiences in production and operation since they have been growing together with Great Wall Motor's expansion in the past years. The professionals that Great Wall Motor has paid a high price to hire from abroad, the special technical experts and the so-called 'foreign brains' are yet to be the backbone of the company's R&D team.[23] Generally speaking, the company's R&D activities are still at the stage of experience-based research, and a standardized and module-based R&D regime is being constructed.

With its success in the market, Great Wall Motor has in recent years made huge investment in R&D and established a sound and comprehensive auto testing, trial production, modeling and CAE regime. It has established a safety, engine, emission and vehicle assembly NVH laboratory and an auto grinding tool center, thus largely forming a quite comprehensive auto R&D regime. Thus Great Wall Motor has laid a solid material foundation for its science and technology-based innovation.

The next task of the company is to gradually integrate its internal models and resources together. Driven by the traditional strategy that is market-oriented and focuses on continual launch of new models, the company's different production lines and business divisions are independent from each other and even compete with each other. As the number of product lines increases, especially following the launch of the sedan project, there have been more and more types of products. Therefore, integration of internal resources and establishment of a module-based R&D system and production system has become the key to its next-step development. Currently, the company hopes to establish a general platform for making SUV, pickup and sedan models and carry out module-based design and production to improve its overall corporate competitiveness.

By January 18, 2012, Great Wall Motor owned 792 patents, with 64 of them being invention patents, 269 utility model patents and 459 design patents. Although the company started applying for design patents from 1999, on the whole most of its patents were obtained after 2003, or even after 2006.

5.3.4   Challenges ahead

Great Wall Motor is facing two transitional challenges: transition from SUV and pickup production to sedan production, and transition from reverse imitation to forward innovation.

First, as it moves from the SUV and pickup market to the sedan market, the market competition landscape will be very different. How can it ensure its success?

The success of Great Wall Motor is mainly achieved on the SUV and pickup market. Comparatively, the market for SUV and pickup models is a non-mainstream section that has been ignored by most domestic car manufacturers. The competition in this section of the market is very different from that in the sedan market.

Meanwhile, the recent changes in the domestic market[24] have only a limited impact on Great Wall Motor; this is only accidental and will not last long. Its advantage in making SUV and pickup models will not ensure its success in the sedan market. It is a great challenge for Great Wall Motor to integrate research and development of those models.

Second, how can Great Wall Motor ensure its success in making the transition from a 'guerilla' team to a 'regular army'?

In terms of R&D, the company is facing the challenge of moving from experience-based development to normal science and technology-based development. It needs support from the company's market performance, i.e., in the coming period of time, how much can it invest in R&D activities? How can it ensure the new models it develops are popular in the market? Maybe a better choice is to get cautious about research and launch of new models and even make models that are similar to those popular multinational models, while strengthening quality control to produce high-quality, low-price new models. Another choice is to get listed on the domestic stock market to pool funding for transition and R&D; however, this is only a way to delay solving existing problems for a while and the ultimate solution lies in the first choice. In that process, Great Wall Motor needs to gradually build up its own brand advantage and establish comprehensive and controllable product and supply and sales systems with a cutting edge, so that it can make a transition toward a successful car manufacturer.

5.4   BYD

A car, in reality, is but a heap of iron and steel! No need to feel frightened by car manufacturing; if you have faith, you'll win and hesitation will bring you nothing but lost opportunities. (Wang Chuanfu, chairman, BYD)

5.4.1 Corporate development

BYD is located in Shenzhen and was launched in 1995. Its business activities mainly cover IT, car manufacturing and new energy. In the field of IT, BYD is the world's largest rechargeable battery producer and the world's largest supplier of nickel and cadmium batteries and cellular lithium batteries. Meanwhile, it is also the world's largest supplier of cellphone keypads and cases. In the field of car manufacturing, BYD has rapidly grown into one of the most innovative Chinese car manufacturers with indigenous brand, and with its unique technologies has become a global leader in the electricity-driven car market. In the field of new energy, BYD has successfully launched such 'green products' as a solar energy power station, energy storage power station, electric vehicle, and LED products. It aims at technological innovation and exploration in the new energy field.

After more than ten years of development, BYD had about 200,000 staff by the end of 2010, compared with barely more than 20 staff in 1995, when the company was started. It has set up 11 industrial parks in Guangdong, Beijing, Shaanxi, Shanghai and Hunan's Changsha, and has subsidiaries or offices in the US, Europe, Japan, South Korea, India, China's Taiwan and Hong Kong.

It was in 2003 that BYD entered the car industry through acquiring a car manufacturer in Xi'an, central China's Shaanxi province. On the basis of adopting the car models and technologies of the acquired company, BYD set up an auto engineering research institute in Shanghai the first year it entered the sedan industry. It developed a series of car models, including Flayer, BYD F3, F3R, F0, F6, G3, G3R, G6, S3, S6, S8, L3, M6 and DM. Only seven years after its inauguration, BYD sold 521,232 cars in 2010.

5.4.2 Patent lawsuits

BYD had faced the challenge of two international patent lawsuits in the IT field before it entered China's sedan industry. In September 2002, Japan-based Sanyo sued BYD in San Diego, USA, over patent infringement. Comparative analysis found that the technologies BYD used to make its Li-ion battery were different from Sanyo technologies, and in 2005 the two sides settled the dispute in favor of BYD.

In July 2003, Japan-based Sony sued BYD in Tokyo over patent infringement, accusing BYD of infringing upon two of its patents in making Li-ion rechargeable batteries, namely No. 2646657 and No. 2701347. After continuous efforts, BYD successfully invalidated the two patents, ultimately forcing Sony to withdraw its appeal, and won the case. The two cases in which Japanese companies sued BYD over patent infringement in overseas courts have greatly enhanced BYD's awareness of IPR and it has since strengthened its work in that respect. For example, it has set up an IPR department, devised a corporate IPR strategy, set up an implementation system, become more conscious of accumulating IPR, especially overseas distribution of IPR, and strengthened training of its professionals to help them grasp IPR expertise.

BYD's IPR strategy is a good example. After the two patent lawsuits, BYD has taken measures to continually accumulate relevant experience and expertise, make use of IPR in a flexible manner, make rational distribution of IPR, and effectively prevent IPR infringement, so as to implement its IPR strategy, which is targeted at safeguarding corporate operation and improving its edge in market competition. Continual accumulation of relevant experiences and expertise refers to sustained input to gradually accumulate IPR and enhance the company's IPR capabilities. Rational distribution refers to distribution of more IPR resources in key regions to assist the company's key projects. Effective prevention of IPR infringement refers to, on the one hand, creation of a harmonious business environment through swaps of accumulated patents, and, on the other hand, circumvention or lowering of patent risks through carrying out patent investigation in the process of R&D. Flexible use of IPR refers to making money or containing rivals through licensing of some of its patents to improve core corporate competitiveness.

In terms of corporate structure, BYD has an IPR and legal affairs department, under which there is an IPR section with more than 50 full-time staff. There are also more than 80 people dealing with patent-related affairs in the patent groups of R&D departments. The company has also established an internal patent database, science and technology periodical database, and book database, and researchers can search the patent database for patent-related literary information.

In latter years BYD has not been sued by any other company in the field of sedan manufacturing. Some of its models have been closely monitored by multinational carmakers, but there have not been any formal lawsuits against it.[25]

5.4.3   Technological innovation

As a global technology-intensive manufacturer, BYD has made huge investment in R&D. In terms of IT component industry cluster, the company established its central research institute in Shenzhen to host a large number of high-caliber professionals and conduct basic research and technological innovation in such fields as battery technology, surface technology and liquid crystal technology. In 2003, when it entered the car industry, it established its auto research and development center in

Shanghai, where more than 3,000 auto professionals, divided into more than 20 project task forces, were engaged in the R&D of BYD vehicle assembly, engines, auto electronics, safety devices and electric cars. In 2004, BYD established its auto-testing center in Shanghai for car crash tests, road tests, chassis tests and comprehensive environment tests.

By 2011, BYD had 7,156 patents, among which 2,880 were invention patents, 3,534 utility model patents, and 733 outer design patents. Since 2003, BYD has had 758 patents concerning the car industry, among which 286 are invention patents, 389 utility model patents and 83 design patents.

5.4.4   Challenges ahead

After some years of rapid expansion, in 2011 BYD sold a total of 44,8500 cars, down by 13.95 percent compared with 2010 – the sharpest decline among all domestic car manufacturers, thanks to changes in the domestic car market. The year 2011 was one in which Chinese car manufacturers faced major challenges. After some years of expansion, the growth of China's domestic car market had been normalized and slowed down. In such a market environment, competition based on branding and product quality will become more intensified. Compared with multinationals and their subsidiaries in China, domestic companies still lag behind in that respect. Therefore, those companies all face the challenge of corporate transition.

The adjustment of BYD seems to have begun from 2010, when it started to gradually move from the strategy of market scale and share expansion to a performance-oriented strategy that focuses on quality, branding and profits. It is also making a transition from imitation-based innovation to forward indigenous innovation and from a catch-up and imitation strategy to an indigenous R&D and self-improvement leadership strategy.

5.5   Patent Protection and Innovation Activities of Domestic Enterprises

An enterprise needs to go through complete development processes of developing at least two independent models to become mature in its fostering of automobile development capabilities. Internationally, it takes about 24–28 months to develop an independent car model.[26] Therefore, a domestic enterprise needs at least four to five years to reach maturity in independent product design and development.

The innovation activities of Chinese car enterprises have been started largely from imitation. Such imitation has been realized either through cooperation with specialized international auto design companies, such as entrusted development, or entirely through internal imitation within the enterprise. Why do domestic enterprises not conduct independent development? Why do they stick to entrusted development and imita-tion? The main reason is limited capability and strength, i.e., they are not capable of conducting independent product design and financially they are not strong enough to support such development. Meanwhile, like development of all products, the independent development of car models is very risky. Those newcomers that don't have much capital, technologi-cal strength or indigenous equipment, cannot possibly develop a popular car model within a short period of time. It takes a specialized automobile enterprise 18 months simply to prepare the mold in making a new car. If an enterprise started with independent development, then it would prob-ably fail. Many enterprises have had such experience of failure at their initial stage of development. If they fail two or three times, then all their inputs may be lost. As time goes by and their capital runs out, their confi-dence sags and the enterprise may go bankrupt. Therefore, a better option is to copy the already popular models made by multinationals and put them on sale at lower prices, to grab market share before they gradually develop their own independent models.

Is there development space in China's car industry for domestic enter-prises? In reality, there used to be opportunities for them. When those enterprises first entered the car industry (around the time China joined the WTO and TRIPS, or around 2000), the country's low-end car market was untapped, which provided a fertile ground for learning and imitation. Then from mid-2007, the growth of China's low-end car market slowed down and those enterprises with indigenous brands were facing the chal-lenge of corporate transition. However, the eruption of the global finan-cial crisis provided new opportunities. On the one hand, the government stimulus measures led to the explosion of sales of cars with small engines and low- and mid-end cars, which lasted for two years until 2011. On the other hand, some famous multinational carmakers were bogged down in the financial crisis, which provided the Chinese enterprises with an oppor-tunity to acquire technologies, brands and equipment that they dearly needed. After more than ten years of accumulation and development, those enterprises have gradually acquired the capabilities to enter the mid-and high-end market, which is the challenge they are facing. Among them, Geely was the first to make the transition, starting in 2007. Chery started the process in 2011.

In the process of those domestic enterprises' growth, the protection of IPR has indeed had a great impact on their innovation activities, which are manifest in the following aspects. First, at the stage of imitation, TRIPS and the IPR protection system make it possible for the multina-tional companies to supervise and sue domestic enterprises for alleged patent infringement. Second, patent lawsuits by multinationals also force domestic enterprises to realize the importance of IPR and to form IPR strategies to circumvent such lawsuits, while accumulating their own IPR. Last but not least, as they are more capable of conducting indigenous innovation, the accumulation and protection of IPR have gradually become increasingly important parts of their corporate strategy and therefore they have taken initiatives to voluntarily accumulate and protect IPR.

6.   CONCLUSION: IPR PROTECTION AND INNOVATION

A country's innovation activities are mainly subject to the impact of its economic development level and national innovation regime (Nelson, 1993, 2008; Odagiri et al., 2010; Rodrigo and Sutz, 2000; Malerba, 2002; Fagerberg and Srholec, 2008). The higher its economic development level, the more active its innovation activities are, and vice versa. In the same vein, given the economic development level, the more effective its national innovation regime is, the more its innovation activities. The IPR protection policies and systems, as parts of a country's innovation regime, also have important impacts on innovation activities.

In the more than 60 years after the founding of the republic, China's economy and innovation activities have gone through three major development phases. During the 1949–76 period, when it adopted a very closed planned economy system, China established a diverse industry and national economy system through large-scale technological introduction and imitation. During that period, China did not have property rights or an IPR protection system. In the 1977–2005 period, when it opened up its economy to the outside world, China gradually established a complete IPR protection system in line with general international practice through technological introduction and innovation activities as well as international exchanges. It achieved rapid development in innovation during that period. Since 2006, China has entered the rank of innovation-oriented countries. The whole IPR protection system has been undergoing a gradual transition to encouragement and support for innovation. In 2011, in terms of the number of PCT patents, China has become a major innovation-oriented nation after the US, Japan and Germany.

Case studies of China's car industry further testify to the previous conclusions at the national level.

First, the improvement in the legal and institutional framework of IPR protection provides legal tools and means for the multinationals to safeguard their own IPR. This is why, in the early years of reform and opening-up, the US forced China to join various IPR protection protocols, revise its IPR laws and improve enforcement of them. Meanwhile, case studies of China's car industry also clearly indicate that as the protection of IPR is strengthened, the multinationals are provided with better means to protect their patents. Possibly for this reason, the developed countries, especially the US and its multinationals, strongly advocate IPR across the world.

Second, as a country's economy develops and its production and corporate strength reach certain levels, the improvement in the legal and institutional framework also provides incentives for development of local industries and enterprises. Initially, the local companies and industries learn, accumulate and make use of IPR as means to protect themselves from lawsuits initiated by multinationals. Later, as their accumulation of IPR increases, more and more local enterprises and industries will make use of the legal and institutional framework to gain a competitive edge or even lead the development of the whole industry.

Case studies of China's domestic carmakers indicate that the patent protection system in line with TRIPS, and the lessons they have learned from patent-related lawsuits initiated by multinationals against them, have also forced them to abide by relevant rules. Such an environment, plus the cooperation and entrance restrictions from domestic policies, further strengthen indigenous innovation activities. This is a very unique aspect of the Chinese car industry.

Third, this chapter proves the following hypotheses:

Hypothesis A: The strengthening of the IPR protection system makes it easier for multinationals to carry out rights-protection activities in a bolder manner.

Domestic enterprises mentioned in this article have all been sued by multinationals over alleged patent infringement.

Hypothesis B: The patent lawsuits initiated by multinationals force domestic enterprises to make efforts to protect IPR and conduct technological innovation.

This has been verified by the cases of several carmakers.

Hypothesis C: The environment and conditions faced by domestic enterprises force them to carry out product and technological innovation.

This has been directly verified by cases of researched enterprises. In an interview, the head of a domestic carmaker made it clear that if it is possible, the company will form a joint venture with foreign carmakers. What is behind his comment is that without policy limits and restrictions, domestic carmakers would not have been conducting technological innovation and development so painstakingly.

A fourth hypothesis remains unproven:

Hypothesis D: The more strengthened is the protection of IPR, the more corporate innovation activities there will be.

This is not clearly supported by the interviewed enterprises.

To sum up, this chapter shows that innovation activities of a country or enterprise are mainly determined by the local economic environment. Whether there is a legal and institutional framework of IPR protection has little to do with whether a country or enterprise would carry out innovation activities. Meanwhile, the degree of IPR protection cannot directly determine the quantity of innovation activities by a country or enterprise. In many cases, protection of IPR and patent applications are but a means to obtain information, showcase competitiveness, deter competition and maintain competitive edge. The argument that strong patent protection will definitely push more innovation is yet to receive strong support from this study.

NOTES

1. The major concern of the study is only patent protection, rather than copyright, trademark, geographic indication, industrial design, and integrated circuit.
2. The author thanks Professor Richard Nelson and Sunil Mani for their suggestion for this point.
3. Such cooperation, which is different from the establishment of joint ventures, is beneficial for the introducing party to gradually take the initiative in their manufacturing and operation process, and at the same time, help them gain the full IPR over the two car models. Therefore, Xiali cars, unlike the Santana or VW Jetta cars that use their Western names, use the Chinese pinyin "Xiali".
4. 100,000-unit output was believed to be the lowest scale of car production.
5. The exchange rate of the yuan was 8.3:1 against the US dollar.
6. The Ford Automobile Corporation has also taken a similar strategy. It began joint ventures with Chongqing Changan Automobile Company in 2001, with an investment of less than $100 million.
7. This proportion does not take into consideration the influences brought about by imported vehicles on the country's auto market and is only based upon the whole vehicles sales volumes by domestic automobile factories. Obviously, Volkswagen's market shares in China's auto market in 2002 were overestimated.
8. *The Economic Operations of China's Auto Sector in 2002 and its Prospect Analysis in 2003*, p. 8, China Association of Automobile Manufacture, January 2003.
9. After China's entry into the WTO, the policies extended to the country's auto industry have been mainly as follows: (1) it should not be a sole investment by foreign enterprises and their shares are at most 50 percent; (2) a foreign automobile industry can set up only two joint ventures at most.
10. According to Zhu Yanfeng, then CEO of FAW, interviewed by Cheng Yuan for the

Economic Daily in May 2000; and Zhu's comments in the Dialogue program of CCTV on February 15, 2004. In the second interview, he held that five million units of sales should be the starting point for indigenous development by domestic enterprises.

11.   As a matter of fact, Miao Yu, president of the Second Automotive Industry Corporation, and Hu Yuanmao, president of Shanghai Automotive Industry Group, also held a similar stance and viewpoint ('Speeding up cultivating and developing self-pioneered brand', *Economic Daily*, February 9, 2004).

12.   Carlos Ghosn, chairman and CEO of Nissan, expressed such a viewpoint at a Tokyo auto show in October 2003.

13.   On the contrary, if local enterprises conduct cooperation with specialized transnational corporations, then they can participate in the full process of product development and learn product development technologies. Through such joint development, local enterprises can learn 'why do it this way' as well as 'how to do it'.

14.   During the interviews, many corporate heads said frankly that they were, are and will be willing and prepared to establish joint ventures if they can; however, they also made it clear that if they have to abandon their own brands and indigenous product development, then such cooperation would be absolutely unacceptable for them.

15.   In the 1992–93 period, a small local vehicle manufacturer made several hundred hand-made cars and produced output worth more than 100 million yuan. It shows that the local car market can be very profitable, which has made local government determined to enter the sector.

16.   *China Automobile Industry Yearbook 2004*, p. 442.

17.   GM sent a lawyer's letter to US-based VVLLC, a Chery dealer, in which it said that the brandname Chery was close to Chevrolet's nickname Chevy, and GM opposed Chery's attempt to use it to conduct such commercial activities as registration, sales, and dealership, among others.

18.   In this chapter, the author uses this term to mean the normal type of R&D, comparing with that of reverse engineering. For R&D as forward development, firms or researchers must have their own design and architecture of a new product or process, rather than simply copy or imitate those of others.

19.   It was at the end of 2001 that Geely got the license for making cars, which was near November 11, 2001, when China formally joined the WTO. It has been mentioned previously that China started updating and adjusting its patent system to comply with TRIPS before it joined the WTO in 2001.

20.   Jin Luzhong, former head of the Technical Cadre Bureau at the State Science and Technology Commission, once said: 'As a private enterprise, Geely has had little support from the government, nor has it had the access to the various preferential policies for joint ventures. It took Geely three years to simply apply for the license to make cars; its profit margin is low, but it has to pay a 33% value added tax and invests 300–400 million yuan annually in technological R&D.'

21.   Memoir of the seminar on China's domestic car industry development roadmap by the Ministry of Science and Technology on October 26, 2005; from Sina.com.cn: http://finance.sina.com.cn/hy/20061230/19053211430.shtml.

22.   Nissan later said that the model was not Paladin, but Frontier, a pickup model produced in North America.

23.   It is in line with our observations, i.e., the R&D activities of many Chinese enterprises are still at the stage of experience accumulation and are yet to move to the stage based on science and technology development.

24.   In 2011, the domestic low- and mid-end car market was very inactive while the high-end market was brisk. The domestic carmakers mainly concentrated on the low-end market and therefore they were hit severely. Such a change, however, was not very apparent on the SUV and pickup market.

25.   For example, the popular BYD model F3 is a close imitation of Toyota Corolla, but Toyota cannot sue BYD because BYD has managed to circumvent the patented technologies while adopting those non-patented technologies (Bai Yong, 2010).

26. Estimate by a Hafei Motor engineer; the estimation of Chongqing Changan Group is 33 months while that of FAW is 42 months.

REFERENCES

Bai Yong (2010), 'How far will BYD fare – reshuffling list: transition from a follower to a leader', *Business*, **XII**, 84–8.

China Ministry of Science and Technology (2009), *China Science and Technology Development Report 2008*, http://www.most.gov.cn/ndbg/2008ndbg/ (in Chinese).

China Ministry of Science and Technology (2010), *China Science and Technology Development Report 2009*, http://www.most.gov.cn/ndbg/2009ndbg/(in Chinese).

Fagerberg, J. and M. Srholec (2008), 'National innovation systems, capabilities and economic development', *Research Policy*, **37** (9), 1417–35.

Lan Xue and Zheng Liang (2010), 'Relationships between IPR and technology catch-up: some evidence from China', in H. Odagiri, A. Goto, A. Sunami and R. Nelson (eds), *Intellectual Property Rights and Catch-up: An International Comparative Study*, Oxford, UK: Oxford University Press.

Li Shunde (2000), 'TRIPS and China's IPR legal sysem', *Theory and Exploration*, **VII**, 16–22 (in Chinese).

Liu, Feng-Chao, Denis Fred Simon, Yu-Tao Sun and Cong Cao (2011), 'China's innovation policies: evolution, institutional structure, and trajectory', *Research Policy*, **40** (7), 917–31.

Luo, Yuzhong and Xiuting Yuan (2000), 'WTO, IPR and development and improvement of China's IPR legal system', *Qianxian*, **XI**, 30–34 (in Chinese).

Malerba, F. (2002), 'Sectoral systems of innovation and production', *Research Policy*, **31** (2), 247–64.

Odagiri, H., Goto, A., Sunami, A. and R. Nelson (eds) (2010), *Intellectual Property Rights, Development, and Catch-up: An International Comparative Study*, Oxford, UK: Oxford University Press.

Nelson, Richard R. (ed.) (1993), *National Innovation Systems: A Comparative Analysis*, Oxford: Oxford University Press.

Nelson, Richard R. (2008), 'What enables rapid economic progress: what are the needed institutions?', *Research Policy*, **37** (1), 1–11.

OECD (2005), *Governance in China*, Paris: OECD.

OECD (2008), *OECD Reviews of Innovation Policy: China*, Paris: OECD.

Rodrigo, A. and J. Sutz (2000), 'Looking at national systems of innovation from the south', *Industry & Innovation*, **7** (1), 55–75.

Xibao Li (2012), 'Behind the recent surge of Chinese patenting: an institutional view', *Research Policy*, **41**, 236–49.

Yang Guohua (1998), 'Impact and lessons of Sino–US IPR negotiations', *International Economic Cooperation*, **7**, 59–63 (in Chinese).

Yueh, Linda (2009), 'Patent laws and innovation in China', *International Review of Law and Economics*, **29**, 304–13.

6. Conclusion

Sunil Mani and Richard R. Nelson

In this chapter we summarize the main findings from the country case studies. As stated earlier, the present study is a sequel to the work by Odagiri, Goto, Sunami and Nelson (2010), where the role of patents in catching up was examined. An important conclusion of this study, on the effect of TRIPS, was that it will depend on three things in particular. One is the policy that will be established in countries aiming to catch up, including prominently how these countries use the flexibilities under TRIPS in the determination of their patent law and practice. A second is how aggressive patent owners (in countries at the frontier) are in trying to enforce their patents, and the terms that they demand. A third is how, and how effectively, companies and governments in developing countries respond to legal and political pressures from patent owners in frontier countries and governments that support their interests.

Further, one must also consider the main objectives of TRIPS. This is stated in article 7 of the agreement[1] and reads thus:

> The protection and enforcement of intellectual property rights should contribute to the promotion of technological innovation and to the transfer and dissemination of technology, to the mutual advantage of producers and users of technological knowledge and in a manner conducive to social and economic welfare, and to a balance of rights and obligations.

In the light of these statements, our book has focused essentially on three aspects of TRIPS compliance. The first is the extent to which the countries in our sample have (or have not) used the various flexibilities provided under TRIPS. Secondly, we have examined the extent to which TRIPS has precipitated litigation between firms. The third focus of our book has been on the extent to which innovative activity in each of our countries has increased or not, and to what extent the transfer of technology through the licensing route has increased during the TRIPS-compliant patent regimes. Analysis of the four country cases presents us with a wealth of interesting details about TRIPS compliance, national patent regimes, and innovative activity. Our major findings with respect to each of the four countries on a number of facets of TRIPS compliance are summarized in Table 6.1. In the following section, we discuss in some detail our main findings with respect to the above three issues.

1. USE OF TRIPS FLEXIBILITIES

Although the purpose of TRIPS was to have minimum standards of IPR protection across countries, it did provide a set of five flexibilities ranging from the date on which TRIPS compliance was to be achieved to specifying the conditions under which a compulsory license was to be issued. Countries differ in their actual use of these five flexibilities. However, India, and to some extent Brazil and Thailand, have been rather vigorous in pursuing these flexibilities with respect to the issue of compulsory licenses, having a higher bar on the criteria of inventiveness to prevent especially the practice of evergreening of pharmaceutical patents and in disallowing patents for computer software. In fact, the countries have used the TRIPS flexibilities as a window of opportunity for reducing the deleterious effects of TRIPS compliance on their domestic industry and indeed consumers. This further demonstrates that not all developing countries have been passive in accepting the various provisions of TRIPS.

Of the five flexibilities that are allowed in TRIPS, the countries in our sample have, by and large, used only one, namely the use of a compulsory license to manufacture high-priced drugs domestically. Even on this count, of the four countries in our sample, only Brazil, India and Thailand have used this flexibility and of these three, Brazil has used it at least four times,[2] Thailand about three times, and India has used it just once.[3] The use of this flexibility by developing countries such as Brazil, India and Thailand is significant as the Obama administration in the USA has been consistent in its efforts to stop compulsory licenses (Roderick and Pollock, 2012).

Of the remaining four flexibilities, India seems to be the only one among our sample to have used two more flexibilities, namely the one with respect to the use of transition period and providing exemptions from patentability (see (vi) in Section 1.2 of Chapter 1). It is interesting to note that only India seems to have used the transition period, and that too, to its fullest extent, while all the other three countries have been rather quick to make their national patent regimes TRIPS-compliant. Regarding the flexibility that grants exemptions from patentability, India has inserted Section 3(d) in its amended Patent Act. According to this section, 'the mere discovery of a new form of a known substance which does not result in the enhancement of the known efficacy of that substance or the

Table 6.1   Facets of TRIPS compliance across Brazil, China, India and Thailand

	Brazil	China	India	Thailand
Year of TRIPS compliance	1997	2000	2005	1992
Patent term (in years)	20 from the date of application for invention patents (15 for utility models)	20 from the date of application	20 years from the date of application. A patent has to be maintained by paying the maintenance fees every year. If fees are not paid, the patent ceases to remain in force and the invention becomes open to the public with no risk of infringing the patent	20 years for invention, 10 years for design, and 6 years for petty patent (utility model) with two possible extensions of 2 years each
Patent scope	Discoveries, mathematical methods, and scientific theories are excluded from definition of patentable subject matter, including: • Abstract concepts and literary or other esthetic creations protected by copyright • Commercial and accounting methods • Software programs • Surgical, therapeutic, and diagnostic methods	All inventions since 1992	All inventions, both product and process including those in pharmaceuticals, agrochemicals and food products. However, a number of exceptions to patenting have been specified, notably (i) mathematical or business method or a computer program per se or algorithms; (ii) topography of integrated circuits	All inventions, including those in pharmaceuticals, agrochemicals and food products (invention patents), product/ industrial design (design patents), and new inventions with potential industrial application without illustrated inventive steps (petty patent/utility model)

	• Natural living organisms or biological materials and parts thereof, including genome and germplasm of natural living organisms			
Burden of proof	Burden of proof is reversed in cases of process patent infringement	Patent infringer in the case of process inventions, otherwise the reverse is true	Reversed to be the responsibility of patent infringer in the case of process inventions	Responsibility is on patentee
Pre- and post-grant opposition to granting of domestic patents	Pre-grant and post-grant opposition allowed in Patent Law 9.279	There is no pre-grant opposition	Both introduced and allowed in the amended Indian Patent Act	Both were allowed from the beginning of the Act.
Patenting of traditional knowledge and micro organisms	• Transgenic microorganisms are patentable • Inventions based on traditional knowledge should disclose such knowledge, access to which is subject to contractual agreement of indigenous communities and authorized by Genetic Heritage Management Council of Brazil	Yes	• Traditional Knowledge Library established and access agreements signed with major patent offices in the world. This helps to challenge wrongly issued patents by foreign jurisdictions • Microorganisms are patentable	Traditional knowledge database, similar to that of India, is under construction Only genetically modified microorganisms are patentable
Innovations in domestic pharmaceutical industry/automotive industry	The percentage of firms that introduced product innovations in the pharmaceutical sector has increased, but innovations introduced are often in the form of generics	Has increased, but not entirely due to TRIPS compliance	Has increased in terms of R&D intensity and number of patents granted in India or abroad. Also, there has been a significant increase in export intensity	Mostly limited to process innovations and, to lesser extent, products new to Thailand and/or ASEAN market.

Table 6.1 (continued)

	Brazil	China	India	Thailand
	(products new to the firm or the national market, but not to world markets). Percentage of firms that introduced process innovations rose in the aftermath of the Generics Law but fell during following period. Trends in innovative performance appear to respond more to Generics Law than to the new Patent Law.			Domestic patents mostly owned by foreign firms. Patents granted abroad are limited.
Invocation of TRIPS flexibilities	New patent law and its implementation exploit TRIPS flexibilities by setting high patentability standards and by establishing conditions for the granting of compulsory licenses based on national medical emergencies. A compulsory license was issued for the domestic manufacturer of highly priced anti-retroviral	Has not used	• Full transition period for TRIPS compliance has been used • Compulsory license issued for the domestic manufacture of a highly priced cancer drug • Exception to patent rights by inserting Section 3(d) in the amended Patent Act	Compulsory license issued for highly priced HIV and heart disease drugs. However, due to lack of domestic generic drug capability, main beneficiary was an Indian generic firm, Ranbaxy.

Source: Own compilation.

226

mere discovery of any new property or new use for a known substance or the mere use of a known process are not new inventions' and hence are not patentable. This means that incremental modifications to a known product or process may not lead to the award of a fresh patent in India. By raising the bar on inventiveness the Indian patent regime also runs the risk of discouraging incremental inventions, which have been hallmarks of Indian industry, although there is no consensus that this will be the case. Consequently, while Section 3(d) has the potential to check the practice of evergreening of patents by firms, it has also the tendency to reduce the incentive for incremental innovations. Recently India invoked this section to reject the application of Novartis for patenting a drug called Glivec. This had been the subject of a virulent court battle between the company and Indian courts since 2006, and on April 1, 2013 the Supreme Court of India affirmed the earlier decision by the Indian Patent Office not to grant a patent for Glivec.[4] The 'Glivec case' is thus an important test case in the use of TRIPS flexibility. Neither of the other two flexibilities seems to have been used at all. Even with respect to the three flexibilities that were used, there are considerable variations across the sample countries in the way in which they were used. We begin with what we observed about the use of the transition period.

At one extreme is Thailand, which after an amendment in 1992 had already made its national patent regime similar to that of a TRIPS-compliant regime. This means that Thailand never used the transition period at all; it already had a patent regime that was TRIPS-compliant even before it was required to be so. In February 1992, Thailand, under pressure from the United States, decided to revise the Patent Act in order to avoid trade sanctions under s.301 of the Omnibus Trade and Competitiveness Act 1988. At the other extreme is India, which has used the full transition period available and aligned its national patent regime with the provisions of TRIPS only in 2005. Our analysis of the three amendments to the Indian Patent Act, 1970 show us that India managed to start the TRIPS compliance process only in 1999 and in fact only after it was dragged to the WTO dispute resolution forum by the USA and the European Union. Brazil and China complied very quickly.

Brazil has subsequently taken advantage of the TRIPS flexibilities with respect to compulsory licensing much more than the other countries.

In sum, in using the TRIPS flexibilities, India has been somewhat more aggressive than the other three countries in our sample (see Box 6.1 for a synoptic view of various TRIPS flexibilities built into India's amended Patent Act). Brazil and Thailand too have used one of the five flexibilities while China appears to have used none.

BOX 6.1   TRIPS FLEXIBILITIES BUILT INTO
INDIA'S TRIPS COMPLIANT PATENT
REGIME

- *Exemptions from grant of patents in certain cases* Under Article 27(1) of TRIPS, patents will have to be provided for inventions which are 'new, involve an inventive step and are capable of industrial application'. The agreement however does not define these terms. This provides a flexibility, which India has used to some extent. The Patents Amendment Act of 2005 has provided the important qualification that salts, esters, polymorphs, particle size, combinations and other derivatives of known substances cannot be patented 'unless they differ significantly in properties with regards to efficacy' (explanation to section 3(d)). In other words, secondary patents are not permitted unless these are therapeutically significant.
- *Compulsory Licensing and Government Use* Article 31 of TRIPS, the Doha Declaration and the August 30, 2003 WTO decision allow for the issue of compulsory licenses in various circumstances. India's patent law contains detailed provisions regarding compulsory licenses including those that generic companies can apply for, government use licenses, those issued in cases of national emergency, extreme urgency and public non-commercial use and compulsory licenses for exports
- *Exceptions to exclusive rights in certain cases* Article 30 of TRIPS permits member countries to 'provide limited exceptions to exclusive rights conferred by a patent . . .' The following three are the most significant and common exceptions:
  - Early working: also known as the Bolar exception – under section 107A(a) of India's Patents Act, 1970 use of a patent for development and submission of information for regulatory approval will not be considered an infringement of the patent. Thus generic companies need not wait till the actual expiry of the patents to develop generic products and hence can introduce generics immediately after the expiry of patents.

- Parallel imports: Under section 107A(b), 'importation of patented products by any person from a person who is duly authorized by the patentee to sell or distribute the product shall not be considered as an infringement of patent rights.' Thus, if need be, India can shop around the world and import patented drugs from the cheapest source.
- Research and experimental use: under section 47, patented products/processes may be made or used by any person for the 'purpose merely of experiment or research including the imparting of instructions to pupils'.
- *Opposition and revocation proceedings* Section 25 provides for pre-grant and post-grant opposition proceedings before the Indian Patent Office. Section 64 also allows for revocation petitions to be filed at any time; revocation may also be applied for as a counter-claim during the course of an infringement suit.
- *Limits on data protection* India's Drugs and Cosmetics Act, 1940, which regulates the marketing approval of new drugs, and the amended Patents Act, 1970 contain no provisions relating to data exclusivity. Thus test and clinical data relating to safety and efficacy of drugs submitted by the patent holder can be used by generic companies and the drug regulator for introducing and approving generic products.
- *No links between patent status and marketing approvals* This is not required under TRIPS and India has kept the two issues separate – drug approval procedure does not require consideration of patent status.

Source: Private communication with Sudip Chaudhuri.

Other Facets of TRIPS Compliance

First, all the countries have a uniform patent term of 20 years from the date of application for all products and processes including pharmaceutical, agrochemical and food products. This is a change, which is by itself an important hallmark of TRIPS compliance, as the earlier national patent regimes had exempted these three industries. Although the term 'all products' has been used, an important point to be borne in mind is that the national patent regimes have exempted a number of inventions from being granted patents. Prominent among these exemptions are computer programs and topography of integrated circuits, which need not be granted patents. In none of the countries is this possible. India, which had introduced patenting of software for a brief period, withdrew this after strong opposition from civil society organizations.

Secondly, utility patents have been included in the national patent regime. India is the only country among the four that does not yet have a provision for utility patents, although it is in the process of introducing utility patents into its IPR regime. Thirdly, the burden of proof in the case of infringement of process patents has been reversed. In TRIPS compliant regimes, this now rests with the infringer rather than the patentee. This reversal has important cost implications in the context of litigation, which will now have to be borne more by the infringer until she clears her name. Fourthly, all the jurisdictions except China have introduced both pre- and post-grant opposition to patents. In China, there are no pre-grant oppositions. But again, only in the case of India do we have any data on the number of pre- and post-grant oppositions. Fifthly, all jurisdictions are in the process of creating equivalents of a Traditional Knowledge Library, the existence of which is helpful in preventing wrong issuance of patents based on the traditional knowledge of a country by foreign patent offices. As far as the patentability of microorganisms is concerned, TRIPS itself is very clear that they should be patentable. However, the term 'microorganism' lacks a precise scientific definition, and so there are inherent anomalies in patenting these life forms. Though the TRIPS agreement mandates patent protection for microorganisms, it does not define them; thus there is no standard definition for member nations to follow. TRIPS facilitates the provision that the member country may adopt a *sui generis* (adoption of national laws and regulation) system to protect genetically modified organisms and invented biological material. However, it is not clear whether the term refers solely to genetically modified organisms or whether it includes naturally occurring substances also. Consequently, most of the countries in our sample allow patenting of microorganisms only if it is the result of genetic modification procedures. But Indian law seems to allow patenting of microorganisms.

2. PATENT LITIGATION AND PRE- AND POST-GRANT OPPOSITION

A significant finding of our study is the emergence of patent litigation, although such litigation is still limited in number. We have identified three important features in it. First, such litigation is taking place increasingly between domestic companies and less between MNCs and domestic companies. Secondly, it is taking place not only in the pharmaceutical industry but also in the automotive industry. Thirdly, such litigation can also happen between the country governments and MNCs – especially in the case of Brazil. In fact, the government there has used the threat of compulsory licensing as a way of preventing MNCs from charging exorbitant prices for AIDS and cancer drugs. These three findings indicate that patents are not just a measure of appropriating returns from own research efforts, but as argued earlier, are increasingly used to deter entry and prevent competition.[5] Of all the countries in our sample, this seems to be more frequent in India than in other jurisdictions.

In the following section, we attempt a countrywide summary of our findings with respect to patent litigation.

Brazil is a relatively young patent litigation forum, with comprehensive patent laws introduced only in 1997. While complex patent litigation has not developed rapidly since then, disputes over patent validity, which are handled by attorneys at law, have helped to generate a competitive legal market. More recently, the booming economy has attracted attention from foreign investors and companies which seek to protect their innovations; patent applications, filings and consequently disputes are all on the rise. The unique Brazilian pipeline patents are also an area of interest and concern for players from overseas. Pharmaceutical companies are making use of the most valuable technology coming into the country and, as ever, are taking steps to protect their innovations from local generic companies. Elsewhere, the natural resources, steel and telecommunications sectors are also thriving. Regarding trends in patent litigation, the data is fragmentary. Goulart and Ahlert (undated) count 80 patent infringement cases filed before the Brazilian courts in 1997, but by 1999 this increased to 200 new filings. According to Ehlers (2012), a cumulative total of 176 litigation cases seem to have occurred during the six-year period between 2006 and 2011. What is interesting is that the majority of both the plaintiffs and defendants were national firms. It is also observed that the majority of the cases were decided in favor of the plaintiff (namely the patentee). This is in sharp contrast to India, where the decisions were mostly in favor of the defendant (the patent infringer) in patent infringement cases.

China is host to the largest number of patent litigation cases in the world, reflecting the country's position as both a leading manufacturing center and a major consumer market. TRIPS compliance of Chinese patent laws includes provisions for an increase in the maximum amount of recoverable damages for infringement. In general, confidence has grown significantly in China as a jurisdiction for patent litigation, though challenges remain for rights owners. Although administrative channels still handle many patent infringement claims (as well as questions of patent validity), patent owners from China and further afield are increasingly pursuing compensatory remedies via judicial litigation. Forum selection can also play a major part in a patent owner's quest to enforce its rights: Beijing and Shanghai are generally seen as the most favorable venues, as reflected by the locations of the firms. Foreign law firms are prohibited from practicing Chinese law, but nonetheless play an important role in assisting foreign rights holders in engaging local counsel and coordinating litigation, both within China and internationally.

There has been a significant rise in patent litigation in India in the last few years. Needless to say, pharmaceutical companies are very active in litigating their patents in India and enforcing their patent rights. The Indian Patents Act provides for an appeal to the Intellectual Property Appellate Board (IPAB) to any decision, order or direction of the Controller under certain sections of the Act. Revocation petitions are also filed at the IPAB. As of December 31, 2011, 260 patent cases were received by the IPAB, out of which 69 have been disposed (Department of Industrial Policy and Performance, 2012). Litigation trends based on the publicly available reported decisions of the various High Courts (HC) in the country[6] provide valuable insights for strategic decision-making on patent litigation in India. The duration for deciding patent cases in the various HC is typically around three to four years. The average cost of patent litigation in India can range from INR1.2 million to INR2.5 million ($22,000 to $47,000), subject to further uncertainty depending on the engagement of senior counsel to argue the matter. The various HCs in India have decided 64 relevant patent cases from January 2007 to October 2012. The total of 64 relevant decisions includes injunctions as well as decisions on patent infringement and disposal of writ petitions. A detailed analysis of the decisions shows that the majority of these decisions are not in favor of the patentees (Vartak, 2012). However, any aggrieved party can approach the Supreme Court (SC), challenging the order of the HC by way of a special leave petition, and if the SC grants leave, then the matter will be heard and adjudicated by the SC itself. The patent litigation trends also show that the SC had decided only two patent cases from January 1950 to December 2004, but has decided seven cases from January 2005 to October 2012 (Vartak, 2012).

Pre- and Post-grant Opposition

Another interesting aspect has been the introduction of pre- and post-grant opposition to patenting: Brazil, India and Thailand are some of the few jurisdictions where both pre- and post-grant oppositions are allowed, whereas China allows only post-grant opposition. Interestingly, most advanced countries do not follow pre-grant opposition proceedings. India's pre-grant procedure allows any person to file a pre-grant opposition with the relevant patent office. 'Any person' has been interpreted to cover potential generic competitors as well as civil society groups representing interests of, for example, AIDS and cancer sufferers. The grounds on which a pre-grant opposition may be made are also very broad – they include the lack of novelty, lack of inventive step, insufficiency of description, and non-patentability of the invention under the existing law. Data on pre-grant opposition per application does not show increase but only fluctuations; however, post-grant opposition per application granted has shown some increase over time. Pre- and post-grant opposition can actually improve the quality of patents granted. But it may also delay the whole process of granting a patent. If the delay increases the quality of patents that are granted, then the opposition, pre- and post-grant, is justifiable, but not otherwise. However, we do not have detailed data to pass any judgment on the issue. This is clearly an area for further inquiry.

3.   CHANGES IN INNOVATIVE ACTIVITY AND TECHNOLOGY TRANSFER

An important issue for our study was whether there has been an increase in innovative activity as a result of increasing the incentives for innovation, which a strict patent regime would have brought about. But we also noted that an increase in innovative activity might have more to do with supply and demand factors. The period of TRIPS compliance also matches the period of economic liberalization, which all the countries in our sample initiated. The demand-side factors include industrial policy measures for increasing the domestic competition between enterprises, and trade policy measures that opened up domestic industrial markets to foreign competition. Further, most of the domestic enterprises became export-oriented during this time. Increased competitive pressure and intense export rivalry encourage firms to increase their innovative efforts. Supply-side policies include re-tuning of innovation policy instruments like tax incentives, research grants etc. to encourage the supply of innovations, and all four countries have redesigned their innovation policy instruments during this period. Consequent to these demand- and supply-side measures, the number of patents granted has shown an increase in all four countries. But a detailed verification of the ownership of these patents shows us that in all the countries the majority of the patents are issued to foreign companies which have now become confident enough to locate their R&D activity in these countries, taking advantage of the availability of good quality scientists and engineers. In fact, many of the patents are actually granted to such foreign R&D centers located in these countries. Of the four, this trend is more pronounced in China and India. This means that a stricter patent regime may have encouraged the MNCs to relocate their R&D activities, but they might also have been persuaded by the existence of other facilitating factors such as the availability of scientists and engineers at much cheaper prices. But these foreign enterprises are also quick to take IPRs on their inventions. So, a mere increase in the number of patents from these countries need not necessarily mean increased innovative activity if local firms and institutions do not hold the patents.

One of the interesting findings of the study is increased investment in R&D by the pharmaceutical industry in all the four countries. Their performance in the area of generic drugs continued to be good, and generic drugs manufacturers in India seem to have improved their technological capability. This is evident from their increasing share of ANDAs secured from the USFDA and also the increased exports from the country. So the dire predictions that TRIPS would sound a death knell to the generic drugs industry do not appear to have been right. However, the evidence, although fragmentary, does indicate that prices of essential drugs under patent protection have shown significant increases after TRIPS compliance. In fact, the invocation of compulsory licensing is itself indicative of this steep rise in the price of essential drugs after TRIPS compliance, although this proposition needs careful empirical scrutiny.

An interesting aspect of innovation is the evidence of an increase in research activity in the area of so-called neglected tropical diseases (NTDs). This is discernible in the case of both Brazil and India. However, public sector research institutes execute all the research projects in this area based essentially on donor funding. So it is difficult to attribute this increase in research on NTDs to TRIPS per se as there is very little participation by either foreign or domestic pharmaceutical firms. Nevertheless, there is certainly an increase in the level of research in NTDs as evidenced by significant increases in the number of publications in this area. Publications now are a good indicator of the shape of things to come.

Strengthening of IPR regimes was expected to increase technology licensing, especially between MNCs and unaffiliated companies. Evidence from Brazil and India shows that this has not happened. In fact, the number of technology collaboration agreements contracted by domestic enterprises in these countries has come down. Perhaps this has more to do with the imperfections in the market for disembodied technologies, which is increasingly becoming oligopolistic in nature. Most of the technology licensing transactions are becoming intra firm – between MNC parents and their affiliates in these countries. In short, there is absolutely no empirical evidence from any of these four countries that TRIPS compliance has actually increased the flow of disembodied technologies through the licensing route from the northern firms to the southern ones.

In sum, the evidence that we garner from the four countries presents a mixed picture. TRIPS compliance of national patent regimes has had some positive effects, but it does have negative effects as well. However, there is unanimity in one aspect, namely that TRIPS has certainly raised the profile of patenting in developing countries. Increased patenting has also precipitated patent litigation. There is fragmentary evidence to show that TRIPS has raised the prices of certain types of drugs. A number of the positive effects, like increased innovative activity, increased foreign direct investment (FDI), and FDI in R&D etc., may not easily be attributable to strengthening of the patent regime. All these variables are also determined by a number of other factors, such as favorable policies, the availability of incentives and key factor inputs like a well-trained work force, improvements in physical infrastructure etc. Previous studies in this area have been quick to attribute the changes in these dependent variables (increased FDI, R&D etc.) to a strengthening of the patent regime. However, based on the four country case studies, we found very little evidence for such optimism with respect to TRIPS compliance.

NOTES

1. See http://www.wto.org/english/docs_e/legal_e/27-trips_03_e.htm (accessed April 4, 2013).
2. In fact, one of the first Compulsory Licenses (CL) issued was for the Roche product Nelfinavir, and on the very same day of the issuance of the CL, Roche reduced the price of the product by as much as 40 percent.
3. One of the high profile cases in the issuance of compulsory license is again from India. This concerns the compulsory license issued to an Indian generic drug company, Natco Pharma, to manufacture and sell an anti-cancer drug, Nexavar, at INR8,800 (or US$175) for a month's dosage as against Bayer's (which holds the patent for this drug) INR280, 000 (or US$5,500).
4. India has refused protection for Glivec on the grounds that it is not a new drug but an amended version of a known compound. By contrast, the newer form of Glivec has been patented in nearly 40 countries including the United States, Russia and China. Indian law bans firms from extending patents on their products by making slight changes to a

compound, a practice known as 'evergreening'. The Supreme Court reached the conclusion that Glivec does not satisfy a patent's 'inventive step' requirement.

5. The fact that the patent system has veered away from its original purpose of incentivizing was shown by Jaffe and Lerner (2004). Their analysis shows that new laws have made it easier for businesses and inventors to secure patents on products of all kinds, and second, the laws have tilted the table to favor patent holders, no matter how tenuous their claims are. Further, their analysis shows that many technology-based companies make much more income through patent litigation than through licensing their innovations and earning income through royalties and license fees.

6. The highest court in a state in India is called a High Court (HC) while the highest court in the country at the federal government level is the Supreme Court (SC).

REFERENCES

Department of Industrial Policy and Performance (2012), *Annual Report 2011–12*, Ministry of Industry and Commerce, New Delhi: Government of India.

Ehlers, Marc Hagen (2012), 'Brazilian Patent System Seminar. Brazilian patent litigation and practical business', Dannemann Siemsen.

Goulart, Joachim Eugenio and Ivan Ahlert (undated), 'The enforcement of patent rights in Brazil'.

Jaffe, Adam B. and Josh Lerner (2004), *Innovation and its Discontents: How Our Broken Patent System is Endangering Innovation and Progress, and What To Do About It*, Princeton, NJ: Princeton University Press.

Odagiri, Hiroyuki, Akira Goto, Atsushi Sunami and Richard R. Nelson (eds) (2010), *Intellectual Property Rights, Development, and Catch-Up*, New York: Oxford University Press.

Roderick, Peter and Allyson M. Pollock (2012), 'India's patent laws under pressure', *The Lancet*, **380** (9846), e2–e4.

Sampat, Bhaven N., Kenneth C. Shadlen and Tahir M. Amin (2012), 'Challenges to India's pharmaceutical laws', *Science*, **337** (6093), 414–15.

Vartak, Rahul (2012), 'On the up: patent litigation trends in India', *World Intellectual Property Review*, http://www.worldipreview.com/article/on-the-up-patent-litigation-trends-in-india (accessed March 21, 2013).

Index

Titles of publications are in *italics*.